# DEEP AND WILD

Michael Adam Beck

# DEEP AND WILD

*Remissioning Your Church from the Outside In*

*Deep and Wild* Copyright © 2020 Michael Adam Beck

All rights reserved. No part of this publication may be reproduced, stored in a retrieval system, or transmitted, in any form or by any means—electronic, mechanical, photocopying, recording, or otherwise—without prior written permission, except for brief quotations in critical reviews or articles.

Scripture quotations are taken from New Revised Standard Version Bible, copyright © 1989 National Council of the Churches of Christ in the United States of America. Used by permission. All rights reserved.

Scripture quotations marked NIV are taken from the Holy Bible, New International Version®, NIV®. Copyright © 1973, 1978, 1984, 2011 by Biblica, Inc.™ Used by permission of Zondervan. All rights reserved worldwide. www.zondervan.com. The "NIV" and "New International Version" are trademarks registered in the United States Patent and Trademark Office by Biblica, Inc.™ All rights reserved worldwide.

Scripture quotations taken from the New American Standard Bible® (NASB), Copyright © 1960, 1962, 1963, 1968, 1971, 1972, 1973, 1975, 1977, 1995 by The Lockman Foundation. Used by permission. www.Lockman.org.

Printed in the United States of America

*Cover design by Strange Last Name*
*Page design by PerfecType, Nashville, Tennessee*

Beck, Michael Adam.
 Deep and wild : remissioning your church from the outside in / Michael Adam Beck. – Franklin, Tennessee : Seedbed Publishing, ©2020.

   pages ; cm.

   ISBN 9781628247893  (paperback)
   ISBN 9781628247909  (Mobi)
   ISBN 9781628247916  (ePub)
   ISBN 9781628247923  (uPDF)

   1. Emerging church movement.  2. Missional church movement.  3. Church renewal.  4. Christian leadership  5. Church development, New.  I. Title.

BV601.9.B43 2019                     262/.26        2020943432

SEEDBED PUBLISHING
Franklin, Tennessee
seedbed.com

To Jill, you are my person.

# Contents

| | |
|---|---|
| Foreword by Leonard Sweet | ix |
| The Opening Vision: A Tree of Life | xiii |
| | |
| Trailer | 3 |
| Field Interview: June Edwards | 23 |
| | |
| Chapter 1: The New Missional Frontier | 29 |
| Field Interview: Verlon Fosner | 49 |
| | |
| Chapter 2: Post-Everything—Six Shifts | 53 |
| Field Interview: Jorge Acevedo | 87 |
| | |
| Chapter 3: God of Recycling Bins, Not Dumpsters | 91 |
| Field Interview: Travis Collins | 119 |
| | |
| Chapter 4: Wild Branches—Fresh Expressions | 125 |
| Field Interview: Luke Edwards | 159 |

Chapter 5: Deep Roots—The Blended Ecology      163
Field Interview: Mia Chang      189

Chapter 6: (Re)missioning—Time for a Remix      195
Field Interview: Evelyn Sekajipo      227

Chapter 7: Symbiosis—The Hybrid Organism      233
Field Interview: Jonathan Dowman      259

Closing Vision: Tree of Life (Re)Mixed      267
Field Interview: Mike Snedeker      271

Bibliography      277
Notes      287

# Foreword

The best description of Christ to emerge in the second century is this one from the Epistle to Diognetus: "This is the one who was from the beginning, who appeared as new yet proved to be old, and is always young as he is born in the hearts of saints."[1] It is the mission of each generation to help Christ be "born young" in the next generations. Hence the aptness of the metaphor and movement of Fresh Expressions.

The old, old story needs to be told in new ways. Jesus is the same yesterday, today, and forever. But the only way for him to stay the same is that he has to change. No matter how ancient the well, the Living Water must be drawn daily. New water from the old well. The Bread of Life must be baked in the oven, fresh every morning, if Jesus is to feed a hungry world. The water can't be stagnant. The bread can't be stale. Water and Bread must be fresh and in a familiar enough form for people to want to taste and see.

In fact, one of the ways we know the old, old truths are true is their ability to assume fresh, unimagined, and unfamiliar shapes while remaining themselves and without compromising their integrity. "Jesus said to them, 'I am the bread of life; he who comes to Me will not hunger, and he who believes in Me will never thirst'" (John 6:35 NASB).

The Christian faith is meant to be hot-out-of-the-oven bread, always a fresh start. But not from scratch. Rather, from starters of leaven and salt. Each new start is the same but different. What makes it the same is the starter. How did we make bread rise before packets of yeast were available at the local market? Through live-yeast breads. No baker's yeast was used when Egyptians baked bread five thousand years ago or when the pilgrims baked it in the colonies or when gold miners baked it in California and the Klondike.

Sourdough starters are live cultures of naturally occurring wild yeasts, lactobacteria, and fungi. Literally millions of lactobacilli live in one little starter. Carbon dioxide causes dough to rise, and these bacteria produce the gasses that give baked goods their lightness. It feeds on carbohydrates (such as flour or sugar) and produces gas and alcohol (which the old sourdough-miners called "hooch") as by-products. These microorganisms create the rich flavor and add helpful bacteria to our intestines; even when dehydrated the yeast can be fully *revitalized*—just moisten and reheat. Sourdough yeast has bacteria in it that can survive for decades, even centuries. In fact, theoretically, these cultures could live forever. But you have to take good care of your starter. Like a pet, it needs to be fed and cleaned and treated, daily sweetened or freshened. No wonder sourdough starters are called the "bonsai tree of the food world." A starter pot was the most essential ingredient in every wagon on the trail westward.

I am a sourdough, a sourdough-disciple of Jesus. The term *sourdough* arose to describe the frontier cook who religiously guarded his sourdough starter and used it to make the daily bread. The starter is the faith "once delivered to the saints" (Jude 1:3). The starter is the Scriptures, issuing in tradition, revealed by reason, yoked to experience. The creative genius of Christianity is not that every generation starts over from scratch, or creates something from nothing, but from a starter bakes fresh bread that feeds the hungers of the culture—whether those hungers be for pumpernickel, rye, challah, buns, boule, biscuits, potato bread, corn bread, chocolate cake, pizza, pancakes. An endless possibility of remixes is possible with every starter.

God invents from scratch and discovers the new. Humans innovate from starter and make the old new or discover the new or combine the old with something else so that something new happens that can be put into practice. According to the most recent research on creativity from a composer and a neuroscientist, the old becomes new mostly in three ways: by bending, breaking, and blending.[2] *Bending* involves altering a property. *Breaking* involves taking something apart and reassembling the ingredients. *Blending* entails mixing the ingredients in new ways. Michael Beck will do all three in this inspiring book. He is a true frontier practitioner of remixing the starter kit in fresh ways.

Fresh Expressions is a sourdough strategy for church revitalization, and this book is a starter pot. But every starter pot should come with a warning: BEWARE. Sourdough yeast EXPANDS. Whatever container you choose to keep it in—plastic or glass or ceramic (never metal)—make sure it's big enough to expand. Biblical faith is a yeast culture, an expansive culture. You can't contain it. You can't predict it. It's organic, but it's explosive. It's the original flour power.

Dr. Leonard Sweet
Charles Wesley Distinguished Professor of Doctoral Studies, Evangelical Seminary
Visiting Distinguished Professor, George Fox University
E. Stanley Jones Professor Emeritus, Drew University
Distinguished Visiting Professor, Tabor College

# The Opening Vision: A Tree of Life

# The Blended Ecology

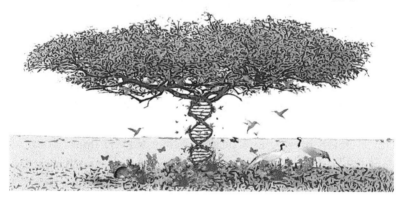

Welcome back to our three-course picnic at the tree of life! In Book One, "the appetizer," I offered bite-sized pieces of what I now provide here in Book Two as full, heaping portions of a "main course." Book Three, "the dessert," is a workbook with practices, tools, and processes. The three books were created to complement each other in the following sequence: Book One (seeing), Book Two (understanding/assessing), and Book Three (action/implementation), with some blending of the three.

This opening vision is intended to help us enter fully the scriptural imaginarium of the blended ecology. Scripture begins by calling us deep into the imagination of a pioneer God. God imagines what can be, and then speaks it into being by God's own word and will. All of creation starts in God's imagination before it has any substance.

Then the Spirit playfully sweeps over the swirling waters of chaotic nothingness and brings forth elegance, beauty, and life (Gen. 1:2). Later, God gets down in the newly watered dust of creation and plays around in the mud. One of the first images we see of God is God at play. When God plays in the sandbox of his imagination, we get a universe. When God makes mud-pies, we get human beings. God gets dirt beneath his fingernails, then breathes into us the breath of life (Gen. 2:6–7). Beautiful news: God invites us to get down in the mud and play too! With sanctified imaginations, we can play forth new possibilities for our local communities.

Jesus told stories that harnessed the power of imagination. His teaching style was not one of simply sharing data, but in using imagery and metaphor to help hearers enter a fresh kingdom vision from which they could see the world through new eyes. Our Western paradigm is heavily reliant on the impartation of data. When data has taken us as far as it can go, we must trust the power of metaphor. *Metaphor* is derived from the Greek roots of *meta* (over, across, or beyond) and *phor* (to carry), hence literally "to carry across." Interestingly enough, the Bible never explicitly defines what the church is; rather, it shows us a kaleidoscope of images for what the church is like. To break us free from the death spiral of the same-old church questions and church answers, we will use a metaphor to carry us across the bridge into new vistas of possibility.

While this is a serious project based in scholarly research, it is also an exercise in play and imagination. We have been using

Newtonian logic for a couple hundred years in our attempts to reform the church, treating her like a machine in which we need only trade out the broken parts. Let's give imagination a shot. We've been crammed into serious stuffy spaces with whiteboards and gurus long enough; let's try play! Let's get down with the God of mud-pies in the sandbox of our communities and try some missional mess-making.

Creativity, imagination, and innovation are what allow human beings to lean into the future and remake the world. As reflections of the creator God, we generate alternative realities by following the Spirit into the imagination of God and asking "what if?" I want to invite you to ask "what if" with me and engage the Scriptures with a fresh imagination that may open us to what the Holy Spirit is up to just outside the walls of our churches.

Once again, we find ourselves at the tree of life. The tree is a sign of the faithfulness of a God who doesn't waste anything. A God of the remix. It is a symbol of the continuity of God's plan for the renewal of the cosmos, and one of the most consistent images of God's faithful presence. Our story starts at the tree (Gen. 2:9), starts over at the tree from which our Savior hung (Gal. 3:13), and continues eternally back at the tree in the urban garden of new creation (Rev. 22:2). As we journey through the modes of how God dwells among us, we will find the tree—in Eden, tabernacle, temple, synagogue, church, and new creation. Eden remixed.

This tree is the central image of the blended ecology. Across the desert landscape of a post-Christendom US, a network of trees is flourishing on the backdrop of the sweeping waterless void. Springing from the root-balls of these resilient shade-offering organisms are emerging life-forms, new species never seen before, bursting with life in all their splendorous weirdness.

There is a life-giving exchange happening between the *inherited* church, with its rootedness and depth, and these new wild life-forms, the *emerging* church. In this main course, let's look at this organism a little closer. Can you see the double helix trunk of this tree?

This is also an image of the personhood of God, the diverse singularity of the Trinity, inherent in the DNA structure. There is a blended ecology, a "togetherversity" of inherited and emerging modes of church life (form), because there is a Trinity, who is the diverse singularity of one and three persons (source).

God is our central story, the reality from which all other stories and structures flow. That story is manifested most fully in our time-space reality in the person of Jesus of Nazareth. The fully-human, fully-God one, who is the very life of the tree in all deserts. God's way is the way of resurrection, the remix, the making-all-things-newness. God's way is the life-giving "withness" in the desert times.

This is an image of the past-present-future church. We are a manifestation of that withness. We are the life-giving shade tree in the parched communities of drought. Our ecclesial structures, and the shape of the church, must be derived from the person of God. The God story of Immanuel, a "God with us," a God who is both fully human and fully God, attractional and incarnational, one and diverse. We are a both/and community, drawn from the very life of the triune God. A new creation community. This is an image of the forgotten story, but it is coming alive again.

The future of the church is *not* fresh expressions. The future of the church is the blended ecology of fresh expressions *and* traditional congregations—a manifestation of not only Jerusalem *and* Antioch, Gathered *and* Scattered, Tabernacle *and* Temple, Digital *and* Analog, Deep Roots *and* Wild Branches, but of the God who is Father, Son, *and* Holy Spirit. We now embark on a journey together, that may allow our churches to join again into the circle dance of the Trinity.

## Mixing Our Metaphors—Tree of Life (Re)mixed
*Romans 11:16–24*

Let us start with some metaphor mixing. Paul himself is quite adept at mixing his metaphors, so let's take his lead by remixing some of his own.

This is a complex passage. At the simplest level, Paul is speaking to the marvelous thing God has done in Jesus Christ, making Jews and Gentiles one living organism. He is using the image of the olive tree as a warning about unbelief, which causes branches to be "broken off." Therefore, his Gentile hearers should not boast about this new scenario, lest they too be broken off. Paul does some of his trademark metaphor mixing here.

> If the part of the dough offered as first fruits is holy, then the whole batch is holy; and if the root is holy, then the branches also are holy. But if some of the branches were broken off, and you, a wild olive shoot, were grafted in their place to share the rich root of the olive tree, do not boast over the branches. If you do boast, remember that it is not you that support the root, but the root that supports you. (Rom. 11:16–18)

The movement from the image of a whole batch of dough being holy to a tree being holy may seem confusing, but the key point here is the status of "holy" bestowed upon a "whole" through the condition of a "portion." This reaches back to the idea that by offering "the first of your dough," the whole batch is consecrated (Num. 15:20). In this image, the deep roots of the tree (Patriarchs, Matriarchs, Torah, Covenant . . . now through Messiah Jesus) confer a status to the whole, but individual branches can be broken off or grafted in by God.

Gentiles, then, are the "wild branches" *grafted* into the very same root system as the Jews. They are now one tree. Paul, the city boy, acknowledges this is "contrary to nature," for in the logic of horticulture, cultivated branches were grafted into wild trees, not vice versa (Rom. 11:24). Thus, this is a *supernatural* process. A new creation organism has emerged through a process of grafting, but humans cannot accomplish this. It's God's resurrection power, the mysterious importation of his presence, that gives life, grafts, and breaks off.

Paul goes on, "For if you have been cut from what is by nature a wild olive tree and grafted, contrary to nature, into a cultivated olive tree, how much more will these natural branches be grafted back into their own olive tree" (Rom. 11:24).

These diverse species of olive trees have been grafted together into one tree. The blended-ecology way requires us to do some grafting.

Later I will discuss grafting at length. Our closing image to illustrate this process is called "Ketchup n' Fries," an example of symbiosis and "grafting gone wild."[1] Can the same plant grow colorful tomatoes up top (ketchup) and potatoes (fries) in the root ball? Yes! Can the same local church grow inherited and emerging forms of church? Yes!

The tree of life is for both Jew and Gentile, indeed for all people. We will gather together around this tree in the new creation. The church is a living composite organism. Paul was operating in a liminal time of in-betweenness. As communal life in Jesus began to take on new forms among the Gentiles, it was being grafted back into the inherited ways of their new Jewish family members.

Once again, the church of a pandemic world is in a liminal space, a threshold between times. Once again, the Spirit is up to something with the denizens of this strange new world. New forms of church are springing up across the globe, quite distinct from what many of us have known as church. For churches to experience revitalization, there will need to be some grafting. Once again, only the supernatural power of God can accomplish what needs to be done. Once again, we need to *believe*, and not *boast*.

There is a grove at the foot of the Mount of Olives in Jerusalem, believed to be the garden of Gethsemane where Jesus agonized in prayer the night before his crucifixion. The olive trees there are reported to be around two thousand years old. I prayed in that garden and touched those olive trees, trees that maybe Jesus himself touched.

There I made a fascinating discovery: the gnarled hollow shell of the root ball had multiple younger shoots springing up and blending together. An olive tree can be cut down to a stump and will still rejuvenate. While the ancient part of the tree is still there, and the root system is largely unchanged, the tree renews itself by reproducing these new branches. The olive trees survive so long not by staying the same, but by continually supporting the emergence of the new shoots.

The tree itself is a blended ecology!

The olive-tree-of-life is an organism of deep roots *and* wild branches. Rooted in God's faithful activity in the past *and* growing

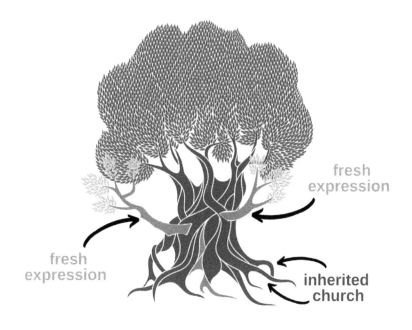

wildly toward God's promised future manifesting in the present. The deep roots of *inherited congregations* must be grafted together with the wild branches of the *fresh expressions of church*, forming new creation ecosystems in our neighborhoods and networks. We are indeed tree-of-life and vineyard people.

In Jesus' parable of the vineyard, he himself is the living organism, the *true vine*; his life flows through the whole complex network of the vineyard. What if local congregations could find their deepest story again and base themselves, structurally speaking, on Paul's olive tree or Jesus' parable of the vine, rather than some corporate entity? What does the local church look like as a living, composite organism that is an interweaving, organic, polycentric, dispersed, networked system?

We will graft these images together throughout the book until we finally arrive at the remixed tree of life. Please take some time to prayerfully inhabit this scriptural space, meditating over these passages.

## Some (Re)mixing . . .

Any book about Fresh Expressions should *be a fresh expression*. A fresh remix of what was, what is, and what's to come. I've blended in some fresh elements as we journey through the old, old tree story.

**Field Interviews**: Following each chapter you will find field interviews. This is the collaborative work of a collective intelligence. These are interviews with nine actual blended ecology pioneers from diverse denominational, theological, and ethnic backgrounds. These are practitioners on the missional frontier who are living out these concepts in real time. Nothing gets a congregation's blood flow pumping again like resurrection stories of lives transformed by Jesus. Many of us learn more through stories than taking in data, so I will offer up both options for you.

**Missional Travel Glossary:** *A clarification of terms, with definitions, functioning like a kind of search engine for the journey.* Few things are more frustrating than when an author uses words we can't define, forcing us to pause, snap our computer or cell phone out of sleep mode, and Google it. I will not force that horribly disruptive process onto you. Hence, the Missional Travel Glossary terms are included in the chapters as you go along.

# DEEP
AND
# WILD

# Trailer

I want to know Christ and the power of his resurrection and the sharing of his sufferings by becoming like him in his death, if somehow I may attain the resurrection from the dead. (Phil. 3:10–11)

Come, Lord, stir us up and call us back, kindle and seize us, be our fire and our sweetness. Let us love, let us run.

—Augustine

Thirteen years ago, First United Methodist Church of Fort Myers, Florida, was a thriving congregation. Founded in 1872, for most of 144 years the church was a spiritual powerhouse of the community. During that century-and-a-half season of ministry, many people connected to Jesus, worshiped the living God, and served others. In the 1950s, large buildings were constructed as the church thrived. In the '70s, a preschool began, and in the '80s a large family life center was constructed to keep pace with the church's numerical growth.

In 2016, no longer able to financially sustain the congregation, First UMC, Fort Myers held its final worship experience and closed its doors. They voted to become a campus of a thriving multi-site church nearby, Grace UMC. Just last week of this writing, the awe-inspiring steeple of this church was demolished, leveled to the ground. Compared to the thousands of churches that simply fail and must close their doors every year, this is a graceful way to die. Offering the property up to the hope of a brighter future for the next generation.

The story of First UMC, Fort Meyers is not unique. It is the new normal of US churches across denominational boundaries. We live in a time coined "Post-Christendom," "The Great Decline," and the "Post-Christian United States." We live on a new and uncharted frontier. The land of the so-called "nones and dones," the "de-churched and the no-churched." The United States is now the "largest mission field in the Western Hemisphere and the third largest on earth."[1]

Yet as the COVID-19 pandemic exposed, there is an incredible spiritual hunger among the masses. We find ourselves on the edge of the greatest missional opportunity in the history of the United States.[2]

While the church of Jesus Christ will never die, the church as we know it is dying. You are most likely reading this book because you are convinced that this shouldn't be the case, and there must be a way to revitalize existing congregations.

The big idea of this book is that local congregations that plant fresh expressions of church can indeed experience forms of revitalization from the outside in.

**Nones:** People who claim no religious affiliation or practice.

**Dones:** People who once practiced a religion but no longer do.

Churches across denominational lines have poured endless resources into the problem of decline. Many books have been written, attempting to give the silver bullet to church growth and the seven keys to revitalization. Many denominations have doubled up strategies on planting churches, hoping to outpace the rate they are closing. While some of these efforts have proved hopeful, we have, at best, merely stemmed the flow of decline.

In *Structured for Mission: Renewing the Culture of the Church*, Alan Roxburgh poses the question, "Why have we spent so much energy and resources in processes of restructuring, reorganizing and renewing, but see little actually change?" He proposes that simply restructuring is not enough; we must deal with the "legitimating narratives" from which our structures emerge, join what God is doing in our neighborhoods, and release local collaborative experimentation.[3]

**Legitimating Narrative:** An overarching story that provides a group (a small unit or a whole society) with a way to express its underlying values, beliefs, and commitments about who they are and how life is to be lived.[4]

The church in the US embraced the legitimating narrative of the twentieth-century corporation. Now for many congregations, the foundational story that undergirds the institutional church has been buried beneath sedimentary layers of bureaucracy and irrelevant structures. We will explore how the blended-ecology way is the deepest legitimating narrative of the church, which flows back to the diverse singularity of the triune God.

Alan Hirsch and Dave Ferguson discuss the theory of "blue and red oceans" from the corporate world to describe the 60:40 dilemma. Corporations often compete for the same small base of existing customers in the blood red waters of the 40 percent, while ignoring the potential with that larger 60 percent. The 60 percent are reached through value innovation that unlocks new demand.[5]

For the church, the 60:40 scenario can be understood as a twofold problem. The *missionary problem:* There is currently 60 percent of the population (or more) that the attractional church model will most likely never reach. The *strategic problem:* Most churches are fighting in the blood-red waters for the same 40 percent of already-Christians. These churches best their competitors by "doing church better." Better facilities, better bands, better coffee. There is an entire wider, deeper, blue ocean of people, the 60 percent, who will remain beyond our relational bandwidth through the current attractional only mode.[6]

Amid this scenario of decline and death as a new normal for the church in the West, Michael Moynagh, in reference to the Fresh Expressions movement, says, "We are at the frontier, it seems, of a new wave of Christian outreach and impact."[7]

**Fresh Expressions:** A fresh expression is a form of church for our changing culture, established primarily for the benefit of those who are not yet part of any church.

The Fresh Expressions movement is church out in the blue waters, and it is transforming existing churches in profound ways.

So, I want to heed the wisdom of Roxburgh and not get caught in what he calls the "Cul-De-Sac" of church questions and church answers. I want to follow his lead on envisioning a "different kind of church" that the Spirit is breathing forth for a new world.[8] I want to stretch you to think beyond revitalizing churches and think about how churches can play a role in creating renewed ecosystems. In the imaginarium of ecosystems, we will see the fresh expressions of church as green spaces that invite communion, rest, worship, and play, giving fresh air and life in the larger community.

**Inherited Church**: A form of church passed on as a precious gift by the saints of generations past, as in our parents leaving us an incredibly valuable inheritance that we must now learn how to steward well. Sometimes compared/contrasted with the "emerging church." Also referred to as "traditional, attractional, gathered, analog" church.

**Emerging Church**: A contextual form of church that reaches and serves people currently outside the inherited church. They are shaped from a relational interaction between people, cultures, and the gospel. Sometimes compared/contrasted with the "inherited church." Also referred to as "modern, missional, scattered, digital," and fresh expressions of church.

**Emerging Missional Church:** Alan Hirsch uses the language of *emerging missional church* to describe what the Holy Spirit is up to today.[9] I am aware that there is a distinction between the *missional church* and the *emerging church* movements. As Chris Backert says, "In truth, they are parallel movements that have intersection through key figures and ideas."[10] While the Fresh Expressions movement flows clearly in the stream of the missional church movement, there are certainly some intersections that blend the streams together. Thus, I will engage thought leaders from both streams, whose DNA is apparent within Fresh Expressions.

We need to think beyond asking church questions and seeking church answers, but we need to resist the extreme of leaving the inherited church behind in the rearview mirror. It is a place between the extremes where we find the sweet spot of the Holy Spirit—the grafting God at work.

Many argue there is a false dichotomy between ecclesiology (study of the church) and missiology (study of mission). Scholars across the theological spectrum have been closing that gap for decades now.[11] As Paul Avis writes, "Given the decline of Christianity in the West and the need to re-evangelize 'Christendom,' it seems likely that ecclesiology will take its bearing from missiology more strongly in the immediate future and that the two approaches will increasingly be seen as two sides of a coin."[12] Let's (re)envision them in the form of a Möbius strip, as a continuous loop of co-creation, flowing into each other.

What I will attempt to do here is offer a blending of ecclesiology and missiology, remixed into a mash-up of the same song: "ecclesio-missiology," if you will, more widely known as *missional ecclesiology*. Much like we will see how (re)missioning is a remix of inherited and emerging modes of church.

**(Re)Missioning:** A process of awakening and practically focusing the efforts of the congregation on the Great Commission locally. By engaging the local context, a transformation is catalyzed from the outside in. Where revitalization often involves internal adjustments—an inside-out approach (better preaching, better coffee, better programs, etc.)—(Re)Missioning involves an outside-in approach. As we join what the Spirit is up to in our communities, cultivating fresh expressions, the congregation experiences positive transformation through this symbiotic relationship (i.e., feedback loops).

## New Thinking—Beyond the Cul-De-Sac

If you're looking to put butts in pews, there are probably better books.

This is not a trick. This book really is about revitalization. However, the revitalization conversation with many of its fundamental assumptions is quite flawed. At this point in world history, amid the significant decline of the US church, no effective revitalization strategy has yet emerged. There are *many* revitalization strategies; the key word is *effective*. If there was an effective strategy, clergy wouldn't be quitting in droves, dozens of churches wouldn't be closing every week (thousands per year) and only 15 percent reporting growth.[13] The fundamental flaw of most approaches is that they fall into Roxburgh's description of the cul-de-sac of church questions and answers.

We've been trying to solve the problem of decline with the same thinking that created it. Most revitalization strategies are focused on making internal changes to a congregation.

Churches in decline don't just need more or better inherited mode leadership. That is a large part of the problem that created the decline to begin with. The concept of leadership itself, among many other foundational concepts, must be reconceptualized. The pioneer leadership emerging in the UK over the past several decades, as well as a shared leadership approach based in the relational dance of the Trinity, will be explored.

Much of what we thought we knew was wrong. David Bosch took up the slippery but necessary language of "paradigm shift" to describe the emerging scenario.[14] In the US, upcoming generations are having a qualitatively different experience than our ancestors just one or two generations removed. At the dawn of the third millennium, Bosch observed "a growing awareness that we live in an era of change from one way of understanding reality to another."[15] Discoveries in biology, chemistry, and most particularly in physics have challenged long-held fundamental assumptions about life and the universe.

Leonard Sweet, in this same period, began to speak of a "postmodern science," repudiating the assumptions of all previous paradigms, "an emerging cosmology that is now as revolutionary as once were the Copernican and Aristotelian-Ptolemaic cosmologies."[16]

Sweet speaks of quantum physics enlivening a spiritual perspective of the universe, a "quantum spirituality."[17] This nascent way of thinking is what Margaret Wheatley calls simply the "new science."[18] Sara Savage and Eolene MacMillan write of the new sciences, "in particular, quantum and chaos theories—have opened the doors for a more fruitful dialogue between science and religion."[19] Michael Moynagh uses the term "complexity thinking" to describe a variety of theories emerging from various disciplines in this vein.[20]

Mechanistic Newtonian assumptions are being replaced by the complexity thinking of the strange new quantum world in science. This paradigm shift, along with technological advances, have contributed to the restructuring of society. Western culture itself, amid a now globalized (increasingly interdependent and integrated) network society, has undergone a dramatic transformation. As we examine this reality in the next chapter, we will see how the church has largely failed to adapt to these changes and is still living under the spell of old assumptions.

One place the implications of this new science is yet to be fully realized is in the revitalization of churches. We are discovering that while churches rarely experience renewal from the inside out, we are witnessing a phenomenon of churches experiencing (re)missioning from the outside in.

A warning here—revitalization might not be what we think it is. The bare understanding of revitalization is simply something that once was vital, that no longer is vital, is made vital again. This describes the action of imbuing something with new life and vitality. If it's measured by a return of butts to the pews on our featured Sunday morning worship experience, *revitalization* is the wrong word to use. Planting fresh expressions in the community may not result in butts in pews—but a form of revitalization often will. Let's start with redefining revitalization itself.

> **Revitalization**: A force of remix, in which God uses a community of persons as conduits to unleash the power of resurrection in a given ecosystem. This is a form of emergence, in which the Spirit reconfigures old and new components of a living system in a new amalgamation.

## The Big AND

There is a big hairy "and" I will ask you to hold together in creative tension from start to finish in this book. A fundamental paradox, if you will. Fresh expressions are new forms of church established to reach those not currently involved in any church; they are not designed to revitalize inherited congregations *and* . . . inherited congregations that cultivate fresh expressions of church are experiencing revitalization.

As John Drane noted more than eight years ago, "Actually many people who connect with church through Fresh Expressions do then find their way into traditional worship, and that is one of the benefits of the 'mixed economy' concept with its recognition that there are many different ways of being church, with the traditional and innovative being of equal value."[21]

> **Mixed Economy**: In business, an economy in which some industries are privately owned and others are publicly owned or nationalized; or an economy that combines elements of capitalism and socialism, mixing some individual ownership and regulation.
>
> In church, a diversity of ecclesial forms in which fresh expressions of church existing alongside inherited forms in relationships of mutual respect and support.[22]

Furthermore, Lynda Barley, in studying church attendance trends in the UK, writes, "A more cautious interpretation then is that fresh expressions of church are making a significant contribution towards arresting the decline in church attendance and, in particular, the decline in traditional Sunday church attendance across all denominations." She also notes how fresh expressions spread worship activities over a whole seven-day week, allowing local churches to embrace a "multi-congregation model." She highlights the potential of fresh expressions to significantly change the fortunes of church attendance in the twenty-first century.[23]

This book is based on a growing observation across the Western church that inherited churches can and are being revitalized by adopting the fresh expressions approach in the mixed-economy way. While revitalization is not the goal, it is an effect of joining God's disruptive cause amid the fragmentation and isolation of human lives.

Revitalization is a reaction in a series of more complex chain reactions. As we travel through multiple disciplines, stopping for a brief foray in the field of complexity thinking, we will seek to understand revitalization as a manifestation of *emergence*: synergistic relationships occurring between inherited and emerging modes of church that result in a new complex system.

> **Emergence**: Under the broader umbrella of complexity theory, emergence refers to novel and coherent forms (structure, pattern, order) arising from the dynamic self-organizing interplay among elements at successive layers within a complex adaptive system,[24] and the irreducibility of the properties of the whole to the characteristics of its parts.[25]

Exploring the phenomenon of emergence will steer us clear of the pitfall of approaching revitalization as a result that can be engineered or managed by the right quality of heroic solo leader. It is helpful in seeking to understand how impactful even small missional adaptations can be. For instance, one local church's simple decision to offer breakfast to people experiencing homelessness catalyzed a radical transformation of the church and served as a case study of emergence for researchers in the field of organizational management.[26]

This revitalization can take many *forms*: from simply the awakening of a congregation to the spirit of evangelism; an inherited congregation birthing a network of fresh expressions; a congregation birthing a fresh expression that becomes the congregation; a fresh expression that forms organically on the edge is grafted back to an inherited congregation in a mutual exchange of life; a congregation with multiple inherited and emerging modes of church transforming each other; and so on. All of these possibilities can be described as a "re-missioning" of the inherited congregation, and the key word in each equation is *and*.

### *"Andness"*—The Power of Symbiotic Relationship

Fresh expressions of church enable existing congregations, no matter the size, to become in a sense "multi-site." When local churches plant fresh expressions and live in a mixed-economy relationship for a period, a transformation begins to occur. A *blending* takes place as the inherited and emerging modes interact together in a life-giving exchange of *andness*.

The term "mixed economy" traces back to Archbishop Rowan Williams, who appropriated the term from the business world to describe the larger model of ecclesiology emerging in the UK in which inherited and emerging forms of church could function in a symbiotic relationship. This is now embraced as the dominant missional strategy there.[27]

At the simplest level, the mixed economy assumes that no single form of church life is adequate to the missional task before us in the West. We need traditional and new forms of church operating together, not in competition, but as complements. This is a conjunctive form of church, a both/and way.

Stuart Murray, in *Church after Christendom*, writes, "The brightest hope for the church after Christendom is a symbiotic relationship between inherited and emerging churches."[28] Murray uses the term *symbiosis* to describe a relationship that involves two organisms interacting together for the benefit of both.

It is quite easy for us to immediately draw our focus to these exciting new forms of church. Often, we do so at the expense of this principle of "symbiotic relationship" implicit in the mixed economy, which is about a "relationship" between "inherited and emerging churches." As Archbishop Williams has said, "In all kinds of places, the parochial system is working remarkably."[29] Very little attention has been given to the effects on traditional congregations that launch fresh expressions, or the result of that sustained interaction. There exist very few resources on how local churches can successfully cultivate this kind of relationship. This is what I hope to offer in the Deep Roots, Wild Branches series.

## Toward a Blended Ecology

The term "mixed economy" is used for the larger strategy of the Church of England, and US denominations are catching on. However, Archbishop Williams himself has spoken openly about his regretfully ever having coined this term.[30]

The scriptural basis for the language of "mixed economy" is obscured by the prevailing cultural understanding. In the US it unnecessarily creates a false dichotomy and frames the conversation within the corporate narrative of capitalism. The church needs a divorce from that narrative of consumerism to rediscover our own core story. We are stuck in a bad metaphor; let's get out. We need to return to the organic language and images of Scripture, leave behind the sign house of the industrial West, and rediscover the person at the center of our story, in whom the diverse singularity of the church has its being. Jesus is that person; he is the why of our existence.

So, let's leave behind the mixed-economy terminology and proceed with "blended ecology," which is more faithful to the organic language of Scripture and descriptive of the emerging cultural scenario.

While it is never an easy path to change accepted language or enhance an already defined concept, it is the necessary remixing work of pioneering ventures. Jonny Baker, in a discussion about the term *pioneer*, references the problematic nature of finding language on the edge of change. He says, "Language makes and remakes the world, so this is not surprising—finding language is a huge part of the journey to the new."[31]

> **Blended Ecology:** Fresh expressions of church in symbiotic relationship with inherited forms of church, in such a way that the combining of these modes over time blend to create a nascent form. Early in the Fresh Expressions US movement, we began to use the language of "blended ecology," which speaks more potently to the new prevalent family forms, creative process, current cultural realities, and the ancient agrarian language of Jesus' teaching. This will be the primary language of the current work.

Time is the fertilizer of good relationships. Perhaps no one could have foreseen the transformation that would occur as inherited and emerging modes of church lived in relationship together over time, or the blending that would take place.

In *Runaway Species: How Human Creativity Remakes the World*, Anthony Brandt and David Eagleman describe three primary ways that all ideas evolve: breaking, bending, and blending. They propose this threefold way of creativity is the basic framework that divides the landscape of cognitive operations. Human creativity and innovation can be explained through the lenses of these three phenomena. *Bending* is associated with the modifying or twisting out of shape an original. *Breaking* is associated with the dismantling of a whole. *Blending* is the merging of two or more sources.[32]

While some bending and breaking will be necessary in the task before us, revitalization of existing congregations is primarily a work of *blending*. We take the best of both attractional and missional modes and *blend* them together in a new configuration. This allows every local church to simultaneously harness the power of missional innovation (disruptive solution), while cultivating less drastic change in aging congregations (incremental solution).

My wife, Jill, and I have a blended family of eight children. We have taken these once little people who come from different biological and cultural origins, blending them together in one larger body over time. While they have maintained their own individuality and the unique defining characteristics of their biology, now, twelve years later, they have been reconfigured and woven into a new diverse singularity. We have become *one* family, in the deepest sense, no more or less one than any other non-blended family. As challenging as revitalization ministry can be some days, blending our family has been the hardest thing we have ever done. It has also been the most rewarding.

The local church also has some blending work ahead of us. While it is difficult blending inherited and emerging forms of church together in a wonderful new creation, I have discovered it to be the most rewarding work any church could do.

When churches break free from the brick-and-mortar paradigm and embrace the language of ecology, we can see the local church as a habitat within the unique ecosystem of our local community, perhaps within an even larger denominational ecosystem. Leaders of local churches will need to become mini-bishops, who equip, authorize, and release the people in our pews to become ecosystem cultivators in our communities.[33]

Every church will become a church-planting organism. These church plants may look very different from the inherited church that seeds them in the community, but they have the capacity to become the fullness of the church in their own right and give life back to the sending center.

## Starting with the Right Why

Let me be clear: planting fresh expressions to revitalize dying churches is not the right motivation. Fresh expressions are not another save-the-denomination plan. It's the very breaking-pieces-of-the-body-of-Christ-off-and-giving-them-away-to-a-hungry-world plan. The church is not in the self-preservation business, but the self-donation business. The church should always be about cultivating communities of Jesus that are missional, contextual, formational, and ecclesial. Even if the church was not in decline this should be a primary focus of our activity. In fact, declining congregations, plateaued congregations, and thriving congregations that plant fresh expressions are experiencing new forms of life.

Again, the inherited and emerging modes operating together is in the church's very DNA, rooted in the personhood of God.

So, while the purpose of fresh expressions is *not* to revitalize existing congregations, but to reach people the church is not currently reaching, we are witnessing a transformation occur through that sustained interaction.

All over the nation, churches are closing. There is no question we need to plant more churches, replant more churches, revitalize existing churches, merge strategically, and so on. The blended ecology is not a pure revitalization strategy; rather, it is an awakening to the primordial form of the church. It's not a pure church-planting strategy either. The main idea there is usually still about training qualified church planters to plant more churches. The churches they plant are typically expected to construct a building at some point.

*The blended ecology is about releasing the priesthood of all believers within existing churches to plant new ecclesial communities.*

It's not about hiring outside church planters, it's about equipping the so-called laity to plant the seeds of the gospel in their contexts. The gospel can grow in wild, indigenous ways in those soils. Every church becomes multi-site, not by calling in the gurus with their whiteboards and vision statements—but by releasing the pioneering apostles, prophets, evangelists, shepherds, and teachers already in our pews—to cultivate fresh expressions of Jesus in the community. Therefore, this process is meant to be explored in community, by the community that will journey through it. It needs to be shared with a cohort of the willing, no matter how small at first.

We have seen some very small (and even very dysfunctional congregations) completely transformed by adopting this approach. In *Mission-Shaped and Rural*, Sally Gaze observes that not only are small rural churches cultivating fresh expressions, but the inherited congregations that do so are experiencing revitalization.[34]

The only guaranteed way a congregation will surely close its doors, or even a denomination for that matter, is an unwillingness to go through a cruciform process of self-giving death and resurrection, so a new creation can be birthed by the Spirit.

## For the Practitioners—From the Practitioners—Who Eat Their Own Cooking

This book is written for both traditional *and* emerging local churches. I'm writing as someone serving the local church, sharing learnings with other local church persons.

Nassim Nicholas Taleb, speaking of fragility and having skin in the game, highlights a powerful truth, "At no point in history have so many non-risk-takers, that is, those with no personal exposure, exerted so much control."[35]

An unfortunate by-product of the hub-and-spoke corporate denominational structure that helped us thrive for so long is that leaders at the center of a power hub can become entirely out of touch with local realities while still making decisions for them. Revival movements are released from disruption, experimentation, and risk-taking from the bottom-up, not the top-down. The top of a pyramidal structure is dependent on the base, not vice versa. Denominations cannot cultivate renewal in local churches, but local churches can cultivate renewal of denominations.

What I mean by this is not to diminish the existence of denominations, but to release the paralysis of local churches who are waiting for denominational authorities to address their local declining condition. I believe God is asking the local church the Moses question, "What is that in your hand?" (Ex. 4:2). The God who can turn sticks into snakes can breathe new life into dying churches. Revitalization will not come from above at the top of the pyramidal bureaucracy. Each local church is the fullness of the church, or as Bosch says, "the universal church actually finds its true existence in the local churches."[36]

The blended-ecology way offers a way forward in the 60:40 dilemma. *Strategic problem*: allows every local church in the *attractional* mode to continue to form disciples of the 40 percent *and* release them to reach the 60 percent. *Missionary problem:* puts us in the blue waters of the 60 percent to form *emerging* communities of Jesus where people live, work, and play. It restructures the local church to embrace the polarity that Gil Rendle describes between *institution* and *movement*. Every local congregation can maintain the stability and support of an institution (deep roots) and recover our movemental nature (wild branches). To engage a mission field that's "increasingly differentiated by generational, geographic, and global niches and which is constantly morphing with the speed of technology."[37]

When institution and movement learn to live together, something incredible is on the horizon. When local churches can harness the rootedness of the institution, while experimenting in wild movemental ways, dual transformation can occur . . . the blended ecology.

While journeying through the research from many fields, I will also lean heavily on the case study approach. The field interviews are examples of case studies where we can see the blended ecology at work on different scales. Also, I will draw from my own experiences of pioneering fresh expressions, cultivating the blended-ecology way in several declining congregations, and how the Spirit catalyzed revitalization in those communities. My primary living laboratory will be the church I currently serve, Wildwood United Methodist Church, Wildwood, Florida.

While Fresh Expressions has been ecumenical from the start and continues to be so, I will be speaking from my tradition as a United Methodist clergy person, and I will weave the history of the Wesleyan movement throughout this work.

As the cultivator of Fresh Expressions for the Florida Conference and director of (Re)Missioning for Fresh Expressions US, I do also serve in both a national and denominational capacity. In the North Central District (NCD) of Florida where I have been appointed as cultivator for the past four years, I've had the joy and responsibility of working with eighty-six churches on holistic vitality and cultivating fresh expressions.

Most of these churches have been in significant decline for extensive periods of time. The majority of those that are growing are taking advantage of demographic trends, like retirement migrations or urbanization—already-Christians moving into an area—but not by forming new Christians. This is not unique to our area; of the

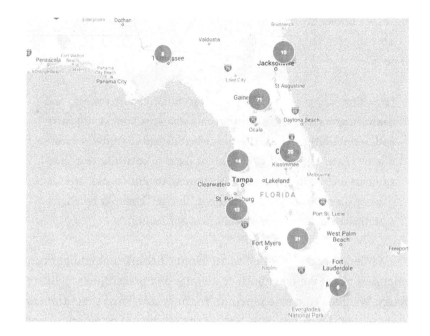

approximately 33,000 United Methodist congregations in the US, only five, or .01%, have been able to maintain an annual growth rate of 10 percent for the past ten years.[38] However, the NCD is now the hub of fresh expressions in the US, with more than eighty fresh expressions in our district alone. Another way to think of this: we have added an entire new district of fresh expressions of church in four years.

I've heard some who adamantly oppose fresh expressions say, "I'm not ready to give up on the church yet." This is a widespread and profound misunderstanding of the movement. I must say I'm not ready to give up on the church yet either. That's why I pioneer fresh expressions. Frankly, I believe some have gone too far to the extreme, as if the church as we know it suddenly has nothing left to offer the new world. It is specifically my love for the inherited church that shapes my passion for this work.

Most books are not written by practitioners. Nassim Nicholas Taleb captures this paradox by identifying primarily two groups of people:

> [The first category consists of] academics, report-writers, and commentators who study future events and write books and papers; and, second category, practitioners who, instead of studying future events, try to understand how things react to volatility (but practitioners are usually too busy practicing to write books, articles, papers, speeches, equations, theories and get honored by Highly Constipated and Honorable Members of Academies).[39]

While I agree with Taleb to an extent, I think he highlights an emerging need. We need both academics *and* practitioners writing books. We need to create pipelines for busy missional practitioners to share their learnings. This book is the product of a community of blended ecology practitioners, failing forward, living in the trenches of real-world revitalization every day. We each follow Taleb's practitioners' ethos; we "eat our own cooking."[40] We are not attempting to provide a one-size-fits-all revitalization approach. We are only sharing the recipes we have concocted in the process of cultivating our own gardens. We hope you find one that will nourish you in your particular place in God's vineyard.

As practitioners, we are grateful to Fresh Expressions US and Seedbed Publishing to have been given the opportunity to publish this book.

FIELD INTERVIEW
# June Edwards

District Superintendent
North Central District, Florida Conference UMC

For June Edwards, the one constant in her life besides her family has been the Methodist Church. She has the Cradle Roll certificate to prove it. The denomination that she has served as a child, youth, and adult, as both lay and clergy, has been an integral part of her life experience. In August 2016, she began one of the most exciting and daunting roles of her pastoral ministry—that of district superintendent—and was appointed to the North Central District of the Florida Conference of the UMC. There are currently eighty-six churches in the North Central District where she is charged to serve as the chief missional strategist. The majority of these churches are experiencing the decline that the rest of Western Christianity is facing, which proves to be a great challenge.

### Can you briefly describe the fresh expression(s) of your district?

When I arrived in the North Central District, I was fortunate that my predecessor, now a bishop in our denomination, had already begun plowing the ground for fresh expressions. Creating a part-time position for someone who was already cultivating and leading fresh expressions, Rev. Michael Beck, and inviting pastors and churches to consider the possibilities of fresh expressions, I found myself joining a conversation that was already in process. Building on an image that arose out of a sermon I preached at my Service of Installation, a district-wide event was planned. A district Fresh Expressions team was formed and soon planning for "From the Steeple to the Streets—13,628 Going" was underway. Every church in the district was asked to mobilize the average worship attendance of their congregations in order to visit identified locations in their communities and do three things—Pray, Observe, and Encounter. This was preceded by a district training event focused on the fresh expressions process to prepare the churches to begin to envision and explore this whole idea of fresh expressions. Now from gatherings in restaurants, pubs, tattoo parlors, and dog parks to yoga, tai chi, prayer on the porch, and dinner church, people have begun the journey to move beyond the walls of the church to those Jesus would have them meet. We are only at the beginning, barely having started the journey into the new and unknown territory. But the vision and energy of Fresh Expressions has begun to take hold, and I have no doubt it will continue to put down deep roots and bear fruit in that future to come that we have yet to know.

## Explain the blended ecology dynamics between the inherited church and your fresh expressions. What kind of tension, if any, goes on between the two?

The challenge before those churches whose pastoral leaders along with the pioneers that join them face when they seek to engage in fresh expressions is the challenge that faces every entrenched system and institution that moves toward innovation and change—there is resistance. The notion that the pastor will be spending time in the community with those that they do not know, nor wish to venture out to get to know, is mystifying to many in the church as we know it. It is counterintuitive to consider that the church would commit resources—both human and financial, for the purpose of creating groups that are not intended to regularly participate in formal worship or in other ministries of the church that take place on their campus. The cry goes out, "Why them? What about us?!" So, ultimately, the blended ecology can lead to conflict as persons fear the loss that comes from change. However, knowing that from the outset helps in riding the rapids of conflict when it does come. It is possible to hold in tension both the ministry requirements of the inherited church and fresh expressions. One image is that of a new church start within an existing congregation. The necessity of the continued vision casting of the kingdom, combined with a large dose of prayer and patience, goes a long way in helping people embrace a new way of being and sending in the church. Another important factor is the need for solid support by denominational leaders who provide oversight and accountability for local church ministry. This provides much-needed cover for pastors who are ready to respond to the call of innovation and creativity to move beyond the church property into the mission field of their communities. To have a foot in both worlds is hard and exhausting work, but it is possible and necessary.

## How have you seen that fresh expressions have a positive impact on the existing congregations? In what ways?

If anything, just having the conversation about fresh expressions has begun to raise the consciousness of some of the need to be the church in the context where they are located. Beyond that, churches that have established ongoing fresh expressions are experiencing renewed energy and vitality, and it is making a difference in their individual personal faith journeys as they discover a much greater and expansive vision of the kingdom. It is shifting the vision outward and opening the door for imagining possibilities for ministry that had not previously existed. And though the intention is not to grow worship attendance or membership, Fresh Expressions has given permission to form new relationships outside the church and created an environment for learning to authentically share one's faith gently and gracefully and can result in some folks coming into the sphere of ministry as well as part of the worshiping community.

There are several examples that come to mind of churches experiencing a positive impact through initiating fresh expressions ministry. The most prominent example would be Wildwood UMC. A small congregation located in what was a sleepy little town until a large retirement development was established nearby now has multiple fresh expressions that have been launched. Though there are those that have resisted this notion, there have been many benefits as a result, and the inherited church is growing because of them. Another small church located in a nearby small community has begun a dinner church. Through this fresh expression, new teams of people have been formed, and they have found a place to share their gifts of hospitality through preparing meals for guests that come to dinner. This church has a food pantry serving clients who are not part of the church. These folks are the ones receiving the invitation to come to dinner and worship. Nearby, the much larger church in the retirement development is reaching seniors in assisted living and skilled nursing facilities, a senior population that their church cannot reach. Residents have accepted Christ that have never done so before. At a large church in a university town, an associate pastor has initiated a runners' group that is connecting with the fitness culture and reaching millennials the inherited church cannot reach.

## Knowing that launching fresh expressions in your congregation involves time, sacrifice, resources, and people power, why do you believe it's worthy to pursue?

Fresh expressions brings us back to what it means to be the church. It's a wake-up call for congregations to take stock and consider what really is their missional purpose. In the Florida Conference, as is the case across the Methodist connection, if it's fall, it's Charge Conference season. In an effort to provide a visual demonstration of the situation most congregations are facing, I took a very unscientific poll asking persons in the churches gathered at the various charge conferences a series of questions:

- *Raise your hands if you have been committed to Christ and/or a member of a church for fifty years or more.* In every case, close to half of those present raised their hands.
- *Raise your hands if you have been committed to Christ or a member of a church for twenty-five years or more.* Again, another large group raised their hands.
- *What about ten years or more?* Maybe eight to ten people responded.
- *What about five years?* Two or three responded.

I then said, "Did you pay attention? What will your church look like in ten years? This is the challenge of the church before you right now." There is no question we must learn to move beyond the walls of the church to connect with the communities around us. I have challenged both pastors and leaders in our district to consider Jesus' ministry as described in the Gospels, asking them to show me the place where it says that Jesus made his way to temple and put a sign out front that reads, "If you want to get to know me, you are welcome to come any time between 11 and 12 on Sunday mornings." Jesus did no such thing. He went to cities, countrysides, crossed bodies of water, and met anyone who came his way. We are called to do the same.

Elaine Heath tells a story of a pastor going into a declining church where she was asked to lead a significant transformation process. As she walked into one of the Sunday school rooms, she described it as smelling of "old hymnals and despair." I'm sure each one of us knows both that image and that smell quite well. We are experiencing great forces at work around us as the new expression of church is being formed in the crucible of transition of generations and culture with no clear path or outcome before us. With the unmistakable smell of old hymnals and despair, of declining churches in our nostrils, we stand atop the mountain Tod Bolsinger describes in the book *Canoeing the Mountains*, where the Lewis and Clarke expedition reaches the summit and gazes out at the unexpected expanse before them. What they saw was not the great waterway they expected to find. Instead, stretched out as far as they could see was more mountains. They realized that from then on, they were "off the map" and would have to innovate and trust their guide, Sacagawea, to find their way. We stand at the same summit and must do the same—let go of our assumptions, presumptions, and plans we now have about the church and innovate and seek guides that can take us to the places we do not know.[41]

The primary work of the church is outside the walls of the church. Fresh expressions give us a vehicle to join God there. We have done a good job teaching churches how to be good institutions, but in so doing we have taken our eye off the ball. The challenge before us now is to do just as thorough a job teaching churches to be missional, because that is our core value and purpose. It does not mean that we let go of the institution that has brought us to this place and time. It just means that we put mission at the center of the primary purpose of the church again and put the institution in its proper place of supporting the work of mission. The mixed economy allows every local church to meet that challenge.

CHAPTER 1
# The New Missional Frontier

> Moreover, that whole generation was gathered to their ancestors, and another generation grew up after them, who did not know the Lord or the work that he had done for Israel. (Judg. 2:10)

> I had to plant the seed in the Masai culture, and let it grow wild.
> —Vincent Donovan (referring to sharing the gospel in a foreign context)[1]

## Good News First

Surely a book attempting to speak an explosively hopeful word in a scenario of decline should start with good news. So, I want to give you that good news right up front: the church of Jesus Christ will never die! At Caesarea Philippi, Jesus told his disciples, "On this rock I will build my church, and the gates of [hell] will not prevail against it" (Matt. 16:18). On a fallible community of Peters and their shaky confessions, Jesus is building his church. Nothing in this world, under this world, no demographic trend, no cultural shift, can ever kill the church of Jesus.

Now unfortunately, my church might die. Your church might die. Denominations might die. The 1950s time-capsule worship as we know it might die (the 2000s time-capsule worship as we know it might die as well). But the church of Jesus Christ, a Spirit-filled body of believers of every race, culture, and nation, the *ecclesia* infilled and equipped by God's own power, and founded and sustained by Jesus himself, that church will never die.

Why, you might ask? Well, that's what this book is all about. As long as there has been a church, the church Jesus is building is always expressing itself in fresh, contextual, formational, missional, and ecclesial ways. In fact, the most consistent aspect of Christian tradition is innovation.

To get outside the cul-de-sac of church questions, we need to explore the complexity thinking of new fields of knowledge. Asking the same old questions will only result in stale answers, no matter how we polish them. I want to lean very much into the wisdom of John Wesley, who said "the world is my parish."[2]

If we dare to dream that the whole earth is our church, and God is already at work there, then what is God doing in other spheres of knowledge? Rather than getting stuck doing doughnuts in the traditional field of religious research, we will follow the Holy Spirit's movement through multiple frameworks: creativity, innovation, entrepreneurialism, sociology, design thinking, organizational management, technology, semiotics, urban planning, ecology, music, and other fields. We will integrate principles from these fields into the readaption of local churches to the shifting mission field.

## The Strategic Problem
*Disruptive Change and Innovation*

Returning to the 60:40 scenario, the strategic problem shows us that, at best, church in its current dominantly attractional form can only reach 40 percent of the people. The twenty-first century has been a time of seismic shifts. We currently live in the post-industrial, knowledge-based era now described as the Information Age. Technology has made the world smaller, in that humanity is now a truly global community. Microelectronic and communication technologies serve as flows that enable us to connect across geographies and time. The new organization of this global community is a complex series of interconnected networks. This new societal order has been termed the "network society."

> **Network Society:** Manuel Castells originally posited that at the end of the second millennium, a new form of society arose from the interactions of several major social, technological, economic, and cultural transformations. Network society consists of a social structure made up of networks enabled by microelectronics-based information and communications technologies.[3]

> **Flows:** Castells posits that the network society is constructed around technologically enabled *flows* of capital, information, organizational interaction, images, sounds, and symbols. Flows are the means through which people, objects, and information are moved through social space. These flows are the social organization, the expression of processes dominating our economic, political, and symbolic life.[4]

While the church exists in a network society, we remain operating under the assumptions of a neighborhood society. Faithfully engaging this emerging societal structure requires an adaptation of our missional approach.

Lesslie Newbigin wrote, "The idea that one can or could at any time separate out by some process of distillation a pure gospel unadulterated by any cultural accretions is an illusion. It is, in fact, an abandonment of the gospel, for the gospel is about the word made flesh."[5] David Bosch also speaks of the "illusion" of a pure gospel unaffected by culture and society. Theology will always interact with and emerge from a specific context with its implicit assumptions.[6]

For instance, eighteenth-century Anglicanism blended the scientific method and rational empiricism of the Enlightenment project with natural and revealed religion.[7] Vincent Donovan shows the church and priesthood as we know it is an example of culturization, which originated from the Greco-Roman and Eastern Byzantine world, not necessarily the servant mentality of Jesus or the New Testament.[8]

Every historical iteration of the church, while maintaining fundamental characteristics, reflects the epoch in which it exists. Leonard Sweet reminds us, "Christianity must bring to every culture an indigenous faith that is true to its heritage with Christianity's becoming a culture faith."[9] All faithful expressions of the church should be a result of this culturization process, a faithful interaction between gospel and context.

The dominant Eurotribal form of the US church is the amalgam of a culture that is fading from view.

**Eurotribal:** Refers to a form of Christianity emerging from Western culture, based in Euro-American imperialism and colonialism. The Eurotribal church resulted from the enculturation of the faith by European Christians, an ethnic expression of the inherited traditions from their countries of origin.

Perhaps it is easy to provide an overly critical analysis of the institutional church with language such as "immobile," "self-centered," and "introverted," or even "an invention of the Middle Ages."[10] Yet, the inherited mode of church is still quite capable of reaching a large share of the population.

Bosch discusses the idea of paradigm shift, which originated with philosopher of science Thomas Kuhn. This is an essential idea for our time. Kuhn shows that when one theoretical framework replaces another it is not an "overnight" event but a process that may take "decades, sometimes even centuries, to develop distinctive contours." Bosch says, "The new paradigm is still emerging . . . For the most part we are, at the moment, thinking and working in *two* paradigms."[11]

Thus, there is a liminality between paradigm shifts, an in-betweenness, while in a sense, the church "in the world but not of it" is never *not* in a liminal space. For "a sharing and intimacy that develops among persons who experience liminality as a group" is the very essence of our *communitas:* the spirit of the community. The church's every present occurs "betwixt and between" God's faithful action in the past and God's promises toward the future.[12] Yet, there are times in history when civilizations themselves are at a threshold, when there is a transitionary phase, marked by instability, ambiguity, and paradox.

---

**Liminality:** From the Latin word *limina*, which means a "threshold." Liminality refers to the transitionary process where change occurs. In anthropology, it's a phenomenon marked by the ambiguity or disorientation occurring in the margin (*limen*) where a subject is described as having no particular place, in between a pre-ritual and post-ritual status. Or simply, "in-between-ness, the stage in the middle of change."[13]

While the church is no stranger to liminality, this is most particularly where we find ourselves today. The coronavirus pandemic accelerated this transformation. Following a relatively stable period of Christendom, the church is in a place of disorientation, in-betweenness, and paradox, called post-Christendom. Anything defined "post-" means it exists in liminality, "after something" without clearly knowing what the "next something" will be.

In the postmodern scenario, we live in a creative tension between two ages, even between two ways of understanding the universe. In the early twentieth century, physicists noted numerous discoveries that challenged the core assumptions of scientific materialism. This "gaping hole" in our understanding of matter led to the field of study called quantum physics.[14]

For example, the idea of an "unbiased observer," a fundamental premise in experimental science, has long been questioned by the *observer's paradox*. Quite simply: results are driven by the observer's methods, goals, etc. Quantum physicists have proved patently false the possibility of an unbiased observer. By many variations of the same "double slit" experiments, they discovered that light or matter only behave like particles in the presence of an intelligent observer—the "observer effect." The oversimplified highlight, the *intelligent observer paradox* shows that even measurement by an intelligent observer causes matter-waves to behave differently.[15]

We are learning there is so much more to reality than what we can observe, test, and replicate. Most of our systems and institutions still function in the mechanistic, reductionist framework, while the "new science" develops further, transforming many of our long-held foundational assumptions. Societally speaking, we see the monoliths of the Industrial Age existing together in the emerging Information Age.

In the appetizer, I suggested every church could create a "disruptive innovation department." Let's go further with this concept.

In the 60:40 problem, the "blue and red oceans" of the corporate world, when companies begin fighting in the red ocean for the limited segment of an established consumer base, the 40 percent, they often die cannibalizing each other. The companies that can get out into the blue oceans and innovate value are the ones that often thrive.[16]

One of the ways companies can reach out into the deep blue and thrive in virtually untapped markets is by catalyzing the powerful process of disruptive innovation.

> **Disruptive Innovation:** A technology whose application significantly affects the way a market functions. A term pioneered by Clayton Christensen, "disruptive innovation" brings disruptive solutions to the market that serve a new population of consumers, thus creating a new market and value network and eventually disrupting an existing market and value network.[17]

For instance, Blockbuster, Kodak, Borders Group, and many others were displaced by this phenomenon. One of the ways an organization harnesses the revolutionary power of disruptive innovation is by finding a path to the consumer, outside and beyond the established hierarchy and institution.

Proactive corporations have created disruptive innovation departments within the larger structure of their organizations. This allows continued focus on developing quality enhancement for existing customers (those in the red ocean), while at the same time releasing the potential of disruptive innovation to reach new customers (those in the blue ocean). Rather than being potentially displaced by a smaller entrant harnessing an innovative technology, established incumbents can out-disrupt the disrupters! In the business realm this is called dual transformation; in the ecclesial realm it's called the blended ecology.

**Dual Transformation**: Dual refers to two simultaneous transformations that reinforce each other, rather than a monolithic process of change. Transformation refers to a fundamental change in form or substance. At the simplest level, dual transformation involves (a) finding ways to better service existing customers, (b) while simultaneously finding ways to reach new customers outside core markets, and (c) then combining the leveraging of a company's valuable assets for new entrepreneurial ventures.

There are three key components involved in the process of dual transformation. For a business, this (a) refers to repositioning and improving the business model to maximize resilience, (b) involves creating a new growth engine, (c) the "capabilities link" involves building on the relevant mix of critical assets, brand, and scale, and managing the interface between the core and the new.[18]

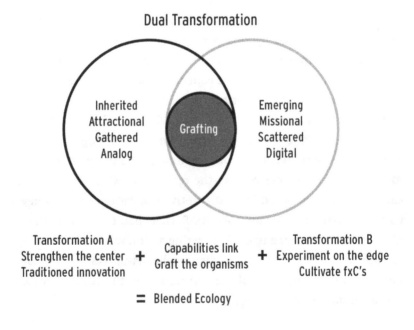

This creates a thriving scenario for corporations, in which existing customers can be properly cared for, while simultaneously harnessing emerging technologies to reach new customers who have been priced out of the market.

The church is perhaps the original pioneer of disruptive innovation, and most renewal movements can provide powerful examples. Adapting the local church in the blended-ecology (dual transformation) way allows every church to have a disruptive innovation department in house, which can catalyze revitalization by reaching new segments of the population. Even churches that have been in existence for hundreds of years can be futurefitted for mission in this way.

> **Retrofitting:** Refers to the addition of new technology or features to older systems. In urban planning, engineers are tasked with retrofitting cities with new green technologies and green spaces to minimize pollution and improve the quality of life.

> **Futurefitting:** Refers to the planting of fresh expressions in communal ecosystems, and (re)missioning inherited congregations in the blended-ecology way, to create a sustainable future. Futurefitting is a more appropriate description of the Spirit's work of cultivating colonies of new creation in existing communities, rather than retrofitting.

More on this later. For now, I am simply making the point that while all the world has shifted around us, the church has failed to adapt. While civilization has been moving at blazing 5G speeds, we have continued to try to attract people to wander the aisles of our rentable materials, desperately attempting to survive through charging late fees and "Be Kind. Rewind." campaigns.

Part of the decline of the US church is exactly because denominations adopted the corporate business model of the twentieth century and continue to employ it, even though it is growing less relevant in a globalized economy. Thriving institutions are learning to adopt a more fluid structural organization to harness the power of these changes.

The church is an institution in the pure sense of the word. In the current perception, institutions are bad and the enemy of postmodern, revolutionary communities of innovation. But this is simply not true. As Alan Roxburgh argues, institutions are formed from the underlying narratives that give meaning and purpose to our lives.[19]

Institutions are good and needed, but they can often become museums. The inherited church, particularly mainline denominational manifestations, has been a central institution of North American society for much of its existence. Institutions that are responsive to the seismic shifts can adapt, grow, and thrive. Institutions that try to preserve the idealized status quo of ages past typically die. Rigid institutionalism is never a good thing.

Some have described an honest acknowledgment of institutional realities and the kind of innovation needed in the church as "traditioned innovation." L. Gregory Jones reminds us, "For most of American history, faith-based communities led the way in innovative approaches in sectors such as education, health, housing, food, just to name a few." He calls for a rediscovery of Christian social innovation, in which the church takes an active role in building, renewing, and transforming institutions to cultivate human flourishing.[20]

Jones goes on to list the Fresh Expressions movement as a strategy deeply rooted in the kind of disruptive innovation the church needs to adopt—traditioned innovation.[21] He catalogs some of the various past social innovation projects of the church, which have become the major institutions of today's society: hospitals, universities, schools, and so on. The Fresh Expressions movement is an entrepreneurial approach that demonstrates the reemergence of Christian social innovation. Traditioned innovation is the way forward for the inherited church; it is the blended-ecology way.

> **Traditioned Innovation:** Is a way of thinking and living that holds the past and future together in creative tension, a habit of being that depends on wise judgment, requiring both a deep fidelity to the patterns of the past that have borne us to the present and a radical openness to the changes that will carry us forward.[22]

Every church can be futurefitted with a traditioned innovation department to unleash dual transformation. Dwight Zscheile, a teacher and author in missional leadership, challenges the Christendom assumptions of the church in the West. He speaks of the "The Great Disintegration" combining a plethora of resources to describe the severity of US church decline. He suggests that inherited churches must challenge long-held assumptions, including dedicated buildings and professional clergy, and refocus energy on reaching disaffiliated neighbors.[23]

He proposes innovating simpler, experimental, more cost-effective and contextually specific expressions of church. Zscheile echoes Jones and others in arguing that the church, largely dependent on sustaining innovation, will need to embrace "traditioned innovation." He describes "the innovator's dilemma" referring to the position clergy in declining systems now find themselves: the challenge of sustaining the established organization while simultaneously embracing and harnessing disruptive innovation. Zscheile describes a process that has parallels with the fresh expressions journey: listening to neighbors, iterative small experiments, failing forward, and improvisation. He also suggests this activity can revitalize inherited congregations.[24]

Let's do some imagining and proceed with the metaphor of a time capsule to illustrate the need for traditioned innovation.

## Time Capsule Church

Charles Taylor suggests in *A Secular Age*, "Most epochs posit a golden age somewhere in the past; and sometimes this is seen as something which can, in favorable circumstances, be recovered."[25] I am quite aware that there has never really been a golden age of Christianity. The New Testament preserves divisions among the disciples over greatness (Luke 22:34), in the book of Acts we see different factions of the faith having disputes right in the genesis of the movement (Acts 6:1), and Paul's letter to those crazy Corinthians deals at multiple points with the dysfunction of the early church.

While there is no golden age of a perfect church somewhere in the past, there are essential ingredients that make the church the church, and if we can strip down to those first principles, we have a better chance at engaging the new missional frontier.

Some of the greatest contributions to the decline of the church have been of our own making. Our self-inflicted wounds have been some of the most painful. The underlying narratives that undergird the institution have been corrupted and lost. The church in the West has become a kind of time capsule, preserving the artifacts and narratives of a specific brand of Eurotribal Christianity. The problem is, what we have preserved in that time capsule consists of some primarily misguided content. The Christendom version of the church is not exactly the right model for all cultures and all times.

> **Christendom:** The iteration of Christianity that began with Emperor Constantine and is now fading as the dominant form of Western Christianity today. It assumes Christianity as the state religion and is primarily attractional in nature. Bolsinger calls it "the seventeen-hundred-year-long era with Christianity at the privileged center of Western Cultural life."[26]

Imagine today, if someone were to take some cassette tapes, pagers, fanny packs, parachute pants, a Sega Genesis, Walkmans, and a Bible, write a note that said, "Hello from 2020!," place them in a time capsule, and bury it. At some point, someone in a future generation would recover that time capsule. They might behold those artifacts with awe and say, "So this is what 2020 was all about!"

However, those items would not be accurate reflections of 2020, more like accurate reflections of the 1980s or '90s. (Let's hope this time capsule wouldn't spark a '90s renaissance based on those artifacts!) In a sense, the church has become that time capsule. Some of what we are preserving as the "church" is not an accurate reflection of the church at all, but a finite, culturally specific brand of the church, from one perspective in time and place. Primarily, what has been preserved is a marred North American imperial form of Christianity that now has a fragmented connection with the culture. There is a deeper narrative that has been somewhat buried.

We will always need pants, not necessarily parachute pants. We will always need music, but not always listen to it on cassette tapes and Walkmans. Bags of some sort to transport everyday personal items—yes; fanny packs—no. Now some of the contents of the time capsule, like the Bible for instance, are an accurate reflection of an essential ingredient of the church. Those essentials can be boiled down to what one of the first organized groups of Christians discerned back in AD 381 in the Nicene Creed (amended from the earlier version in AD 325).

When they were developing their essential identity and institutionalizing the narratives that gave shape to their lives, they decided upon the words used to describe God the Father, God the Son, and God the Holy Spirit. When they got to the church, they captured it in four words, or what we call the four marks: *one, holy, catholic,* and *apostolic*. Perhaps they demonstrated profound wisdom in choosing those simple words. This allowed the church to travel light, to remain reflexive, and to become incarnate within the various cultures throughout time and space.

The church in the West, currently existing in this world of *andness*, among the many dualisms, has largely failed to adapt to these changes and find cultural embodiment. This is where the power of the blended ecology comes into view, where both the inherited and emerging modes of church can harness the conjunctive potential all around us.

## The Missionary Problem: "Another Generation Grew Up"

Once again, we are in a situation similar to Judges 2:10, "Moreover, that whole generation was gathered to their ancestors, and *another generation grew up* after them, *who did not know the L*ORD *or the work that he had done for Israel*" (italics mine). A famous quip attributed to Mark Twain states, "History doesn't repeat itself, but it often rhymes." The missionary problem is concerned with the increasing 60 percent of the population that have no connection with the church.

Len Sweet and I propose in our book *Contextual Intelligence: Unlocking the Ancient Secret to Mission on the Front Lines* that in these times, we need Issacharian leaders, "Of Issachar, those who had understanding of the times, to know what Israel ought to do" (1 Chron. 12:32).[27] In this passage, the people are in a liminal space, a time between the times, various constituencies of the tribes are rallying around David in the wilderness. The tribe of Issachar shows up; the semioticians—known as the sign readers—could see the signs and "knew what to do." We need some semioticians to arise, some Issacharian sign readers, who can read the shifts and know how to engage the culture. IQ (intelligence quotient) and EQ (emotional quotient) are important, but some CIQ (contextual intelligence quotient) is sorely missing and needed in the church today.

**Contextual Intelligence:** From the Latin *contextere*, which means "to weave together"; and the conjunction of two Latin words: *inter*, which means "between," and *legere*, which means "to choose or read." Contextual Intelligence is literally about "accurately reading between the lines" (the threads that intertwine to form a context). So, the ability to accurately diagnose a context and make the correct decisions regarding what to do.[28]

What does it mean for the church to develop some contextual intelligence in this scenario of in-between-ness?

The Greek word for "signs" is *semeia*, from where we get the word *semiotics*. Len Sweet defines semiotics as "the art of making connections, linking disparate dots, seeing the relationships between apparently trifling matters, and turning them into metonymic moments."[29] Sweet goes on to remind us that Jesus instructed us to do semiotics: "You know how to interpret the appearance of the sky, but you cannot interpret the signs of the times" (Matt. 16:3).

Has the church lost our semiotic prowess? How can we awaken from our apostolic amnesia, pay attention, see the signs around us, and attune ourselves to the disruptive work of the Holy Spirit? How can we cultivate some contextual intelligence?

Perhaps the greater challenge is to know what to do. If we take our cues from Jesus and the early church, some adaptation is before us. Jesus and his disciples read the signs, immersed themselves relationally in the context of the people's daily lives, and became a community of transfiguration within it.

Hans Küng demonstrates how throughout various epochs of history, the church has mirrored the culture. Christianity is always "shaped by the particular concrete form it takes at a period in history." He writes further, "Every age has its own picture of Christianity which has grown out of a particular situation, lived out and formed by particular social forces and church communities, conceptually shaped beforehand or afterwards by particularly influential figures and theologies."[30]

We can see strong parallels between the church and dominant societal structures from age to age. The rise and decline of various iterations of the church reflect global cultural movements, as "new forms of faith grow alongside cultural developments."[31] So denominations in the US structured after the twentieth-century corporation can learn from the emergent structures and forms of a globalized network society.

Küng also provides caution that cultural adaptation can of course go too far, when the church "adapts itself and becomes enslaved by the present age or culture, and so abandons itself equally uncritically to the disasters of total changeability.... It must not identify itself completely with the programmes and myths, illusions and decisions, images and categories of any particular world or era."[32] This is both a description of exactly what has happened to the church in the US, and a warning for the task of adaptation before us in a network society.

Authors of *Missional Church* write, "There is no cultureless gospel. . . . the church is always bicultural, conversant in the language and customs of the surrounding culture and living toward the language and ethics of the gospel."[33] Perhaps H. Richard Niebuhr missed something in *Christ and Culture*. It's not Christ *against, of, above, in paradox,* or even as *transformer* of culture. Christ and culture are not equitable concepts. Jesus was *with* culture, incarnate within, while embodying a holiness that transfigured it from the inside. Through *withness*, God uses the fallible church to draw people into the *perichoresis*—the circle dance of the Trinitarian life.

Jesus shows us to "empty ourselves," come fully into the space of the other, and incarnate God's love amid a spiritually hungry world (Phil. 2). We can make this love accessible in new ways, if we don't bury our head in the sand and ignore the changes around us.

We can listen, engage, and find fresh ways to offer communal life in Jesus.

So, while the content of fresh and vintage forms of gospel wine don't change, the delivery mechanism—the wineskins of the church's structures—are always changing within a certain spectrum (Matt. 9:17). These forms must be derived from the very life of Jesus. The gospel must be planted to grow wild in ever-changing contextual soils.

The significance of decline calls for some deep contextual intelligence and some prayerful sign reading. A massive 2010 study by the American Church Research Project, surveying more than 200,000 churches, discovered that about 17 percent of the population attended church on any given Sunday. It is not a secret that the overall population growth rate far outpaces the church's rate of growth. These figures are even more disconcerting than other research that puts regular church attendance much higher (around 40 percent). Unfortunately, numerous studies demonstrate people report going to church more than they really do.[34]

Robert Putnam notes that careful survey comparisons reveal that parishioners "misremember" whether they attended services, overreporting attendance to a tune as high as 50 percent.[35] In clergy circles the term *Chreaster* (those who attend church on Christmas and Easter) has been used to describe these "regular attenders." What some data are really measuring is whether North Americans think of themselves as regular attendees.[36]

Furthermore, Thom Rainer's research demonstrates that 65 percent of current church attendees come from the "builder" generation, those born before 1946.

These staggering statistics, and the convergence of other forces, led Lovett Weems to write of a coming "death tsunami" for the United Methodist Church. Weems's work can be easily applied to churches across the theological and denominational spectrum.

## Churchgoing in the United States[37]

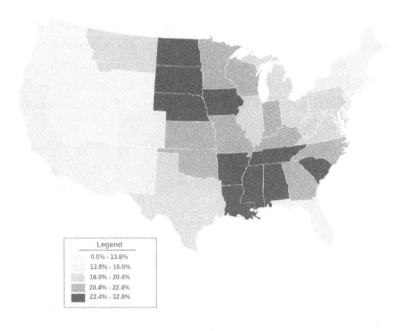

## Generations Involved in Church[38]

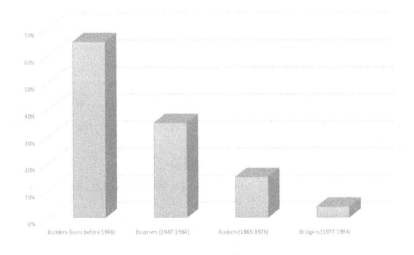

He advocates for churches in a decline spiral to reset their financial baseline and to reorient their congregations around a new criterion, "reaching people, and the whole system needs alignment toward that goal."[39] Adopting the fresh expressions approach helps churches realign in this way. This is partly what creates the melee that Travis Collins describes as "mecessary," as many churches in decline are primarily focused on taking care of their own, preoccupied with money to keep the church alive.[40]

Weems offers staggering statistics showing decreases of what he calls the "people down" trend in United Methodism (decreases of percentages from 1968 to 2009):

| | |
|---|---|
| Number of churches | 80% |
| Worship attendance | 78% |
| Membership | 71% |
| Professions of faith | 57% |
| Children and youth | 44% (from 1974 when reported for first time)[41] |

He makes a sobering statement: "Aging members with increased assets and generosity cannot substitute forever for the neglect of the basics on which all giving depends—changed lives and transformed communities."[42] An aging membership, coupled with a projected rise in deaths predicted between 2021 and 2050, places the US church on the edge of a "death tsunami" like something we have never experienced before.[43]

The new missional frontier requires a both/and approach to neighborhood and network.

FIELD INTERVIEW
# Verlon Fosner

Pastor of Westminster Community Church,
Pioneer of Dinner Church Collective

Doctor Verlon Fosner has lead Westminster Community Church in Seattle, Washington, since 1999. In recent years, the congregation transitioned from a traditional proclamation church into a multi-site dinner church. Verlon holds a doctorate of ministry from Assemblies of God Theological Seminary and has written several books: *Dinner Church, Dinner Church Handbook,* and *Welcome to Dinner, Church.*

### Can you briefly describe the fresh expression(s) of your church?

Our fresh expressions churches are developed around the dinner table theology that was historically employed during the Apostolic Era. We serve large feasts at dinner time in community spaces located in sore neighborhoods, along with worship music, artists painting sketches from the gospel, and a speaking segment focused on something from the Gospels. Following the speaking and group prayer, the Christ-followers who are eating and sitting among the guests engage in discipleship conversations as the opportunity presents itself and the Spirit leads.

## Explain the blended ecology dynamics between the inherited church and your fresh expressions. What kind of tension, if any, goes on between the two?

Though our church was a traditional church for eighty-five years, we have now shifted to make our dinner churches the front burner congregations of our ministry. Our only traditional gathering is held on Saturday nights, a worship service to strengthen our pastors and core teams so they can go strengthen their dinner congregations throughout the week. There is not any tension, because the traditional congregation has taken on a supportive and supply-line role for our front-lines congregations.

## How have you seen the fresh expressions have a positive impact on the existing congregation? In what ways?

Our congregation had become hopelessly ingrown. However, once we started our first fresh expression (FX) congregation, a new sense of mission began to flood into the existing congregation. Missional envy (in a healthy sense) started to form, and soon everyone wanted to get out to the front edges of evangelism and work in one of the dinner churches. We started to say, "Attend the weekend gathering for yourself, but attend the dinner church for the benefit of others. And if you have to miss one, make it the weekend gathering." That repeated phrase changed us all. Our FX congregations were on the frontlines of evangelism, and that is where the most potent sort of mission exists. Once our long-term saints went to the frontlines, they brought that same spirit back. Soon it was dominating our weekend gatherings, our classes, our leadership meetings, and even our boardroom. It truly was like leaven that spread through the whole ministry.

## Knowing that launching fresh expressions in your congregation involves time, sacrifice, resources, and people power, why do you believe it's worthy to pursue?

For a church to rediscover its mission and calling, it needs a praxis to form them. All the talk in the world simply will not reshape the soul of the church; a Great Commission environment is needed. And if a FX congregation is anything, it is a Great Commission environment.

# CHAPTER 2
# Post-Everything— Six Shifts

> Now all the Athenians and the foreigners living there would spend their time in nothing but telling or hearing something new. Then Paul stood in front of the Areopagus and said, "Athenians, I see how extremely religious you are in every way. For as I went through the city and looked carefully at the objects of your worship, I found among them an altar with the inscription, 'To an unknown god.' What therefore you worship as unknown, this I proclaim to you." (Acts 17:21–23)

> Christians are hard to tolerate, I don't know how Jesus does it.... I'm one of them.
>
> —Bono

I want to further explore the sketches of the major shifts that have contributed to the decline of Christianity in the US I introduced in the appetizer. These shifts are moving at an unprecedented rate of speed in human history. The multiplicity of change is pushing us into a post-everything age. There is no going back to "normal." We must now learn to live into a new normal. The future has come in the night and we are here now. COVID-19 thrust us toward the new world that was forming beneath the surface for quite some time.

Every church had to become a distributed church overnight, whether we liked it or not. Distributed simply means "spread" or "shared." It has been a word that we of the Fresh Expressions movement have often held together in creative tension with the collected church. We have also used the words "gathered and scattered," "centered and dispersed," "attractional and missional," or "digital and analog." The key word for us has been *and* as we have advocated a blended ecology of church, where these modes of church live together.

This chapter is meant to be purely descriptive. Some of these emerging realities are a result of the fragmented nature of sin-broken humanity. Missional adaptation does not mean accepting these changes wholesale or letting culture trump scriptural truth. It means changing our missional posture so we can engage these realities in a Jesus-faithful way. We will return to each one of these sketches later to demonstrate how the blended-ecology way is capitalizing on the energy of these shifts and utilizing the emerging societal structure to seed the gospel in the soils of this new frontier. Much more could be said here. This section is not meant to be an exhaustive list, only a primer to the conversation of how God is bringing forth a new world amid these changes.

I work from the assumption that change is not bad. Life is a process of change. If something is not changing, it's not alive. If we as the church grow in our contextual intelligence and understand these changes, we can avoid more self-inflicted wounds and begin the process of adaptation and healing. What if we saw each of these shifts not as problems to be solved, but opportunities to join what God is doing in the world? What if we could somehow get into the stream of the Holy Spirit's disruptive work, releasing ourselves to that power?

To understand the dynamics of the change requires us to keep one foot in what is, and one in what can be. In our rigid bureaucratic institutionalism, we are watching profound missional opportunities pass us by. Alan Hirsch writes, "We are living at the end of Christendom (the settlement) and peering into the rest of this century, a frontier filled with challenges, dangers, and opportunities."[1] So, while the church is unraveling as we know it, the Spirit whispers of a new reformation.

Ultimately, we will need to abandon the safety of research about people and risk entering relationship with people. We can learn about people from statistics and surveys, but we cannot know people until we enter their world as listeners. Later I will share a process for how we can do that; for now, let's clean out the clutter of our time capsule and get down to the essentials.

There are currently four major US adult living generations. While I'm aware there is much debate about these broad categorizations, for our purposes, following the lead of Paul Taylor and the Pew Research Center, we simply label them in the following manner:

**The Millennials**: Born after 1980; the first generation of digital natives

**Gen Xers**: Born between 1965 to 1980; entrepreneurial rebels, loners, distrustful of institutions

**Baby Boomers**: Born between 1946 to 1964; exuberant youths, led countercultural upheavals

**Silent Generation**: Born between 1928 to 1945; builders, endured World War II, largely conservative.[2] (These descriptive words are commonly accepted generalizations.)

## 1. Church Identity Crisis

*From Constantine, to US Imperial Corporation, Back to Caves*

The first shift is within the church itself. In a sense, the US church is in the middle of an identity crisis. We suffer from a kind of missional amnesia, in which a fundamental aspect of our identity has been lost. This problem has a deep history. The North American version of Christianity that most of us inherited goes back to Emperor Constantine in AD 313. Up until Constantine, Christians were a rogue, and periodically illegal, religious movement that experienced several rounds of imperial persecution. At times, the primitive church met in secret spaces, subversively scratching the fish symbol (*Ichthys*) on cave walls to identify meeting places. They riskily met under threat of death.

This small renegade movement, with no buildings, no professional clergy, no committee meetings, between the time of Jesus' death on the cross in the 30s and Constantine in the 300s, grew numerically across vast geographical distances. With no program of evangelism, no formal mission statements, and very little resources, they became a force to be reckoned with. Alan Kreider offers a wonderful and extended analysis of what he terms "the improbable growth" of the early church in those days. He says, "the expansion of the churches was not organized, the product of a mission program; it simply happened."[3]

While the growth of the church up until that point is difficult to explain, the explosion of growth after AD 312 is quite explainable. Emperor Constantine, with his vision of a cross and voice from the sky saying, "in this sign conquer," changed the course of history and the identity of the church forever. Elaine Heath and Scott Kisker remind us that Constantine had a history of self-aggrandizing visions and that "this vision with several military victories got him into power."[4] Perhaps the emperor was operating more out of a political necessity than spiritual conversion—he was not actually baptized until he lay on his deathbed twenty-five years later in AD 337. Regardless, he transformed the faith like few individuals in history.

Emperor Constantine's adoption of Christianity as the state religion birthed the Constantinian system that continues into our inherited US version of the church.[5] Initially this adoption had an incredible and powerfully relieving effect for those early Christians. First, they no longer had to be arrested or killed for following Christ. Secondly, confiscated properties were eventually returned. The blending of religion and state power also had negative effects. The church devolved at times into a hotbed of scandal, gross extravagance, and hypocrisy. The professional clergy model was born and, in a sense, Jesus was dethroned, replaced by the emperor. Vast church building projects were launched of unparalleled grandeur in human history.

In 1517, Martin Luther nailed his 95 Theses to the door of the Wittenberg Castle Church. Inadvertently, he created a major fresh expression within the stream of Christendom. Thus, in the sixteenth century this began a fragmentation process that resulted in the multitude of competing mini-Christendoms of denominations today.[6] Now, the "protest-ant" (from the word *protest*) movement has been largely domesticated and functions in the greater, attractional only, Christendom mode.

As we define these terms, remember these are generalizations, but they describe the dominant language and thinking of our day. Please note, a "come to us" approach can be missional in some contexts.

**Attractional Model:** A model that consists of a "come to us" kind of marketing strategy. "If you build it they will come" is a motto of the attractional church.

**Missional Model:** A model that consists of "we go to them" kind of strategy. An incarnational and relational approach where we enter the world of the other and stay.

The version of Christianity we have inherited in the West is not the fish-scratching, secret-meeting-in-caves version. It is primarily an *attractional only* model—*build it and they will come*—overseen by professional clergy, who receive special tax exceptions from the empire. It operates in the Christendom assumptions that we are a Christian nation and most of the people are already Christian. There is expectation in this arrangement that good people will go to church, as it is a cultural norm. The empire and the church work together as complementing institutions that shape the behavior and societal norms. Gregory Boyd calls this "the myth of America as a Christian nation."[7]

In *God, Neighbour, Empire: The Excess of Divine Fidelity and the Command of Common Good*, Walter Brueggemann identifies three "markers of empire" that recur in ancient and modern imperial iterations: (1) Extraction: empires extract wealth from the vulnerable and transfer it to the powerful. (2) Commoditization: empires reduce everything and everyone to a disposable commodity, bought, sold, traded, possessed, and consumed. Everything and everyone has a price. (3) Violence: empires enforce imperial policies and practices of commoditization and extraction with violence.[8]

Brueggemann goes on to say that while there are other empires in the global arrangement, globalization is primarily spearheaded by the United States, "with its inexhaustible consumerism, its unrivaled military power, and its growing economic gap between haves and have-nots, is a forceful, willful practitioner of extraction and commoditization."[9] While globalization brings great benefits overall for most of humanity, a small handful of very powerful people are benefiting disproportionately.

**Globalization:** Michael Moynagh and Richard Worsley define this simply as the world becoming "more interdependent and integrated," with physical, cultural, and virtual dimensions.[10] This is the movement toward a single global community through integration of markets, trade, nation-states, communications, and technologies, which implies the opening of local and nationalistic perspectives to a broader outlook of an interconnected and interdependent world with free transfer of capital, goods, services (and now viruses) across national frontiers.[11]

Some see imperial parallels between the United States and ancient Rome, the environment in which the early church took shape. For instance, they compare the oligarchy of Rome's world-dominating power, with the corporatocracy of the United States, and the church as its "compliant acolyte" functioning in much the same way as Caesar's imperial cult.[12]

Brueggemann's most disturbing implication is that empires legitimate their practices with religious allegiances: the imperial cult as the handmaiden of empire. In this arrangement, the power of God and state are combined. In the US, the Christian church has been used in this way going back to our founding forefathers. Slavery, racism, and the subjugation of women is legitimated using Scripture. The church backed and gave credibility to the empire in these practices. God encourages us to be champions of violence, commoditization, and extraction, in God's name, as God's chosen people.[13]

In the *World Development Report 2006*, the World Bank directly acknowledges the inequality of global markets, "and the rules governing their functioning have a disproportionate negative impact on developing countries."[14] Just ponder for a moment how in 2014 more than 2.1 billion people were overweight, compared to 850 million who suffered from malnutrition. In 2010, famine and malnutrition killed around one million people; obesity killed three million.[15] Hidden from the sight of the general populace is the global exploitation that has taken place to feed the cycles of extravagance. Some are disturbed by this North American version of Christianity, one where flags and crosses are seen as equally powerful symbols on sanctuary walls.

Gen X and millennials seem to be questioning this amalgamation of Christ and empire. They overwhelmingly describe the church in survey data as "too concerned with money and power, too focused on rules, and too involved in politics."[16] The way the church has been used to authorize exploitive capitalistic practices seems to be disturbing for younger people. They report the hostile, politically divided, and hypocritical nature of so-called Christians is not appealing.

The images of gun-wielding patriots, with crosses around their necks, killing in the name of God is being significantly questioned. Perhaps one way to understand the Constantinian shift is this: in the second century, *no* Christians could be soldiers; by the fourth century there was a mandate that all Roman soldiers must be *only* Christians.[17]

Gregory Boyd says, "The truth is that the concept of America as a Christian nation, with all that accompanies that myth, is actually losing its grip on the collective national psyche, and as America becomes increasingly pluralistic and secularized, the civil religion of Christianity is losing its force."[18] The Christendom model as we know it, our Western institutional version of the faith, is disintegrating. The attractional model is not connecting with a growing number of the population.

While the church's form has always grown out of its interaction with context, the danger is the corruption of the church. As Hans Küng notes, cultural adaptation is not always good, "for that could mean adapting itself to the evil, the anti-God elements, the indifferentism in the world."[19] Emerging generations describe the vast disconnect between the Jesus of Scripture and the church of North America. The church seems to have lost its prophetic street cred, and even more damaging, our legitimating narrative.

Alan Roxburgh discusses at length how Protestant denominations in the US adopted the organizational structure of the twentieth-century corporation and benefited greatly. Adapting this corporate structure helped churches to thrive in that season, as the legitimating narrative of United States culture became a perfect bedfellow for the church. Churches took up the language of rationalized efficiency, professional management, and bureaucratic structures.[20]

Gil Rendle refers to this season in which the US church flourished as an "aberrant time." An aberration is not the norm; it is in fact "a departure from the normal state of affairs."[21] The conditions that caused the Christendom, largely attractional, corporate iteration of the church to thrive in the US have changed. Rendle proposes that this is not a technical problem with a technical solution; this is an adaptive challenge. Perhaps it's like learning to live in an entirely new ecosystem. The church, planted in jungle conditions, must now learn how to live in a desert. This identity crisis is centered around a mental model formed in the aberrant time; the deeper legitimating narrative has faded from living memory. It seems in the shadow of post-Christendom; the church is back in the caves again.

Of course, while the church has many blemishes, she also has many beauty marks. Much of the hyper-critical stereotypes of emerging generations fail to take into consideration how the church has transformed the world for the better in incalculable ways. As mentioned earlier, through social innovation the church has gifted the world with hospitals, universities, shelters, and food banks— not to mention the movements like abolition, women's suffrage, civil rights, and so on, each largely pioneered by Christian leaders. Christians have served as the moral leaven in ancient and modern times, lifting the gaze of humanity to the higher virtues.

In the ancient world, where greed and power were often unchecked and newborn babies were left to die on the side of Roman roadways, the church brought the radical countercultural values of charity and the sanctity of life.

David deSilva describes the New Testament culture of honor and shame, and how the story at the center of the church's faith forces a decision concerning the reliability of the world's estimation of these concepts.[22] To live as a slave (a Jew under the yoke of Roman subjugation) and be crucified (an intentionally degrading death reserved for the criminals at the lowest end of the shame spectrum) would not be a story celebrated as honorable.[23] In fact, it completely inverts the dominant cultural values.

Philippians 2, for instance, captures the shame-honor reversal that Paul describes more fully elsewhere as a "stumbling block" and the "scandal of the cross" (1 Cor. 1:18–31). DeSilva calls Philippians a "fine study in the application of the ethos of unity and harmony" in which the "mind of Christ" shows that "only a spirit of humility, a willingness to sacrifice what we may hold dear for the sake of love for the other, a willingness to 'die to self' will contribute to restoring unity in the church where it has been breached and preserving it where it is now threatened."[24]

Even today there are churches all over the world exemplifying these values.

## 2. Emerging Economy
*From Big Faces to Bitcoin*

We are amid a time of incredible economic change. The Dow Jones Industrial Average suffered the largest point drop (2,997 points) in history on March 16, 2020. The 2020 Stock Market Crash was precipitated by concerns over the ongoing 2019–20 coronavirus pandemic. Even before the current crisis, millennials were inheriting the worst economy since the Great Depression. While the poverty of the 2020s is certainly different than the poverty of the 1930s, there is a real crisis. The financial system itself is unsustainable even before the current skyrocketing rates of job loss and the closure of businesses. The housing market crash, persistently high unemployment, rise in wealth for the minority, income inequality for the masses, and stagnation in standard-of-living growth are the persistent North

American hardships for more than a decade. Furthermore, there is a rising problem of generational equity. For instance, the young are paying taxes to support a level of benefits for the old from which they themselves will never benefit.[25]

The economic dilemma of this emerging generation is created by a convergence of unemployment, globalization, automation, foreign competition, a faltering education system, and massive educational debt.[26] With the 2008 economic collapse still prominent in the rearview mirror, and now the 2020 crash, anxiety is the norm. The postindustrial, digital age has dawned. The late twentieth-century corporate model is being made mostly irrelevant, and so are the denominations who structure themselves after it. Anthony Brandt and David Eagleman say simply, "In recent decades, the world has found itself transitioning from a manufacturing economy to an information economy."[27] We are living in the middle of that transition.

With this globalized and knowledge-based economy as the new financial reality, there is a growing chasm between the super-wealthy and everyone else. One percent of the world's population now controls over half the world's wealth.[28] This shift from a localized economy to a globalized economy is having an impact on the church. The massive unbalanced distribution of wealth has significantly decreased the existence of a middle class.

Globally speaking, there is less extreme poverty than in the history of the world, and for the first time, poverty is not growing just because the population is.[29] However, in the context of the West, a small percentage of the population is creating categories of super wealth never seen in world history. Perhaps there is a dark side to progress. Smaller, vulnerable nations are being exploited to create super wealth for a tiny minority. The effect on North American society is what Paul Taylor calls "a hollowing of the middle."[30]

From a practical standpoint, the eroding of the middle class has destroyed the once solid volunteer base of churches. Members no longer enjoy relatively steady 9–5 jobs, pension plans, paid vacations, and weekends off. The emerging North American economic landscape has created a 24/7 work culture, where an increasing share of the population works on weekends to get on top financially. What little free time is afforded is not likely going to be spent at the church.

The emerging economy has changed societal structure and the rhythms of community itself. Globalization creates conditions that encourage migration, resulting in a disconnection of peoples with native culture and place.[31] With the growing elimination of extreme poverty, increased mobility, and mass access to decentralized education, people no longer base their identity in a town. Locally, increased mobility is allowing longer commutes, pursuit of jobs, and decreased loyalty to a central space where we would live and work our entire lives.[32] It is becoming unusual for someone to stay in the town where they were born. Industry has shifted to a networked, knowledge-based model, and people follow their vocation. The volunteerism that was the lifeblood of the local church for the past fifty years is disappearing. Churches have not adapted to these massive changes.[33]

An example of the kind of seismic shifts that are occurring financially, particularly the kind of decentralization on the horizon with the growing reality of globalization, can be illustrated by Bitcoin. Ultimately, the technological forces that are transforming the world are leading toward access, collaboration, and sharing, and away from possession and ownership narratives. Globalized civilization is moving toward redefining and potentially abolishing the center of all current economic systems . . . money itself. In our lifetime, we may see the decentralization of minted currency. Physical currency is becoming impractical in a global economy.[34]

**Bitcoin:** A type of digital currency in which encryption techniques are used to regulate the generation of units of currency and verify the transfer of funds, a blockchain structure operating independently of a central bank.[35]

Bitcoin was the first attempt at a decentralized, distributed currency that needed no central bank. There was no institution tasked with accuracy, enforcement, or regulation. Bitcoin is a shared, networked system of currency, powered by a mathematical technology called "blockchain." This radical technology has the capacity to decentralize most systems. This distributed database served as a disruptive innovation to the entire economic system.[36]

This is currency whose power lies in math, not governments. While some see Bitcoin as a failed attempt (unfortunately it was immediately harnessed and used illegally in the trafficking of narcotics), it planted the seeds of a disruptive innovation yet to be comprehended. The blockchain technology now being developed in various systems experimentally may become the new normal of a globalized economy. Eventually, the failing inherited economic system will be replaced.[37]

The church can interpret this sign as a step in a coming transformation and realize that networking, accessing, sharing, and stewarding is the language of our core narrative, rather than possessing, extracting, commoditizing, and violence. Throughout history, the church has adopted and transfigured the societal structure to offer communal life with Jesus. The church can appropriate the polycentric blockchain structure at a local level to futurefit existing congregations for mission. What would be the implications if we learned to restructure ourselves appropriately in a networked, globalized society? Would this perhaps even move us more fully toward a scriptural design for human community?

One of the greatest threats in this church age dubbed the "great decline" is a financial one. Closure is the outcome of local churches that become financially unsustainable. While some churches can be spiritually dead yet remain propped up financially by endowments, low expenses, and a handful of folks that tithe faithfully, many churches die because they can no longer afford to operate. Once a church can no longer support a "professional clergy" person in the current model, they typically cross the line of sustainability.

Older congregations have accumulated properties and buildings over the years that are left primarily empty. As those buildings wear down, the price of renovation becomes greater than a congregation can sustain. The strategy of many denominations is to close those churches, sell the often highly valuable properties, and use the resources to plant new congregations. In many cases, this may be simply rearranging the chairs on the *Titanic*. Conventional church plants often grow by attracting already-Christians away from declining congregations. Very few churches are growing by reaching not-yet-Christians.

How can the church lead the way of reconciliation in the current economic scenario? Can there be healing between the growing resentment between generations? Can we reclaim the shifting language of networking, accessing, sharing, and stewarding as our own again?

## 3. America (Re)mixed

*From* Leave It to Beaver, *to* The Brady Bunch, *to* Modern Family

One of the greatest shifts in the West at large has been in the family itself. Many churches have not adapted to the restructuring and transformation of family units. Even the need to have a family in the sense of settling down and having children is undergoing transformation. While using the term "post-family" would be going too far, "post-familialism" is an accurate description of the reality the church must engage in a missional way.[38]

The definition, structure, and societal expectations of family have changed. The *Mission-Shaped Church* report, borrowing data captured in a variety of statistical surveys published in *Social Trends*, notes several shifts that translate across Western society: rises in divorce, single parents, stepfamilies, adults who decide not to have children, cohabitating couples, and single persons, all contribute to the decline of the inherited church.[39]

Just consider the evolution of a prevalent North American cultural phenomenon—the sitcoms, or situational comedies—that have portrayed family life being broadcasted into US homes for seventy years. *Leave It to Beaver* is almost beyond generational memory now, but it captured the 1950s ideal nuclear family structure (i.e., two parents—a man and a woman—and usually two children). This show featured two sons, Wally and Beaver, who kept audiences laughing with simple comical debacles common to 1950s North American families.

By the 1970s, *The Brady Bunch* burst onto the scene, in some ways ahead of its time but reflective of the newly emerging reality of divorce and the remixing of familial structures. Carol and Michael Brady bring their families together with six children (three boys and three girls), plus a dog and their housekeeper, Alice. While the blended family unit was somewhat of an emergent improvisation then, this is no longer the case.

At the genesis of 2010, *Modern Family* was released. This family is complete with adoptions, cohabitation, straight, gay, multicultural, and blended traditional. This is an accurate reflection of the change in familial dynamics to date. The blended family, where parents bring children together from previous relationships, and the single-parent family have been growing steadily as the prevalent family forms in the US. The blended family as a dominant form presents massive challenge and opportunity for the church today.[40]

This is America (re)mixed. While society is interracial, multicultural, blended, and predominantly inclusive of people who identify as LBGTQ, the church is faltering on how to share the transformative gospel in these new soils. Interracial relationships were taboo only decades ago. In the 1960s they were actually illegal in sixteen states. Today about 16 percent of all marriages in the US are a blending of races and ethnicities and are considered simply normal by the general populace.[41] Furthermore, the tens of millions of Hispanic and Asian immigrants who have made North America home since 1965 are not creating a melting pot of stew but a completely different blended flavor of soup. New remixes of humanity are emerging that fall outside our common definitions. The idea of a checkerboard kind of US, with black, white, and a couple minorities, is over.

As an "xennial cusper" born in 1980 (a blend of Gen X and millennial), I experienced an '80s elementary school that read about segregation and the civil rights movement as history. We associated, dated, and formed friendships across racial boundaries. We listened to heavy metal, gangster rap, and pop with equal appreciation. Those inherited narratives of racism were already dissolving. Where my generation was at least "multi-racial" growing up, my children are now "interracial."

There is only one race—the human race. But today when we drop our kids off at school, or have their friends over, I am wondering what blending of ethnicities created these new marvelous humans. What was history to us is now ancient history to my children. They don't seem to even think about skin color the way we did just thirty years ago.

In our blended family of eight children, my stepdaughter Kaitlyn and our son-in-law Kemar have created a newly minted human that transcends all current categories of beauty named Gabriella

Gracelynn. Kaitlyn has a mixture of Native American and German on her biological father's side, with German, Irish, and a touch of Swedish on my wife's side. Kemar comes from native Jamaican ancestors. Hence, Gabriella has light golden eyes, with caramel skin and curly hair, a blend of her Jamaican-Native American-German-Irish-Swedish ancestry. She is literally an entirely new category of splendid, a new creation indeed.

Our adult children are appalled at things like the 2017 Charlottesville incident, which shocked them into the awareness of a lurking sickness of racism beneath the cultural surface, preserved in the highest levels of institutional leadership.

Among this big, beautiful, blended, and remixed United States, the Sunday morning church hour continues to be the most segregated hour of the week. In an interracial society, we are still using words like "multi-racial" in the vision statement banners hanging in our sanctuaries. The categories of race that defined our cultural reality themselves have changed. Emerging generations report the lack of diversity and the segregationist nature of some local churches is unattractive.

This is not to mention the mounting tension among the generations themselves. There are two trends significantly shaping our future. In the US, people are not having as many babies, and they are living much longer. Because of the wonderful advances in science and medicine, the old paradigm of high infant mortality and short-life expectancy has been replaced by low infant mortality and long-life expectancy.[42]

Leading scientists speak of revolutionary technologies that will extend life even further. Through advances in nanotechnology, they claim we will be able to restore and replicate organs and heal any disease. Neuroscientists speak of a day when our consciousness will be downloaded.[43] The graying of the population is a trend unlikely to change. This is having a huge impact on the nature of families.

For the most part, the church continues to function, structure, and program to the *Leave It to Beaver* days. Our systems are designed for the nuclear family model. Essentially, we have not discerned how to missionally engage *The Brady Bunch* yet, much less *Modern Family*. How can we lift up the life-changing message of Jesus in the cultural milieu? How do we adapt our missional approach in the turbulence of these changes? The US church is not exactly wired for adaptation or speed.

For example, one place we have largely failed to respond to and offer graceful habitats is for divorcees. Single parents have described a sense of alienation in some traditional worship settings. They feel awkward, as if they are in a 1950s rerun. There is also a rise in young people without kids, who don't connect to the nuclear family–based activities of the church. Beyond the whole seemingly odd time-capsule reality of the church, there are simply logistical challenges with these emerging shifts.

One practical implication for the church is the reality of visitation in these new parental arrangements. Most children in single, blended, and divorced familial contexts have shared custody arrangements in which they are with the non-custodial parent on rotating weekends. This disrupts any regular Sunday morning participation and the kind of communal bonds that need to form with children and youth if they are to sustain a relationship with the church.[44]

Many churches are still dying on the hill of the single Sunday morning worship experience. The amount of weekend family activities the church must compete with include youth sports leagues, social functions, working parents, Disney World parents (those who make up their absenteeism with endless recreational weekend experiences), and working people that only have one day to sleep in! The family has changed all around us; the gospel the church bears has the power to transfigure the fragmented aspects of these realities. It requires adaptation on how we reach people and invite them into a life of discipleship.

## 4. New *Mayflower*
*From Christendom to Pantheon*

On November 21, 1620, a ship called the *Mayflower* carrying a group of English Separatists, known today as pilgrims, landed on the tip of Cape Cod at what is now Provincetown, Massachusetts. These brave Christian pioneers and entrepreneurs journeyed to the new world partly to freely practice their nonconformist brand of Christianity. The Separatists had given up attempting to reform the Anglican church, and so a fresh expression was born in the North American colonies as they sought to create a new environment where they could live and worship freely. Those forbears also held that desire together with the deep conviction of religious freedom for all. This is the impulse that created our inherited version of the US church. A new *Mayflower* attitude is sailing across the United States religious ocean.

North America has become the most religiously diverse nation in the world. The Pew Research Center reports that all Christian groups are declining, while the fastest growing demographic is the so-called "nones," those that report "none" when asked to identify religious affiliation. (Between 2007 and 2014 this group increased from 16.1 to 22.8; that's up 6.7 percent in seven years.) The only other growing demographic according to this data is "non-Christian faiths." That means 23 percent of all adults and more than a third of all millennials now find a home in the tribe called "none."[45]

The US population is growing tremendously, but conversely the number of Christians is shrinking. To clarify, between the years of 2007 and 2014 North America's population grew by 18 million people, while the number of adults who identify as Christian declined by 7 percent. There are 17 million self-described agnostics and atheists and 39 million nones. To put it bluntly, this is a seismic shift that indicates the potential death of Christianity as the leading religion. The data show this trajectory will continue.[46]

We must carefully seek to understand the perspective of these so-called nones and the growing tendency of disaffiliation. Certain myths are perpetuated about this group that are not exactly accurate. A 2012 survey offers some interesting insight. Of the 46 million unaffiliated adults, 68 percent believe in God, 37 percent self-describe as "spiritual but not religious," and one in five reportedly pray every day (21 percent).[47] Many are open to spiritual practices, and have a receptivity to Christ but not the church. Again, they are not particularly hostile toward organized religion, although their critique is it's typically "judgmental, homophobic, hypocritical, and too political."[48]

Kenda Creasy Dean analyzes Christianity's "fall from faith to religion" and the Moralistic Therapeutic Deism that is overtaking Christianity as the dominant form of religion in American churches.[49] Christianity itself has become "almost Christian, and Christian-ish." More a relic-like belief system than way of living, loving, and being.

Dean, through conducting large studies with teenagers, concludes that while they are not hostile toward religion, they just have little concern for it. It is in some sense irrelevant to their lives. The Christianity that they have encountered is frankly not very engaging. It's a "nice thing" that promotes doing good to others. What is this Moralistic Therapeutic Deism that has supplanted Christianity as the leading religion of the United States?[50] Dean pulls together the research and some of the guiding beliefs.

**Moralistic Therapeutic Deism—Guiding Beliefs:** (1) A god exists who created and orders the world and watches over life on earth. (2) God wants people to be good, nice, and fair to each other, as taught in the

Bible and other religions. (3) The central goal of life is to be happy and feel good about oneself. (4) God is not involved in my life until I need God to resolve a problem. (5) Good people go to heaven when they die.[51]

Perhaps we are seeing the emergence of a new nonconformist movement, the cult of "spiritual, but not religious." Entire movements, like Richard Jacobson's "Unchurching: Christianity without Churchianity," are springing up and attracting millions of people, harnessing the technology of a network society.[52] People are open and even hungry for spiritual meaning, but the common assumption is that it cannot be found in institutional religion. There is a particular push against denominational Christianity. The emerging spirituality is once again "protest-ant," protesting and pushing against the established hierarchies. There is a little bit of *Mayflower* running through our spiritual veins, where many are opting out of trying to reform the inherited systems and leaning into creating new spiritual movements.

At least two generations have grown up in a rapidly secularizing and pluralistic culture. Today, the next generation is growing up with a predominantly minimal experience of church. Again, most congregations' primary constituency are "the builders" (about 65 percent), those born before 1946, who endured the Great Depression and World War II.

Within the living memory of some North Americans, and in a tiny minority of locations, is the time of the "Blue Laws," those restrictions designed to ban Sunday activities to promote the observance of a day of Sabbath. The time of Blue Laws is over. The age of Christendom is passing; the age of the new pantheon has come.

I'm borrowing the term *pantheon* from our Greek and Roman ancestors, which describes the constituency of all the gods collectively, or their temple. The Roman pantheon syncretized worship to include the noteworthy gods from subjugated peoples. For instance, in Bath archeologists unearthed a temple where both Sulis, a local British god, and Minerva, a Roman god, were worshiped together. There are numerous similarities between ancient paganism and contemporary relativism.[53] The new US religious landscape is moving beyond pluralism to post-pluralism. Pluralism suggests a situation in which people of different races, cultures, and religious perspectives share in a society together.

The idea of "acceptance" associated with pluralism, or the possibility that all religious paths lead to the same divine, does not fully describe the zeitgeist of emerging generations, which Gibbs and Bolger call "a smorgasbord form of spirituality."[54] The concept of two or more religions with mutually exclusive truth claims being equally valid is perceived as an unnecessary dichotomy. All religious paths being accepted as true manifestations of the same greater divine reality is only a starting place for nascent spirituality in the West. Competing claims of spiritual truth and falsity have fallen into obscurity.

For younger generations, the concept of pluralism is evolving. It is more in the line of pantheon thinking, where all the gods share the same mythical space. The practices associated with their worship are acceptable and viewed by many as superstition. Of course, they are equally able to meet the spiritual hunger and add value to our lives in the same way. Which god or combinations of gods one chooses is more a matter of personal preference than a matter of eternal destination. Racial, religious, and cultural diversity are a fact of life to emerging generations. Ideologies that fracture social harmony are assumed as archaic. Spirituality has been privatized and consumerized like all other aspects of life.

What's emerging is in some sense more along the lines of syncretism—a merging of different faith traditions into a new North American configuration. The common perspective of emerging generations is to see the Judeo-Christian God as one of many gods, who share equal claims over creation. In this scenario, all paths may lead to God, but you don't need to pick one. In this eclecticism, they all can offer value to your life. Even most Christians in the US now report that "many religions lead to eternal life."[55]

I know a young person who claims the Muslim faith, goes to yoga class once a week, prays to Mary, and occasionally drops in for traditional Methodist worship! The posture of emerging generations is to learn from all religions collectively. The idea of devotion to one path is being lost. Further, emerging generations no longer commit to a single institution. They will contribute and move freely through multiple institutions. This causes problems for denominational churches built upon the concept of membership.

Another underlying assumption is that most of the institutions of the world religions are bankrupt. Being "spiritual, but not religious" means you don't have to belong to an institution to be spiritual. Many millennials see themselves as the most enlightened generation in human history, with religion as a subject that is studied in the pursuit of education. That subject may or may not have practical value to their lives.

As with all generations of the human species, there is a narcissistic and hedonistic tendency to seek pleasure, avoid pain, and define your own morality. That mind-set, coupled with technological innovations and social media, has created a new normal of unchecked consumerism, and hookups with no emotional entanglements. This is a self-defined morality that borrows from religious truths without committing to any one truth.

In that sense, the US is also increasingly post-atheist. That description has its connotation in a tension that no longer exists. In a society where Christianity was the dominant religion, those who did not believe in a creator God self-identified as atheist.

Quantum physics continues to disrupt enlightenment assumptions, and we learn more and know less. Agnosticism is the new default mode of the clear majority. There is a greater awareness of some power beyond rational understanding. Many churches are moving away even from the language of "conversion." A sense of Christian responsibility to convert atheists is moving into a mindset of relationship with those who are spiritually open.

The monocultural nature of Protestant congregations across the US is a huge detriment to their growth. The church was complicit in preserving racism, sexism, and anti-cultural practices. Emerging generations are highly suspect of this reality and intentionally disassociate with Christianity because of the current imperial form that pervades North America.

In this strange old-new religious environment, the growing reality among millennials is "none." No religious affiliation. You can keep the church—millennials don't want to be limited by those traditional confines. Rather than competing for the dwindling population of already-Christians, fresh expressions are focused on reaching the growing demographic of "nones and dones."

Fortunately, the New Testament emerged in a very similar environment. Paul and the early church offer us a model to engage a new pantheon kind of culture.

Len Sweet wrote almost thirty years ago that we are always "playing away" now, "the church no longer will be playing home games to home crowds."[56] Being that Christendom has "lost the home field advantage," we must adapt and respond to these massive shifts and reclaim a missional DNA, culture, and structure.[57]

## 5. The Digital Ecosystem

*From Morse Code to Virtual Reality*

Perhaps the most underestimated shift of all is the technological revolution unfolding before our eyes. COVID-19 wreaked havoc, but Christ-followers responded by loving their neighbor through social distancing. Many churches who had never streamed their services before were forced to do so under strong suggestions and ordinances resulting in breaking the Internet! The Internet is nothing new, but streaming church services was a new wineskin for many congregations as a response to a global pandemic. Churches were thrust into the digital ecosystem—for many, a new frontier.

This is wildly hopeful and true in many ways. On Easter Sunday 2020, perhaps more people heard the gospel of Jesus Christ for the first time than any other day in history. Churches were figuring it out as they went along, experimenting with new technologies, taking risks, failing, and learning. For the first time, many churches discovered the value of digital forms of worship enabled by technology.

Indeed, technology is not only changing every industry, it is changing society and the organization of community itself. These advances in technological capability can be described as moving from rolling stone wheels to spacecrafts in a single generation.

Look at the history of broadcasting, for instance. Morse code (the wireless telegraph) burst onto the scene in the late 1890s. Commercial radio broadcasting was emerging in the 1920s. In 1939, theater audiences were dazzled by *The Wizard of Oz* as Dorothy walked into Technicolor and realized she wasn't in Kansas anymore. Up until the 1950s most US families rallied around a radio for weekly broadcasts. By the 1960s, color televisions were becoming widely available. Since that time, Americans have gathered around their televisions to get their news from the three national broadcasting networks: CBS, NBC, and ABC. New technologies have destroyed that oligopoly, splintering into millions of pipelines. Social media has created a new digital society where anyone can disseminate news.[58]

Millennials don't need to watch news; it comes to them through social media. If something important is happening in the world, it lights up Facebook, Instagram, and Twitter in real time. Through the various livestream features you can experience momentous events as they unfold. Televisions themselves are becoming obsolete. Now, experimental technologies in virtual reality are not simply providing a one-dimensional optical and aural experience, but full sensory immersion, taking people backward and forward in time. The first virtual reality church services already began back in 2016.[59]

Manuel Castells describes how the web and wireless communications are more than traditional media; they are a global means of interactive, multimodal, mass self-communication creating online communities that are not in a virtual world but "real virtuality." This creates a hybridized version of everyday life for emerging generations in which they experience virtuality as reality.[60]

In the 1970s, the clunky personal computer was becoming available; today, we carry around miniature super computers on our wrists or in our pockets. So, here's a typical day for a millennial in relationship to technology. Our phone alarm wakes us, and by simply looking at it through facial recognition technologies it displays a calendar with all the day's appointments. For me, after a time of prayer and meditation (an anomaly for most households) and a cup of coffee, I check into our family group text to catch up with what our adult children are doing and check out the latest high-definition pics and videos of our grandchildren. I have experienced my grandchildren talk, crawl, walk, and pitch fits, all enabled through the advanced capabilities of my iPhone. I can then, in seconds, see what my network of friends are doing across the globe, through various social media platforms.

Next, I pull up the daily Scriptures in a Bible app, then using another voice recorder app, send a voice reflection from my phone to hundreds of people through my e-mail. Each morning my congregants receive a mini-sermon right in their inbox when they wake. They hear my voice and I reflect on Scripture as they sit in their pajamas drinking coffee, lying in bed, eating breakfast, or driving to work. Unlike Paul, who used the innovation of Roman road technology and courier systems, my messages arrive in seconds rather than weeks/months.

My watch tells me how many hours I slept and measures the quality of my sleep through recording biometrics. I can look back over the past week at my activity report to see how well I stewarded my "temple of the Holy Spirit." My heart rate, steps, hours slept, workouts, and calories burned are all available on my wrist.

After cleaning my teeth with two electronic devices—a toothbrush and Waterpik to provide superior gum care, specifically designed for my braces, a technology currently reshaping my once uncorrectable 99 percent overbite—I get ready to sweat. Most days, there are fitness groups focused around some particular practice (yoga, cycling, HIIT, Zumba, CrossFit, and so on) that I can join, sending out alerts across social media.

I go out for my morning run. With a voice command, my watch begins to record the data of my workout. With another voice command, my watch begins my running playlist through wireless earbuds. All this technology is already more advanced than some of the first space satellites.

The collective superintelligence suggests a playlist based on my previous selections over the past ten years. Sometimes I choose my own playlist and, other times, to sustain the spiritual practice of randomness in my synchronized life, I choose the one the supercomputer on my wrist has designed just for me. The playlists tailored to the cumulative choices of my past are typically just as good as the ones I would have organized for myself, only I no longer waste my time creating them. This is the artificial intelligence that previous generations only dreamed about in sci-fi films, fitting neatly in my watch.

While running, my Siri can suggest different running paths, screen my calls, and alert me to incoming text messages and e-mails. After a shower, I am ready for my first meeting of the day. A day's worth of meetings may be held in digital rooms like Zoom, GoToMeeting, or Skype. Technically, one could work all day without ever having to leave one's bedroom. Sometimes these meeting rooms are filled with people spanning the globe, connecting and collaborating across space and time.

If I have some old fashioned, face-to-face appointments, I jump in my car, now guided by the navigation system that tells me alternate routes, traffic delays, and weather patterns. I collaborate with other Waze app users, as we "outsmart traffic together," alerting each other to accidents, road debris, and law enforcement in real time. I know within minutes when I will arrive at my destination. The only random possibility in this scenario is inferior performance on another driver or myself to cause an accident. Soon, automated cars may eliminate that possibility and save millions of lives and countless amounts of digital currency.

This is what is already right now, but again, the digital revolution is progressing ever more rapidly. Consider the music industry, for instance. Some would argue that the Rolling Stones were revolutionaries who changed the music industry. The Stones were edgy, rebellious, and untamed, often in comparison to the Beatles, with their more conservative mass appeal. Mick Jagger and the Stones are now eligible for retirement benefits. Their legacy of edginess has been overshadowed by generations of provocative performers.

Yet the emerging shift occurring in the music world today is not about doing what previous bands did better, louder, or edgier. Technology is transforming the way music is created and disseminated, as well as the conventional understanding of bands and musicians. The "mash-up" we will discuss later, for example, is one recent music revolution. Master mixers digitally combine and synchronize instrumental tracks with vocal tracks from two or more different songs and genres, creating endless possibilities of remixes. For example, consider the late Swedish DJ Avicii (Tim Bergling, 1989–2018) whose song "Wake Me Up" was named the highest charting dance track of the decade, reaching a global audience of billions . . . his primary instrument was a laptop.

Artificial intelligence may create music in the future with more precision and beauty than ever. The whole concept of ownership has been replaced with sharing. Technology allows a kind of collaboration never thought possible. We are creating a collective super intelligence like the world has never known every time we Google. Yet the church has not even made the transition from Beatles to Rolling Stones, much less moved into the age of the mash-up. What churches define as "contemporary" is already ancient to emerging generations.

There is much to learn from these technological revolutions, and we will spend some time doing that later. For now, the church's time capsule stuckness is a contributing factor to the decline. There is an uneasiness about these technologies with the people I serve. We are hesitant to embrace innovative technologies and the last ones to harness the power of even outdated ones.

In a profound sense, this caution is appropriate. Not everything about technology is positive. The optimism surrounding technology ten to fifteen years ago is falling on hard times lately. Just consider the mental health epidemic in millennials and Gen Zers, political positions and intrusions of tech companies and data collection companies, economic disparity fueled by global capitalism, forfeited privacy, loneliness, ideological polarization, and so on. These are all dimensions to the digital culture and our information age that should be acknowledged and warrant our caution.

Neuroscientist Susan Greenfield combines scientific studies, news events, and cultural criticism to convincingly dispute the assumption that our technologies are harmless tools. Our digital habits are rewiring the chemical landscape of our brains, in ways just as damaging as compulsive engagement in rewarding stimuli despite adverse consequences. This harm is equal to that associated with different forms of addiction. The dependence on technology is limiting our ability for critical thinking and genuine empathy.

However, Greenfield also shows how these technologies can be used appropriately as a force for good in the world.[61]

And yet, for the church to refuse to get on the digital highway at this juncture is like rejecting horse and buggy technology in a world of automobiles. Churches are just beginning to imagine the implications of these technological revolutions. Some of the hurdles we must consider from the perspective of a none: Why would a newcomer wake up early, on most likely their only day off, and drive to a church to hear a highly contextual message for a group of people they may have never met? Is it the amazing choir that would make the trip worth it? Is it the band? If we had a sudden hankering for Christian music, there are very few songs we could not experience immediately and without cost . . . on our watch.

There is no shortage of inspiring messages available at the command of our voice; it only takes two words, "Hey, Siri." Immediately, more sermons by professional, polished speakers not contextually confined to local parishes are available than one could possibly view. Consider the banquet of TED Talks alone, which can be deeply spiritual, maybe even transformative, not as long, and with no plea for money in the end!

Or is it the sense of community that the church provides? A healing for the isolation of souls, separated by the digital sea of social media? While it is true that hypoconnectivity is creating a new form of mass loneliness and dislocation from geography, many people in a network society maintain a handful of close personal relationships, which sustain a level of emotional and psychological health.

The idea that technology is limiting real human interactions is not exactly true; it may be enabling them through flows. While people no longer have an allegiance to a place, they form community around practices, connected by these flows. Thus, in a network society culture is now mobile, moving along a complex web of interconnected networks; flows are about the digitally enabled means of movement. Cultures consist of bundles of dynamic practices, connected across space and time through structured flows of information and media.[62] These flows connect people in first, second, and third places, for face-to-face encounter.

Some churches are operating by Morse code in a world experimenting with virtual reality worship services. How can we utilize nascent technological phenomena to form communal life with Jesus in the places where people do life? How can we sustain some of the hopeful developments that emerged from COVID-19? Can churches offer a blended ecology of digital and analog gatherings? How can we use these technologies as tools for the kingdom without destroying our own souls?

## 6. It's a Beautiful Day in This Network
*From* Mister Rogers' Neighborhood *to Neo's Network* Matrix

All these shifts contribute to the final sketch. Community itself has been remixed in a new arrangement. In *Bowling Alone: The Collapse and Revival of American Community*, Robert Putnam describes the shift in the loosening of communal and societal bonds as a "treacherous rip current." Silently, the powerful tide that drove Americans into deeper engagement in the life of their communities for two-thirds of the twentieth century, reversed several decades ago.[63] Putnam analyzes the trend of the erosion of social capital and neighborly good from multiple perspectives and proposes some effects of the isolation. Most of us who live in the United States don't know our neighbors anymore.

I was one of the millions of children impacted by the incredible life of Fred Rogers. From 1968, on and off through 2001, *Mister Rogers' Neighborhood* was a steady force for positively shaping the development of children. Live on public television, Fred Rogers taught generations about the importance of learning and the values of neighborly good, kindness, and compassion. Mister Rogers took us on journeys through real and imaginary places in the neighborhood, teaching life lessons on how to be good humans who live together generatively in community.

I can still sing from memory "Won't You Be My Neighbor." It's no wonder Fred Rogers received every major award television could eligibly bestow, and in 1999 was inducted into the Television Hall of Fame. For my young mind, the potentiality of neighborly good that Mister Rogers inspired was like some of the prophetic visions of new creation. Even though I saw a massive disconnect with that vision and the neighborhood I grew up in, I grew up dreaming that neighbors and neighborhoods like that could and should be.

*Mister Roger's Neighborhood* is no more—both the show and perhaps the potentiality it envisioned. The US is becoming a country increasingly less about neighborhoods, and more a complex matrix of networks. We have moved from Fred Rogers's neighborhood into the fictional computer hacker character Neo's *Matrix*.

The *Matrix* films are prophetic in the sense that the kind of fictional community we see there is becoming reality. Beside the urbanization and clustered but isolated living arrangements of Neo's pre-red-pill world, the film series also captures the sense of people living in two worlds: one the actual, the other digital. One is about creating avatars and escaping into a virtual reality realm; the other is the random daily encounters that happen between the screens we now live our lives on ten hours per day. Television screens, phone screens, work computer screens, dashboard screens, menu screens, watch screens, and so on.

---

**Network:** A basic unit that consists of nodes. The building blocks of modern society. Castells speaks of a network enterprise, "a *specific form of enterprise whose system of means is constituted by the intersection of segments of autonomous systems of goals.*"[64] These networks are enabled by micro-electronics-based information and communications technologies. For our purposes, a group or system of interconnected people, typically centered around hobbies, work, education, sports, food, art, activism, and so on. Typically includes the blending of online and face-to-face gatherings.

Most of the time we are kind of living between the two worlds, as we listen to music and check our social media constantly throughout the passing encounters of the day. There is a dark side to the virtual world technology creates. It supplies a kind of escape hatch, where digital natives can pass through the real world without ever living in it. Perhaps this explains why we now have rehabilitation centers with youth suffering from gaming and social media addictions.

Without the technology that we depend on every day, it would be something like Neo's going through the rabbit hole, awakening in a real-world rebirthing chamber where human lives are being farmed to power a malevolent consumerist system. Many would unlikely survive the cold, unforgiving, rebirth process. Could we live without our screens?

In this new matrix of networks, the makeup of neighborhoods themselves are undergoing a major remix. Households are growing faster than the population, due to the familial shifts described earlier. There is a growing number of new households, yet they are smaller in size. As the population continues to grow, the increasing lack of space is encouraging innovative new communal living arrangements.

For instance, in coming decades, with the trend of urbanization, smaller living spaces in self-contained, dormitory-like structures will become even more prevalent. We are only seeing the beginning of this trend. This is not dissimilar to the living arrangements of ancient Rome where Christianity was able to thrive.

All the factors listed are transforming a society of neighborhoods into a society of networks. In a global network society, communities themselves are beginning to reflect that larger reality.

In the network scenario, "places" becomes secondary to "flows" of communication, information, and mobility. Culture and community become a liquid, moving thing enabled by these micro-electronics-based information and communications technologies. This also creates the new form of dislocation, loss of the value of place, and the fragmenting of relationships.

The COVID-19 pandemic caused us to hunker down and practice social distancing but simultaneously forced us to stay in our place. In many cases we had forgotten that physical space was even there, but exhaustion from the constant fixation on our anxiety-inducing screens caused us to take walks, look around, see our place again. I will offer a reflection on these dual trends in chapter 4.

The *Mission-Shaped Church* reports, "The Western world, at the start of the third millennium, is best described as a 'network society.' This is a fundamental change: 'the emergence of a new social order.'" This report reminds us that networks have not completely replaced neighborhoods, but they are absolutely transforming them.[65]

The church is seemingly still stuck in the Fred Rogers's neighborhood model, while existing in a *Matrix* world. If we want to reach people in the new digital frontier, we are going to have to take the red pill, become vulnerable, and go through a rebirth. This is the kind of vulnerability and kenosis Jesus demonstrates in the incarnation. Leaving the entitled position of divine right, emptying, entering the ordinary mess of a sin-broken world in real human flesh, to save us from ourselves.

FIELD INTERVIEW
# Jorge Acevedo

Lead Pastor of Grace Church, a multi-site
United Methodist congregation
Southwest Florida

Jorge Acevedo was not raised in a Christian home or church. At seventeen, he was addicted to drugs and alcohol. A Campus Crusade for Christ area director led him to Jesus a few days before his eighteenth birthday. Jorge landed in a United Methodist Church in Orlando because they had an amazing youth ministry. From there, he was called to vocational ministry and attended Asbury College (now University) and Asbury Theological Seminary in Wilmore, Kentucky. Jorge is married to Cheryl and has two adult sons, Daniel and Nathan, and four grandchildren, Mia, Levi, Seth, and Zoe. He has been the lead pastor at Grace Church for more than twenty-two years.

Grace Church is a multi-site United Methodist congregation whose original campus is in Cape Coral, with three other campuses in Fort Myers, Sarasota, and a campus under development in downtown Fort Myers. Grace Church is unique in that they are a blue-collar, working-class congregation. Several of their campuses are in under-served, impoverished communities.

## Can you briefly describe the fresh expression(s) of your church?

After a pilgrimage to England with my bishop to see several fresh expressions, Grace Church experimented with our first dinner church in the Suncoast community. Suncoast is the second largest trailer park in southeast America and has hundreds of families trapped in cycles of poverty and addiction. For years, we have been in ministry to an elementary school in that community. On Thursday nights, a team prepares a meal and a simple program for the adults and children. In less than two years, this has grown to 75 to 100 persons weekly. We have seen many first-time commitments to Christ and are developing discipleship ministries in the community.

We also have a fresh expression for adults with special needs called Exceptional Entrepreneurs and a boutique/thrift store where we are experimenting with developing targeted fresh expressions. Several of our campuses have also launched dinner churches and outdoor activity fresh expressions.

## Explain the blended ecology dynamics between the inherited church and your fresh expressions. What kind of tension, if any, goes on between the two?

The staff and leadership for all of our fresh expressions are tethered to one of the campuses of Grace Church. Heather Evans leads all the fresh expressions at the Grace Church, Cape Coral campus, and she coaches leaders from other campuses in developing and sustaining fresh expressions. Funding for fresh expressions comes from the host campus. Accountability for results is also maintained by the host campus. We have not found much tension between our inherited churches and our fresh expressions. I believe this is because of our clear vison as a church.

## How have you seen the fresh expressions have a positive impact on the existing congregation? In what ways?

There is a buzz about fresh expressions at Grace Church in great part because Grace Church is a profoundly outwardly focused church. We exist to transform people from unbelievers to fully devoted disciples of Jesus to the glory of God. Our prayer is "Lord, send us the people nobody else wants or sees and send us to the people nobody else wants or sees." Three hundred sixty-five days a year, Grace Church is making inroads into people groups often forgotten by the church: the addicted, the poor, the under-educated, etc.

## Knowing that launching fresh expressions in your congregation involves time, sacrifice, resources, and people power, why do you believe it's worthy to pursue?

It's simple math for me. Generational statistics clearly indicate that especially younger generations in large numbers will not come to church no matter how cool the music is and how wonderful the lights and coffee are. The Great Commission was a command by Jesus to go. Focusing only on what happens on Sunday morning is a sure sign of congregational drift from the mandate of Jesus.

CHAPTER 3
# God of Recycling Bins, Not Dumpsters

For the creation waits with eager longing for the revealing of the children of God; for the creation was subjected to futility, not of its own will but by the will of the one who subjected it, in hope that the creation itself will be set free from its bondage to decay and will obtain the freedom of the glory of the children of God. We know that the whole creation has been groaning in labor pains until now; and not only the creation, but we ourselves, who have the first fruits of the Spirit, groan inwardly while we wait for adoption, the redemption of our bodies. (Rom. 8:19–23)

It's easier to give birth than to raise the dead.

—Anonymous

The ultimate hope for all the universe is not a dumpster, but a recycling bin. God is not the God of dumpsters, but a dumpster-diving God, who visits them to redeem what's found there. God is the God of recycling bins. He takes what has been thrown away and makes it new creation. The power by which God does this is *resurrection*.

Jesus' resurrection changes everything. Paul reminds us that without it, we are without hope and pathetic (1 Cor. 15:17–19). Jesus is the "first-fruits" of the resurrection (1 Cor. 15:20–28); his risen enfleshed self is the prototype, so to speak, of what all humanity will become and is becoming. Furthermore, the ultimate plan for the entire cosmos is resurrection. In Romans, Paul describes the universe as shuttering in the throes of birth pains, like a woman bearing down, delivering a child. The broken creation is trembling with the force of new creation, by the power of resurrection (Rom. 8:19–23).

For followers of Christ, resurrection is the why of Simon Sinek's "golden circle." *It is what we believe that makes us who we are and drives*

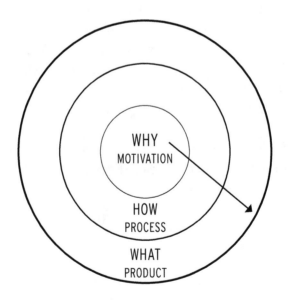

*what we do*. It's quite literally why we exist.[1] We believe in a God who put on flesh and broke the power of the grave, who redeemed creation from the inside out. Resurrection is the way God does business. If resurrection is not somewhere in our why, the center of our motivation, our how and what will never be right.

The recycling bin is a fitting metaphor for the way of God. Churches may find it beneficial to reenvision themselves as a kind of recycling bin among the polluted ecosystems for their communities. How exactly does God make one a new creation now, in the present? It's certainly not that he throws us into a trash can and starts over. It's a force of remix, of working with the existing material, reshaping and recreating.

The hope of creation is not that God will scrap the project of a "very good" universe in a cosmic dumpster and start over from scratch. It is to recycle the content of marred star-and-mud-stuff, to strip it free of all the residue of sin and death and repurpose it in a grand new amalgamation we call new creation. The entirety of Scripture bears witness to this coming new arrangement, which is unfolding as we speak.

Somewhere in the journey of Western Christianity, the narrative of resurrection was replaced with the Greek philosophical idea of the eternal existence of the soul. The body will be discarded and the soul will continue on in some disembodied state. This was one of the marks of the heresy of Gnosticism that the early Christians struggled against.

When you get resurrection wrong, the why becomes about going to heaven when we die, and the what becomes about putting butts in pews. All our processes are aimed at making members of our various denominational institutions.

One of the popular statements among church leaders today is, "It's easier to give birth than to raise the dead." That is not necessarily true; just ask any woman who has given birth how easy it was!

As kingdom people, resurrection from death is just as prevalent as new life. In fact, they are often connected. Dead people, things, institutions, and lives being resurrected are our new normal as followers of Jesus. There are more resurrection stories than birth narratives in the New Testament. The "easier" of this popular statement indicates the illusion we as leaders live in if we think we personally can do either of those tasks.

This is the perversion of our Christian faith with a Western narrative of power. We think quite highly of ourselves and go through life believing that the answer to most problems is the appropriate application of power. When things are broken, we just need better leadership. If we use our power to do this, we can overcome that. If we use our power to solve this problem, we can fix it. If we use our power appropriately, we can "give back to our neighborhood" or "take back our community." What if God doesn't want us to give back but rather stop taking? What if it's not God's desire that we take back our community because, in essence, we would be stealing it from God?

By our own strength we cannot birth new faith communities or resurrect existing ones. Again, only God can do that. Planting churches faster than they are closing is not the way forward. I want to show you how every existing church can birth new churches and how that new arrangement can become a life-giving exchange that transforms communal ecosystems. However, we will have to take a different posture than we are accustomed.

I fear we have too easily dismissed local churches and the resurrection power that is released when we shift orientation, reorganize, and encourage experimentation. Denominations have been all too eager to close them down to utilize the resources for the planting of new churches. This makes sense if you look at the data regarding older churches, the statistics on baptisms, worship attendance, and missional engagement. But what if all churches possess an inner resource that can allow them to experience new life? At the very least, I have seen churches closed that I believe could have been revitalized, and churches revitalized that were by every metric already dead.

I appreciate the wisdom of Lovett Weems, who says, "We are the beneficiaries of this rich witness made possible through sacrifices most of us will never endure. To fail to give our best efforts to such revitalization would be tragic."[2]

I firmly believe that every church that closes its doors is a sad loss for the kingdom of God. I also firmly believe that we are poised for one of the greatest awakenings of the Christian faith in human history.

To recover our story from beneath the sedimentary layers of bureaucracy, this chapter is going to search the Scriptures to reestablish a theological basis in the core narrative of resurrection. Our primary image is the tree of life. A tree thriving in the desert becoming green again is a resurrection image. Our biblical expedition will explore the blended ecology as a resurrection ecosystem.

## You Only Have to Die

Much of Jesus' teaching was wrapped in the agricultural stories of his context. Jesus says in John, "Very truly, I tell you, unless a grain of wheat falls into the earth and dies, it remains just a single grain; but if it dies, it bears much fruit" (John 12:24). Our language of fresh expressions and blended ecologies, new life, and resurrection, all starts with a seed. This truth is often overlooked. A seed that is never placed in the ground never bears fruit. The focus of the gardener, the sower, and the vinedresser are the same. This is again language of the harvest. The people who follow Jesus are people of seeds, vines, trees, and harvests. People who bear fruit.

Jim Harnish, in his book *You Only Have to Die*, reminds us that death is the pathway to new life. We cannot truly live with hope until we are willing to die.[3] In a culture that is fervently pursuing ways to defeat death, utilizing our brightest ideas and greatest technologies and exhausting resources to that end, followers of Jesus are called to die. Jesus teaches us to take up the cross and die to self if we want to follow him (Luke 9:23). This call is no more radical to the selfie generation than to any other. It is completely countercultural to all humanity in all time. However, perhaps our pursuit of not dying is the greatest fear and fixation of our generation, because for the first time in human history, it seems like a possibility.

What would be the implication to humanity if through our advances and technologies we discover how to defeat death? If we believe in resurrection, would it even be desirable? What would it mean if Christians decided to go on living in some scientifically modified state? We will wrestle further with this quandary; for now, let me just say that it's okay to die. It's also okay for churches to die. In fact, many of them need to. They will never bear a fruitful harvest in their current state.

I didn't say churches need to *close*; I said many of them need to *die*. They need to die in the same sense that Jesus describes here. When we are willing to go into the ground, die to our current form, and yield to the power of resurrection, we can emerge fully alive for a new season of harvest. The problem here is most churches are not willing to die. Like someone with a terminal diagnosis, they can get caught in toxic loop of denial. Rather than yielding to the care of potential treatment, they deny the condition and die a slow and painful death.

Phil Potter reminds us, "When the Church of England published the report *Mission-Shaped Church* (looking at new ways of doing church), it first had the title *Dying to Live*. The title was dropped because of the potential for a negative media response, but in many ways it was an excellent one."[4] Potter exposes the undergirding fear that paralyzes churches to death. What the *Mission-Shaped Church* report proposes is indeed a kind of dying for churches in the West.

Churches are convinced it's easier to give birth than to raise the dead, rather than understanding giving birth is a step in the process of resurrection.

Thom Rainer, in *Autopsy of a Deceased Church*, describes some of the signs of a terminal church. Often churches are unaware of the slow erosion taking place within the body. They have idealized the past and get stuck in the loop of thinking, *If we could just do what we did then, we could recreate the golden age*. "We've never done it that way before" becomes a common death mantra. They are unaware of their failure to engage the people in the community where they actually live. Particularly for churches that have occupied the same space within the community for many decades, they completely lose touch with their neighbor. We don't want to reach "those kinds of people" is often the tombstone inscription for these churches.[5]

Often the first response is to cut the missions and outreach budgets and pay only what is needed to maintain the congregation. The congregation falls into a state of apostolic amnesia, forgetting its core identity as sent ones. The church turns into a walled city, where only those who know the secret handshakes and magic words are granted access. Personal preferences of the dwindling population who are providing the funding to keep the church afloat begin to trump everything.

"Visit me. Take care of me. Sing those hymns for me" become the death rattle of these congregations. The clergy become identified as the problem: "If only we had better pastors, they would get us out of this mess." The pastors don't last long. The people stop praying altogether, feeling abandoned by God. We forget the why of our existence; nobody seems to know. Preserving the building becomes the only goal. We have abandoned worship of God for worshiping the facilities. The icon becomes an idol. Finally, the church has become a garden of death—a cemetery.[6]

That is not a good way to die. That is not dying with dignity. That is simply denying our own death as it's happening. I believe there is a better way to die. First, it would mean stopping everything I just described, acknowledging the inevitability of our own death, and making a decision to fight the good fight, going down doing ministry, and "raging against the dying of the light." I appreciate the people I have been with who lived with dignity, joy, and grace in their final days of a terminal diagnosis. The ones who asked, "What experiences do I still need to have, and how do I leave a legacy in this world?"

In each one of the congregations I have been a part of that has experienced revitalization, I have served as a kind of interventionist. One of my roles has been to help the congregations understand that not only were we going to die, we needed to die. In recovery, we use the term "Gift of Desperation" as an acronym for GOD. When people find their bottom and get desperate enough, they become willing to reach up for help from God. Once we reach that place, we must find an alternative metaphor for our life. We must change everything.

Some of the things we will need to do will be counterintuitive. The kind of leadership that's needed is not organizational alone, but shared and adaptive. We need to come to terms with death before we can have a meaningful conversation about resurrection. When churches die for the right things, futurefit their congregation for mission, and decide they are willing to "go into the ground and die" so a harvest can come, amazing things can happen.

Death is nearly a step in a process for those whose core narrative is resurrection. Resurrection is a remix. God takes a fragmented life and makes it new. God takes decaying flesh, dust, and molecules, and breathes afresh and leaves an empty tomb. God takes the DNA of who we are and reconfigures it in a new form. God creates a new version by recombining and reediting the elements of the existing in a splendid work of new creation. Churches that go into the ground will arise as something new, the same but different. The blended ecology is one way that God remixes the inherited and emerging forms of church so that a resurrection harvest can occur.

## Emergence: Resurrection Happening Now

One of the sad ways we have contributed to the decline of the church in the West is what we have done with the Bible. In our Moralistic Therapeutic Deism, where God has become our genie and crisis counselor, we strip out any possibility of the supernatural. We have domesticated Scripture, sanitized its revolutionary power. We have read the Bible through our own US core narratives of consumerism, individualism, power, and control. We dissect the Bible like a dead animal verse by verse and remove parts that we hope to use, rather than respecting it as a living organism of interweaving stories and metaphors. Let's not to do that here; let's enter fully into the core narrative that Scripture has to offer.

What happened to the resurrection? Much of Christian teaching focuses today on the incarnation and the cross. In our kind of functional atheism, we talk about resurrection in two primary ways. One, as something that happened to Jesus, or two, for some branches of the faith, what will happen to us *one day*.

It's kind of like the position Martha takes with Jesus when her brother Lazarus has been dead in a tomb for four days. "Yes, I know, Lord, one day, by and by, pie in the sky, on the last day, my brother will rise again." Jesus immediately confronts her misconception of resurrection with a potent, world-shattering truth, "Jesus said to her, 'I am the resurrection and the life'" (John 11:25). It's as if Jesus is saying, "You don't get it, Martha. Resurrection is not an event for some distant future; it's a person, it's me! I'm about to bring your brother back from death, right now!"

I think the US church has taken up a Martha position on resurrection. Churches die, lingering around the tomb, under the resurrection rhetoric of "I know one day, by and by . . ." We need the fortitude to roll the stone away and deal with the stinky stuff inside. Resurrection is messy but necessary.

We leave out in most conversations the most essential truth of the resurrection: *it's happening now, all around us, everywhere!*

While I believe with Sam Wells that resurrection is a power "beyond description,"[7] I think a helpful way to approach resurrection with fresh eyes, while knowing we will fall miserably short of comprehension, is to borrow from complexity thinking to understand it through the lens of the phenomenon of *emergence*.

**Emergence:** Under the broader umbrella of complexity theory, emergence refers to novel and coherent forms (structure, pattern, order) arising from the dynamic interplay among elements at successive layers within a complex adaptive system.[8]

From the Latin root *emergere*, the word *emergence* means literally "to bring to light." Emergence seeks to describe how new properties and features form when distinct parts are combined. Hence, emergence describes the creation of something new that could not be expected from a description of the parts prior to its creation. In a generic sense, it describes a universal process of creation and is seen across all types of systems. Thus, I appreciate Wells's explanation of resurrection power as "the force of new creation, a significance as great as God's original purpose for the world."[9]

Emergence is literally one way that complexity science gives us a window into the process of creation. For example, a caterpillar becoming a butterfly, a colony of ants working together as a collective living system, the combination of particles that make water wet, or the combination of people that make up an organization. In isolation, there is no clear explanation how the combination of those parts, the synergies interacting between the components, emerge in the new form, or the "irreducibility of the properties of the whole to the characteristics of its parts."[10]

These synergies have to do with relations of interdependence between parts working together, which add value to a combined outcome. The added value of these synergies gives birth to a nascent macro-level organization. There is a mysterious importation of energy occurring in this process, which cause physicists to turn to wonder. Michael Moynagh brilliantly applies this framework to describe the process through which fresh expressions emerge and moves us from thinking simply about church planting to ecclesial emergence.[11]

Thus, the theory of emergence aims to understand a complexity of forms that defy simple explanation. Scientists who work from a position of reductionism—the practice of analyzing and describing a complex phenomenon in terms of simpler parts—cannot account fully for the phenomenon of emergence. There is a living force at work between the synergetic interactions that defy reductionist explanation. I find the phenomenon of emergence not only helpful as we think about resurrection, but also for the process of revitalization, and the kind of nascent communal organism that arises.

In *Star Wars: The Last Jedi*, Luke Skywalker says, "The Force is not a power you have. It's not about lifting rocks. It's the energy between all things, a tension, a balance, that binds the universe together."[12] Emergence demonstrates an "importation and dissipation of energy" involved that challenges the Newtonian paradigm.[13] This importation of energy results in so-called "self-organization," which has been referred to as "the anchor-point phenomenon of complexity theory, a process whereby system-level order spontaneously emerges as a result of dynamic interactions among individual agents."[14] There truly is a living energy involved in the process of emergence that we do our best to apprehend in a rational way.

For Jesus' people—the resurrection people—the universe as we know it is in the process of resurrection. Jesus is not dead, but very much enfleshed and alive. If we hold the complex interactions of Jesus' incarnation, death, resurrection, ascension, and sending of the Holy Spirit at Pentecost together in creative tension, we can realize the risenness of Jesus is not confined to one place, in one moment in time. The risenness of Jesus permeates the entire cosmos, available to be downloaded into every living thing. It was the experience of Jesus' resurrected presence that sustained the early church and enabled their confession of his lordship (1 Cor. 12:3). Furthermore, the risenness of Jesus is the synergistic power at work in the continuous creative activity of God, in every crying newborn, every butterfly awakening from a cocoon, and every opening flower.

The Holy Spirit is not some mysterious force, but a person of the triune God. The synergistic energy we see involved in the transformation of the entire cosmos and all living things is the power of resurrection, guiding all the cosmos to a final form of emergence—the new creation (Rom. 8:19–23; Rev. 22). The power of resurrection—"the force," if you will—is the energy of God's healing, transforming work in the cosmos.

I understand there is no theoretical framework that can fully explain how God is at work in the universe. But the "new science" offers us semantic conceptions that help us recover the early Christian understanding of resurrection and approach what God is up to in church revitalization and the cultivation of new ecosystems. If not, we fall victim to the Martha view, "I know one day . . ." and the absent watchmaker God of deism. Furthermore, we are left with a church that John Wesley warned would have "the form of religion without the power."

The resurrection is not simply a statement about God; it reveals the heart of God. It is the way God's power manifests and disrupts our narratives of power and control. The Holy Spirit is renewing the world. God is engaged in a huge recycling project right now—of the whole universe!

Perhaps we focus on Jesus' life, or perhaps we leave him on the cross because we can manage, own, predict, and control those parts of God's story, much like we deal with reductionist scientific experiments in a lab. The force of resurrection that has been unleashed in the world is something we can't predict, control, or merchandise. Scientific theories fall apart when it comes to the phenomenon of resurrection, in which complexities arise that are irreducible to the lower levels—the risen enfleshed Jesus, the church as the body of Christ, the final renewed cosmos.

Perhaps we also shy away from the reality of resurrection because it brings us face-to-face with our greatest fear . . . death. Death, that old vandal, still evades our attempts to manage, control, and extend life. We don't like to die, and we don't like to watch people or things we love die. Besides on Easter, perhaps the only other gathering where we unpack the power of resurrection is at funerals. When our attempts at control are stripped of their power, we fall back into the arms of resurrection hope.

The church as we know it is dying in the West. That frankly makes us all uncomfortable. There is nothing we can do to stop that, no more than we can stop the death of a loved one who is concluding the current life cycle. We can mourn, weep, yell, curse, shake our fists, eat, and dance, but at the end of the day, the reality of death is still jeering back. Resurrection is not only a topic we present on Easter and at funerals. It is our way of life. It is a force that was unleashed in a new way in Jesus' tomb, that is now transforming creation and society as we know it.

Recovering the narrative of resurrection moves us beyond the cul-de-sac of church questions and church answers. If we take seriously what God is doing in the renewal of a sin-fragmented cosmos, then we can start to see God may be up to something in the world . . . outside the church walls.

"Can the West be converted?" This is the question Lesslie Newbigin asked decades ago, and we are just now beginning to catch up. He wrote, "What would be involved in a missionary encounter between the gospel and this whole way of perceiving, thinking, and living that we call 'modern Western culture'?"[15] When Newbigin returned to the UK after forty years in India as a missionary, he discovered his homeland had become the mission field. The church was having very little impact. Seemingly, the Holy Spirit had left the building.

Realizing that God is already at work outside the church in every human life is a fundamental premise of the missional church movement. It is a different posture of mission, one of joining in "withness" rather than trying to treat people as problems that need to be solved.

From time to time in human history, God does some big, hairy, audacious thing. God uses the world to reform the church. God is working in the world to create a new ecosystem in ways that are often beyond our comprehension. The problem with resurrection is that it defies the causal corporate logic that most churches have subconsciously adopted as their legitimating narrative. You can't whiteboard and flowchart resurrection. You can't tweak programs to make it occur. You can't bring in a resurrection expert to consult with your congregation and form strategic goals for the next five years. It cannot be owned, controlled, or manipulated.

If we accept the premise that a legitimating narrative shapes our behavior as a society, the Western church is living in the wrong narrative. The resurrection of Jesus of Nazareth should be the core of our formational story. The power unleashed in Jesus' resurrection and poured out profusely on all nations at Pentecost—that is the kind of power that shapes us. If we dare dream that God is very much in the resurrection business and is already involved in that work in our communities, then we can listen well to what God is doing and go join it. We can be alongside our neighbor on the journey of life. In fact, we need our neighbors. We are not just there to offer them what we have; they also offer up something that we need. This is a mutual exchange.

Notice the focus is on healing, restoring, and redeeming local communities, not the local church. Also notice the goal is not to fix the community, take the community, or win the community. Healing, restoration, and redemption are a mutual exchange in the social imaginary of resurrection. When local churches understand the role we play in the larger ecosystem, as a kind of green space, something amazing can happen. The community is transformed, new "churches" are formed, and many times the local congregation does experience revitalization.

> **Social Imaginary:** According to Charles Taylor, the ways people imagine their social existence, how they relate to others, how things go on between them and others, normal expectations, and the underlying notions of these expectations.[16]

## Isolation—The Ultimate Dilemma

The church, throughout its history, has colluded with different kinds of power. At times, the church was itself a manifestation of imperial power. The church-state and its god-kings used the practices of extraction, commoditization, and violence to extend this power. In some scenarios, heretics, enemies, and Gentiles were tortured and executed in the name of the Prince of Peace. How does that happen? Samuel Wells reminds us that Jesus is deeply concerned with how individuals and groups use their power.[17]

In the United States, the church has been retrofitted with an alien form of power, primarily corporate power. We have fully embraced the legitimating narrative of the twentieth-century corporate world. Denominations are modeled on that narrative, and local churches are largely dependent on the inherited power systems. Clergy are trained to be efficient, professional managers who belong to the company store, often unbeknownst to us. While the church has always harnessed the culture and societal structures of the day, at times we have used them to replace God.

This is what John Drane refers to as the McDonaldization of the church. In reference to the American hamburger chain, which is now the largest franchise in the world, McDonaldization is the process by which the principles of the fast-food restaurant are coming to dominate many sectors of a globalized society. Drane identifies the four characteristics of McDonaldized systems as efficiency, calculability, predictability, and control, and notes that the McDonaldization of the church is partly responsible for the mass exodus of people.[18]

When a church realizes it is caught in a cascade of decline, often the first reaction is to default to the corporate power models. Break out the demographic charts; we need a new vision statement, we need to cut expenses and increase income, we need denominational intervention to help us navigate the storm. We need to come up with better solutions to our problems. We need to use our greatest faculties of reason to fix this with the wisdom of current leadership gurus. We need to implement new programs and procedures, etc. All these solutions are deeply imbedded in the corporate power narratives.

Samuel Wells offers us a breath of fresh air. He proposes that the underlying fixation of human culture is centered on discovering a solution to the inevitability of death. We are all going to die. Nobody gets out alive. It seems that our culture operationally assumes that the central problem of human existence is mortality. Conquering death seems to have become the defining project of modern humanity. Many of our brightest minds have taken up the challenge of somehow overcoming death through advances in biomedicine, nanotechnology, and neuroscience.[19]

He goes on to posit that if we assume mortality as the fundamental human problem, then most of our institutional power will be focused on solving it. Organizations become committed to helping people overcome limitations and fix their problems. Systems are designed toward that end: service and mission are configured as corresponding terms. We join in the "Millennium Development Goals." We will be creating technologies to help people replace failing organs. We will be building houses for people caught in poverty. We will be creating better medicines that help extend the life of the sick. When the human problem is mortality, all our "mission and service" activities will be aimed at reducing mortality and finding solutions that overcome human limitation.[20]

Wells raises the question, What if the ultimate dilemma of humanity is not *mortality*, but . . . *isolation?* The fragmentation of relationships that leave one alone. Isn't that really what sin and the fall are all about? The greatest brokenness of our human condition is the fragmentation of our relationship with God and each other that resulted from our willful disobedience. If isolation is the fundamental human problem, then our solutions are not based in our power narratives of owning, fixing, and managing. We will not find our solutions in laboratories, biomedicine, and the revolutionary advancements in the fields of neuroscience or nanotechnology. The solutions are already with us, in us, and among us. The solutions are exactly *us*. What we need is one another.[21]

Scripture does not present heaven as simply the overcoming of mortality. Rather, it's a life lived now and eternally onward in which we are healed of our aching isolation.

We are tapping into the real underlying need—relationship. Heaven is a final state of withness. It's about being together with God and with one another in a renewed creation. Wells says,

The heaven that is worth aspiring to is a rejoining of relationship, of community, of partnership, a sense of being in the presence of another in which there is neither a folding of identities that loses their difference nor a sharpening of difference that leads to hostility, but an enjoyment of the other that evokes cherishing and relishing. The theological word for this is communion.[22]

Wells speaks of four models of social engagement: *working for* (a skilled expert who enjoys a concentration of power helps someone less fortunate); *working with* (power is located in likeminded coalitions of interest working on common causes); *being with* (rejects the problem-solution axis of the previous models, which disempowers and reinforces another's lower social standing; rather it is the power of "relationship" "enjoying people for their own sake"); and *being for* (again defaults to the power of doing rather than witness).[23]

One of the central affirmations of the Christian faith is belief in a God who is *with* us (Matt. 1:23). All through Scripture, from the garden of Eden, where God walks "with" humanity in the cool of the day, to being with us in the blazing glory of the tabernacle, to putting on flesh and moving into the neighborhood in Jesus, to pouring out the Spirit at Pentecost, to the final urban garden of new creation where God finally makes his eternal home, God has made a commitment to be *with* us always. The synergism that gives us life, and heals our isolation, is a relationship with God.

Western Christianity has become quite confused between being *with*, and doing *for*. We lean heavily toward doing *for* others. It's neater. It requires no relational commitment. However, if we believe in a God who is ultimately about withness, then shouldn't that be our enactment of this good news in the lives of others? We seek to be with people in the highs and lows of life. We offer comfort not through trying to do for but being with.

Many times, our narrative leaves us helpless: "Well, there's nothing I can do for you." Well, how about trying to *be* with me?

When we are left speechless by the realities of a sin-broken cosmos, where God puts on flesh to be with us and winds up on a cross, it's not our words that bring comfort, but our presence. What if what we really want from each other is not to be fixed, managed, or controlled, but just to have a witness. This doesn't mean that we are now robbed of doing *for* others, but our doing for is shaped by our desire to be *with*. That is the real power, the restraint not to manipulate, fix, or manage, but be with.

What if the cross is really all about Jesus' willingness to experience *withoutness*? In a tomb is he without breath, without life, without love, without us, without the Father? It is the ultimate form of isolation. What if the resurrection of Jesus is not ultimately about what God can do *for* us, but God's desire to be *with* us? What if it is the resurrection that enables us to truly be with God and each other fully once again? What if this is the very way and power that should be unleashed within the church and throughout the whole world?

The resurrection way is our new normal. *Perichoresis*, the interpenetrating relationship of the three persons of the Trinity one to another, is the ultimate expression of withness.

> **Perichoresis**: The "mutual interpenetration," or the way the three persons of the Trinity relate to one another. This is an image of God as "community of being" in which each person, although one remains distinct, penetrates, and is penetrated by the other.[24] Further, perichoresis is used to understand the incarnation of Jesus as fully human, fully God, and because "believers experience union with Christ as a result of salvation provided by Christ, they also participate in the soteriological *perichoresis* with the triune God."[25]

The triune God is a community of loving withness. Jesus draws the believer into this very community of being, and the Spirit indwells the believer. Thus, the church is literally the community of God's loving withness in the earth, in a circle dance that always makes room for the other. This will help us later as we understand the essence and form of the church is, in fact, derived from the life of the Trinity and the two primary modes of God's presence.

If we accept that our real purpose is not to fix death but to embrace withness, it completely transforms our rhythms of being. Our entire understanding of service and mission is transformed. Overcoming isolation does not look to technology to solve the problem, but rather is a tool to create withness. We cannot assume that if we use our perceived power, our greater knowledge, expertise, or skill that we can fix people or manage their problems. If we are seeking to overcome isolation, we realize those capacities of the outdated legitimating narrative may be a detriment. The church is not here to "claim this territory for the kingdom" or to "take back our community" or to "give back to the city." It's to quit claiming and taking, and find ways to be with.

Perhaps we can ask a version of Jesus' question "Who are my brothers and sisters?" (Matt. 12:48). In essence, Jesus is redefining family: "those who do the will of my Father" (Matt. 12:50). Disciples of Jesus are a new form of family, sealed together in baptism . . . water is thicker than blood in the kingdom. Another way to view this is, "And who is my other?" Jesus teaches the disciples to extend this new family to all people, including those outside the reach of the current religious system, inviting them to live under the reign of God.

If we ask who is our *other* and how can we be *with* them, we will stop looking at our community as disadvantaged and in need of our skills and resources, and start looking at them in the same way God does, as people we want to be in relationship with. We won't need to bring our strategies and corporate solutions, but just come empty-handed, ready to form relationship. This will also help us steer clear of the proclivity to deliver our solutions and retreat to our walls. We will come less ready to talk and more prepared to listen. We can leave the tracts, Romans Road, and sinner's prayer behind, and hope that we may find a mutual relationship that will heal our isolation. Our time with others is no longer some means to an end, but it is the end itself. It is the healing balm of our souls.

This does not mean that we will no longer engage in projects for our neighbor. But the purpose of our projects has been infused with new meaning. In the process of alleviating hunger, healing the sick, and clothing the naked, we are forming relationships. The programs will come and go, but the genuine withness will remain. We don't do this because it is the sign of a healthy church, gives us vital statistics to count, or because we are building God's kingdom for him (as if we could do that on God's behalf). These endeavors enable us to join God in being with, as we expand the withness and usness of Immanuel, God with us. The people in our neighborhoods have what we need—themselves. Our community already has everything it needs to experience healing and redemption. If we overcome the obstacles of isolation, the kingdom of God comes, on earth as it is in heaven.

Samuel Wells reminds us that no power in the world is greater than God's power, "which is the power of creation and, ultimately and definitively, of resurrection." The power of resurrection that is available to the church is not derived from systems, properties, and resources; that is power derived from scarcity. This is power that flows from God's abundance. This is power that overcomes isolation and transforms politics. Resurrection is power characterized by God's love, and manifests in forgiveness and friendship.[26]

Mark Mason notes that Wells offers an important theological emphasis for fresh expressions of church. He identifies that these emerging forms of church must attempt to negotiate power at both personal and social levels. He posits that fresh expressions will live in the irreconcilable tension of being "communities of character" (formation in Christ) and "communities of the question" (other orientation, reflexivity, willingness to live in mystery).[27]

Hence, there is a tension within fresh expressions of church, which assume a completely other-oriented posture of listening, while at the same time seeking to encourage formation in the character of Christ. There is also a kind of power balancing act, in that fresh expressions remained tethered to inherited congregations. The inherited forms and emerging forms must seek to maintain withness and resist fragmentation. We can steer clear of the pitfalls of those dynamics if we understand that resurrection power is released through relationship. The work of transformation is God's work, not ours.

The power of resurrection disrupts our corporate narratives. It throws a monkey wrench in our attempts to design a world where love is unnecessary and isolation is the norm. It trips us up as we rush hurriedly through life trying to do for, and not be with. If we can move back into the social imaginary of Scripture, stop fearing the death of our churches, embrace the power of resurrection, and focus on healing the isolation of our communities, a new creation can emerge. We can find a way out of the dead end of implementing programmatic solutions. This is the orientation that can release churches to experience resurrection.

## Revitalization as Resurrection

The first Christians took their belief in resurrection quite seriously. Paul writes, "If you confess with your lips that Jesus is Lord and believe in your heart that God raised him from the dead, you will be saved" (Rom. 10:9). Jesus' lordship and his physical resurrection from death was the centerpiece of the faith. This was not simply some doctrinal statement for the early church. This was their why. This was their legitimating narrative. The first Christians gathered around the confession of Jesus' lordship, a title they believed was conferred on Jesus by God, based on the resurrection (Acts 2:32–36). After they saw Jesus resurrected bodily, they experienced him from then on through the power of the Holy Spirit, as infinitely alive on both personal and communal levels (1 Cor. 12:3).[28] The church of Jesus herself is an *emergence*, a remixed amalgamation of flesh-and-blood disciples, and the risen presence of Christ.

The most spectacular truth about Jesus' resurrection does not stop with his own grave-robbing spectacle, but how it extends to all creation (1 Cor. 15:20–22). Jesus—as the firstfruits of the coming harvest, the resurrection of all humanity—is the preview of what we all will become.

What is fascinating is how the New Testament talks about that becoming as both a present and future reality. "So if anyone is in Christ, there is a new creation: everything old has passed away; see, everything has become new!" (2 Cor. 5:17). This becomes even more interesting when we understand that is the same language that John the Revelator uses to talk of the coming of "new" creation and the old "passing away" (Rev. 21).

Obviously, the way God achieves this making us anew is not in the sense of brand spanking new, like disposing and starting over, but a re-*new*-ing of what is already there. He takes the material he has already made and called "very good," strips it of the pollution of sin, and redeems it. The New Testament extends that hope not only to humanity, but to the resurrection of the entire cosmos, as can be seen, for instance, in the language of Romans 8:21 or Revelation 21–22. In the renovated new creation, we find ourselves back again at the tree of life (Rev. 22:2). This is a recycling project, not a cosmic dumpster. The consumeristic impulse toward brand spanking new, the next shiny thing that creates exorbitant waste, is our way, not God's.

Furthermore, Jesus' preaching on the kingdom of God, resurrection, and eternal life inextricably linked to his person was not about a "postmortem destiny" or an escape hatch from some evil universe, but about "God's sovereign rule" manifesting on this earth, here and now, as it is in heaven.[29] We must hold our understanding of the kingdom of God, resurrection, and eternal life together in creative tension.

Many sadly confuse going to heaven when we die with a bodily resurrection and a massive force of new creation in which God joins heaven and earth together. The modern tendency to permanently separate soul, mind, and body is false and unbiblical. Human beings consist of these distinct parts, but remain whole, created in the image of God.

These bodies will be resurrected from the dead and transformed, again, of which the resurrection body of Jesus is the firstfruits of the harvest, meaning his death-conquering, enfleshed, wound-bearing self is the first look at what we all will become (1 Cor. 15:20–23). Jesus calls us to love God with all our "heart, soul, strength, and mind" (Luke 10:27). Living under the lordship of Jesus includes being a "living sacrifice" unto God (Rom. 12:1).

Displacing our hope for eternal life to some distant celestial shore, disembodied from our current physical state, is again the Martha misconception (John 11:21–27). Jesus, the one who is "the resurrection," comes to give us an eternal life now and share in unending relationship with God.

Furthermore, while each of these concepts are distinct and must be treated so, they are also intimately woven together. The kingdom of God has already been launched, was always here, and is coming soon in all its fullness.[30] Dallas Willard identifies the kingdom of God as the range of God's "effective will," where what God "wants done is done," and the person of God and God's will are the organizing principles of this kingdom. Hence, he says, "everything that obeys those principles, whether by nature or choice," is within God's kingdom.[31]

Willard goes on to use the analogy of electricity to describe the kingdom. The kingdom of God has existed with humanity since the beginning. When humanity figured out how to harness electricity, it changed everything. The entire universe is hardwired with God's kingdom. In Christ, the kingdom that has always been is accessible in a new way. Through Jesus' withness, we can now plug in, translating our ordinary life into an eternal one, and live in the firm already/not-yet hope of resurrection.[32]

In N. T. Wright's masterpiece *Surprised by Hope,* he searches the whole witness of Scripture to unpack the continuity between Old and New Testament hope and how Jesus' resurrection launches that hope.[33] The final awesome hope for the cosmos is not only humanity's bodily resurrection, but that God makes "all things new" (Rev. 21:5) in this way.

The entire cosmos is laboring to give birth to a marvelous new creation (Rom. 8:18–23). Again, God doesn't scrap the project and destroy creation. God's answer is a grand restoration of a marred universe in which we are participating right now. Resurrected and transformed, an eternal life in this new creation in which the fullness of the kingdom of God has come is "life *after* life after death."[34]

While the sequence and details are mind-boggling,[35] we stand on Romans 8:38–39 to conceive the relational reality of eternal life: "neither death, nor life, nor angels, nor rulers, nor things present, nor things to come, nor powers, nor height, nor depth, nor anything else in all creation, will be able to separate us from the love of God in Christ Jesus our Lord." This is ultimate withness. That resurrection power is available here and now as we live as citizens in the kingdom of God.[36] The church is a colony of the kingdom, here in the sin-warped valley. It is a bastion of withness, a community where isolation has been healed and is constantly expanding. When our focus becomes extending that withness, something beautiful can happen.

Revitalization of existing congregations takes place when we release ourselves to the power of resurrection. God takes congregations on the way to the dumpster and remakes them as recycling bins.

## Back to the Tree of Life

The tree of life is a consistent symbol of God's presence from Genesis to Revelation. In the mobile tabernacle, the "holy place" was like a microcosm of Eden, where YHWH's walking around presence was with the people.[37] The menorah, the lampstand that lit the "tent of meeting," was constructed in the form of the tree (Ex. 25:31–37). The lampstand not only symbolized the tree of life but also the burning bush, both which were representative of God's presence. The tree-of-life-lampstand, the ark, and the tabernacle itself were then relocated into the temple (1 Kings 8:1–4; 2 Chron. 5:2–5). Again, an Edenic place of God's presence, centered around the light-giving tree, but now stationary.[38]

The final vision of new creation takes us back to the tree of life (Rev. 22:1–2). It is the ultimate *emergence*. It is a *universal resurrection ecosystem*. The remixed and risen final form of life does not take place in a vacuum, but in the renewed real time and space universe that God called "very good." The resurrection ecosystem is one in which the Spirit's power to disrupt the cycles of sin and death has become fully realized. It is a place in the sense of real time and space. It is a sphere of reality that possesses a physicality and a molecular substance that is actual and imperishable.

The church is called to be a kind of foretaste of this arrangement. A real tree of life, amid real communities. Somehow the church serves a life-giving role, oxygenating the communal ecosystems with resurrection breath. In that sense, the church by its very nature has a purposeful sentness. Read *missional*, if you will. The church is sent to transform the toxicity of sin-broken ecosystems with the death-breaking power of resurrection.

Therefore, we cannot dissect ecclesiology and missiology in any scripturally faithful way. The church exists not simply for itself, but to unleash more fully the force of resurrection already in the atmosphere. The church is a kingdom of heaven, resurrection, eternal life, a green space within the community. Trees perpetuate themselves though seeds. In every seed is the potential of a tree. As the tree of life, it can release seedlings that replicate and create more green spaces throughout the community. These are little oases of hope and withness, scattered across the decaying landscape. The more green spaces that spread across the horizon, the more the atmosphere is transformed.

In the blended-ecology way, the seeds are the fresh expressions of church. The tree is the inherited church. What if we were to understand that every church, no matter how small, has the capacity to replicate itself throughout the community? What if we were to think of our churches as an outpost from which to go forth and plant green spaces in our community? This is where we now turn for the remainder of this book.

Alan Roxburgh, reflecting on the decline of the church, raises the question, "What if nothing is wrong?"[39] What if God is doing exactly what God has always done, disrupting the faulty ecclesiological narratives of settling, managing, and controlling with the power of resurrection? What if the Spirit is somehow working among the seismic shifts that we see as threats to break and reconfigure the world? What if Jesus is even now, by the force of resurrection, shaping a new creation ecosystem?

Are we really willing to die to live? Oh, that we may have the boldness to pray with Paul, "I want to know Christ and the power of his resurrection and the sharing of his sufferings by becoming like him in his death" (Phil. 3:10).

The church is a recycling bin, not a dumpster. The Spirit's power of resurrection is at work through fresh expressions in the transforming of communities in the blended-ecology way. Let us fully join Jesus' recycling project. Let us take our place with the God of the dumpster dive.

FIELD INTERVIEW
# Travis Collins

Pastor of First Baptist Church
Huntsville, Alabama

Travis is the senior pastor of First Baptist Church, Huntsville, Alabama, and director of mission advancement for Fresh Expressions US. He served as a missionary in Nigeria and Venezuela. Travis holds a PhD in Christian Mission and is the author of multiple books. Two of those books, *From the Steeple to the Street* and *Fresh Expressions of Church*, have become basic texts for the movement. Travis got involved in the Fresh Expressions movement during his previous pastorate of a church that began three of these new forms of church—among people in recovery, the international community, and persons trapped in prostitution. In his role at FBC, Huntsville, he is advancing the blended-ecology way to reach people where they are.

### Can you briefly describe the fresh expression(s) of your church?

In October 2017, we launched two fresh expressions of church. One is in the recovery community, and we call it "Bright Star." They gather weekly in a building near our church campus, led by a gentleman who is in recovery. It is an informal time of sharing, teaching, and worship. We experienced a recent influx of creativity when we were joined by new partners from the First Methodist Church of Huntsville.

The second fresh expression of church, launched in October 2017, is in the arts community and is called "Heartfelt Expressions." (I did not encourage names, but the lead teams decided they wanted names.) Heartfelt Expressions gathers weekly at Lowe Mill, a converted cotton mill that now houses all kinds of shops and studios frequented by artists. The gatherings now consist mainly of painting sessions and lessons. They have begun to introduce "gospel kernels" into their sessions, saying things like, "We paint because God is creative and instilled that creativity in us." The devotional time has been well-received, and participants are now invited to a once-a-month prayer breakfast at a local restaurant.

In January 2018, we launched Dinner Church in Butler Terrace, an underserved neighborhood. The Holmes Avenue Methodist Church joined us as partners in the endeavor for a year as they prepared to launch their own dinner church. The partnerships with our Methodist brothers and sisters have been a very cool thing.

In the fall of 2018, we began Gamer.Church, a fresh expression of church among people who are immersed in the video gaming community. That began when students from University of Alabama at Huntsville who were visiting First Baptist expressed their passion for reaching their fellow gamers. Now the point person for Gamer.Church is a student at UAH who grew up in First Baptist. They are still figuring out their strategy.

On the horizon, we believe, is a fresh expression of church among scientists. This could be a thrilling venture. Dr. John Christy, a climate scientist at the University of Alabama in Huntsville, has a master of divinity as well as a PhD in climatology. Here is an excerpt from an article I invited John to write for our church newsletter about this potential fresh expression of church among scientists:

> Our hope is that we can create a venue that attracts those scientists who want to examine the big questions of life and who are open to consider the realm of faith as a pathway for answers. We are putting together a core team to develop this Fresh Expression to touch this considerable, challenging, smart, and influential community.

## Explain the blended ecology dynamics between the inherited church and your fresh expressions. What kind of tension, if any, goes on between the two?

So far there has been no tension between First Baptist as we know it and the new forms of church. I think we are simply too early in the process. But we definitely see a symbiotic relationship.

For example, our church has a huge (40 feet high, 120 feet wide) mosaic of Jesus on our external wall. The mosaic is an icon in Huntsville. The tiles (fifty years old) have been falling to the point that the mosaic was in need of repair. So, we have contracted with Italian artists to restore the mosaic, maintaining the design but replacing the tiles completely. The tiles that have made up the mosaic have such sentimental value to our congregation and community that someone had the idea of making jewelry out of those tiles and donating the profits to a local mission project. The church chose fresh expressions to be the recipients of that project, and we have raised more than $50,000 to support our efforts to launch new forms of church.

As I type this, I am about to head out to the funeral home to be with a young man named Shaun, whose uncle, who raised Shaun, passed away a few days ago. Shaun was the first person to be baptized through our fresh expressions of church. We took our portable baptistery to the parking lot of the venue that hosts dinner church, the firefighters from across the street came and filled it up, and four of us (including the pastor of Holmes Avenue Methodist) baptized Shaun.

## How have you seen the fresh expressions have a positive impact on the existing congregation? In what ways?

I do believe our church has been energized by the launch of the fresh expressions, in these particular ways:

People are thinking more creatively. The fresh expressions initiative has unleashed innovative thinking among us. It's almost as if people have been given permission to think about church differently. Granted, sometimes people use fresh expressions language too loosely—calling any new and creative initiative a fresh expression—but at least they are out of the proverbial box.

People (pioneers) have stepped forward to lead—people who had no real leadership role in the church. All three of our fresh expressions are being coordinated/facilitated/led by people who held no official position in the church before. This confirms what we have been saying: there are pioneers in our pews who simply need to be blessed, unleashed, and given the opportunity to serve.

Our entire church will celebrate this coming Sunday when Trisha will be baptized in our 8:15 service. Trisha came to faith through dinner church, and her baptism will inspire people far beyond the Dinner Church Team.

## 4. Knowing that launching fresh expressions in your congregation involves time, sacrifice, resources, and people power, why do you believe it's worthy to pursue?

These fresh expressions of church do require work and sacrifice. They also involve risk. All of the new fresh expressions of church don't make it, and although I am trying to prepare our congregation for that inevitability, I do wonder how the church will respond when (if) we announce the discontinuation of one or more of our fresh expressions.

It is all worth it, however, given the fact that there are so many people in Huntsville who are almost certainly not going to engage with any church as we know it, no matter how wonderful the music, or how beautiful the facilities, or how creative the programming.

CHAPTER 4

# Wild Branches— Fresh Expressions

Jesus said to them again, "Peace be with you. As the Father has sent me, so I send you." When he had said this, he breathed on them and said to them, "Receive the Holy Spirit." (John 20:21–22)

Christianity is a religion that is less wrapped up in rituals and observances than it is in rapt attention to what God is doing in the world so that we can beat a path to where Jesus is living his resurrected presence.
—Len Sweet

## Back to the Future

I have been to the future, and it was in the deep past. I'm not talking about Marty McFly in the time-traveling DeLorean DMC-12 automobile *Back to the Future* film trilogy stuff here. I'm talking about a time zone–crossing, Spirit journey, in which God's future is coming into the present. The past/future, both/and, urban/garden, deep roots/

wild branches, tree of life stuff. I'm talking about how the Spirit contextualizes the deep traditions of the ancient-future church to new situations.

Throughout church history, renewal movements are not so much about the discovery of the next new-fangled thing, but an awakening to something fundamental from a forgotten past. As H. Richard Niebuhr has famously said, "The great Christian revolutions come not by the discovery of something that was not known before. They happen when someone takes radically something that was already there." The force of resurrection, renewing, transfiguring, and making new is mostly about how God takes us through this process of awakening.

The folks from the United Kingdom are from our future. In England, I had the incredible opportunity to go back to the future. I crisscrossed the country, visiting fresh expressions, and interviewing the legendary scholars and pioneers where this movement began.

There I experienced pure Methodism for the first time . . . just not in a Methodist church. It was with a group of Anglicans, huddled together in the shadows of thousand-year-old London church steeples. There an eleven-year-old fresh expression of church called "Moot"—which identifies itself as a new monastic community—meets in a repurposed guild church, St. Mary Aldermary, around coffee, tea, and biscuits. Started by Ian Mosby and now continued by Rev. Paul Kennedy (an example of a fresh expression that thrived through a succession process), this congregation doesn't have a Sunday morning worship experience. They rent out their facility to a non-Anglican congregation during that time.[1]

However, this youngish group of professionals, many bouncing toddlers on their knees, meets almost daily for some form of worship, including Taizé, Eucharist, small group, and so on. For them, fresh expressions of church are no longer fresh; they are simply church. The new normal of following Jesus in a post-Christian society. As I experienced Rev. Kennedy, an astute Anglican theologian, present the gospel in a simple, relevant way, I had the powerful realization that this is what the first Methodists experienced. Led by Anglican clergy persons, those primitive Methodists gathered in the shadows of the institutional church, tethered to and yet distinct from it. Early Methodism was a both/and movement, where inherited and emerging forms of church were interacting in a life-giving exchange.

During my adventure traveling the ancient-future of England, I spent time in London, Oxford, Cambridge, Ely, Leicester, and Bristol. I visited historic places of worship where people had inhabited spaces for many centuries. I saw cavernous cathedrals of unprecedented beauty and grandeur. Many of those thin spaces were packed with tourists who waited in long lines for hours to pay an admission fee to visit and take pictures throughout the week. Yet, many of those same spaces were empty on Sunday mornings, or hosted a small congregation of people, huddling together in the looming bigness. Secularization and church decline are now advancing rapidly in the US as well.

## To Proclaim the Gospel Afresh

So, what can we in the US learn from our UK sisters and brothers who are from our future? While they are decades ahead of us in the decline of Christendom, they are now out ahead of us in this emerging missional movement, leading the church into a new future.

The preface to the Declaration of Assent that all incoming clergy must confess says, "The Church of England [is part of the One, Holy, Catholic and Apostolic Church, worshiping the one true God, Father, Son and Holy Spirit. It] professes the faith uniquely revealed in the Holy Scriptures and set forth in the catholic creeds, *which faith the Church is called upon to proclaim afresh in each generation.*"[2]

The term "fresh expressions" originated from this statement to describe something the Holy Spirit was up to in a new generation.

Bishop Graham Cray led the team of Anglicans, British Methodists, and others who produced the *Mission-Shaped Church* report in 2004. Rarely do church reports become international bestsellers, reimagine long-held assumptions about ecclesiology, or catalyze the development of thousands of fresh expressions, and similar initiatives in Australia, Canada, mainland Europe, South Africa, the US, and elsewhere . . . but this one did.[3]

In 2014, Michael Moynagh pulled together research that demonstrated that in ten Church of England dioceses, fresh expressions comprised as many as 15 percent of the dioceses' churches and 10 percent of their average weekly attendance. Roughly 25 percent of those who came were Christians, 35 percent were dones, and an astonishing 40 percent were nones (those who had no previous church experience). Most of those have emerged just in the last ten years! Those numbers didn't include Methodists and other UK denominations heavily involved in the movement.[4]

In 2017, Moynagh, summarizing Britain's Church Army Research Unit, reported at that time there were 1,104 fresh expressions of church, an estimated 50,600 people in attendance. Three-quarters of those initiatives were started in the past ten years and were accelerating in multiplication. An estimated 13.5 percent of local churches had at least one fresh expression of church. Average size was about fifty people of all ages, comprised mostly of people who were not attending church previously, and 80.4 percent were taking steps to growing disciples. Further, 37 percent had baptisms, while 43 percent held Holy Communion.[5]

In one sense, there should have never been a time the church was not about forming new communities that were missional, contextual, formational, and ecclesial. Or as we Fresh Expressions Florida folks say, "reaching new people, in new places, in new ways." Proclaiming the gospel afresh in each generation should always be a primary activity of the church.

**Fresh Expression:** These communities are:

Missional: Birthed by the Spirit to reach not-yet-Christians.

Contextual: Seek to serve the context in an appropriate form to the people in it.

Formational: Focused on making disciples.

Ecclesial: A full expression of the church, not a stepping-stone to an inherited congregation.

## Waves of the Spirit

While walking through the London subway, Graham Cray told me something I will never forget. He said, "We seem to have caught a wave of the Holy Spirit. Do try not to fall off!" Bishop Cray was highlighting an important point. Upon the ocean of the church's history, tidal waves of the missionary Spirit steadily come along.

In *Church for Every Context: An Introduction to Theology and Practice*, Michael Moynagh makes a compelling case that fresh expressions of church are one of the most crucial developments in the contemporary church. With the help of Philip Harold, Moynagh provides the undergirding theology and methodology for the movement. They explore multiple iterations of "contextual churches" in history that demonstrate the four characteristics of fresh expressions—missional, contextual, formational, and ecclesial. They start in the New Testament then from Antioch, Saint Patrick in Ireland, Celtic and Roman missionaries, Benedictine monasteries, laywomen Beguines, Ferrar's Little Gidding, John Wesley's class system, Charles Kingsley and the missional parish of Eversley, Dorothy Sayer's missional activity in the pubs, and right up to the fresh expressions of today.[6]

David Goodhew, Andrew Roberts, and Michael Volland similarly demonstrate that throughout Christian history we can point to multiple fresh expression movements, like the rise of monasticism, Cyril and Methodius contextualizing and spreading the faith across Eastern Europe, the founding of Franciscan communities that critiqued and regenerated medieval Christendom, the Reformation, the Evangelical Revival, the Oxford Movement, and Pentecostalism, just to name a few.[7]

I want to further empathize that, while they were missional, contextual, formational, and ecclesial in their own rite, most of these missional waves remained tethered and gave life to the inherited church. They were examples of a mixed economy. When the institutional church has embraced the power of these contextual churches, when stationary and mobile modes live together, the whole church thrives in a fuller way.

One powerful aspect of the Fresh Expressions movement is how it allows us to engage in what J. Todd Billings describes as a "theology of retrieval," which enables us in "hearing the voices of the past in such a way that they are allowed to exceed and overcome the chatter of the present."[8] In short, fresh expressions are a (re)freshing of the various missional innovations that solidify as tradition later. We can point to multiple similar movements in the church's history, of which Fresh Expressions is the latest iteration, enabling a blended ecology. Let us ride the wave of the Spirit indeed.

## Make Methodism Vile Again

Let's take the Methodist renewal movement, for example. Ready for some déjà vu? John Wesley observes that the Anglican Church that he loves and serves is largely failing to reach the vast majority of people. Once again, it is a Judges 2:10 scenario, "another generation grew up after them, who did not know the LORD or the work that he had done for Israel."

Most of the eighteenth-century population was experiencing poverty. They faced a time of enormous social and economic change and dislocation, as the global economy was beginning to emerge. Wesley and his band of rogue ones see a growing disconnect between the church and the people the church were supposed to be reaching. There is a sense that the episcopal bureaucracy of his day had become rigid, unyielding, and lifeless. Wesley's passion to connect with people outside the reach of the current structure of the church drives him to innovate.

On April 2, 1739, in a field just outside what was then the city limits of Bristol, he preaches for the first time outside the confines of a parish or pulpit. He writes in his journal that day, "At four in the afternoon I *submitted to be more vile*, and proclaimed in the highways the glad tidings of salvation . . ."[9] Against the derision of his colleagues and superiors, Wesley begins to take it to the fields, the miners camps, the debtors prisons, street corners, and tombstones. While it doesn't earn him many fans in the inherited church, thousands of people begin to respond to the gospel and accept Jesus for the first time. A movement is born.[10]

Wesley's heart to reach out to the new missional frontier, while simultaneously staying tethered to the Anglican Church, inadvertently creates one of the clearest examples of the blended ecology. John Wesley did not see Methodism as a separate church, but a renewal movement within the Church of England, which he served faithfully as an ordained clergyperson until the day he died. While the emerging Methodist communities with their system of societies, classes, and bands served primarily as forms of contextual church, Wesley intentionally grafted members back into the Church of England.

We sometimes too easily dismiss the relationship between early Methodism and the Anglican Church, or how vigorously Wesley opposed any splintering off. For example, his "Reasons Against a Separation from the Church of England" printed in 1758.[11] Perhaps for those of us in whom the *Mayflower* impulse flows through our veins we tend to easily jump right over to Methodism's formation as a separate denomination. While it certainly had its tensions from the start, people in the Methodist movement, many who were new Christians, were expected to attend worship at the local Anglican parish for Holy Communion and be involved in its life. This created an increase in attendance and a renewed sense of missional engagement in the Church of England. It also had inadvertent societal implications, which benefited the whole church, "lives of the converted changed, drinking was curtailed, family life improved, trades were learned, and money was saved. Social change and conversion were intertwined."[12] It changed the larger missional ecosystem.

Bishop George Sumner writes, "In mission, we are all Methodists now, at least in our root assumptions and many of our strategies." He notes how Wesleyan missiological DNA is deeply embedded in global Anglicanism, as a set of common features: "Lay leadership, Going out to where people are, Evangelistic gatherings, Small groups, Confession, Converted hearts, Singing" have been remixed in many contextual variations.[13] Thus, a common heritage between Wesleyanism and Anglicanism have led to discussions for full communion among the Episcopal Church and The United Methodist Church (UMC).[14]

In its earliest stages, the synergistic exchange caused the greater thriving of the whole church and the transformation of society. Ultimately, a refusal to offer a flexible polity to make room for the Methodist movement contributed to its formation as a separate denomination. We must wonder what could have happened if institution and movement could have learned to live together.

Nevertheless, John Wesley was a true pioneer and an apostolic imagineer. He organized the missional system that is semi-preserved in the polity of the UMC today as itinerancy, conferencing, episcopacy, and connectionalism. Wesley was not just hanging out in cool spaces beyond the walls of the inherited church. He held the missional passion to reach not-yet-Christians together with the structural genius to offer a process of transformation. From the first encounter with Christ, he took believers through a life of sanctifying grace and seeking perfection in love, while simultaneously encouraging participation in the larger church.

Once Methodism spread over to the United States, it took on a life of its own. While many undergirding principles remained the same, the movement had to respond and adapt to the new missional frontier. This fresh expression ultimately became institutionalized as the global organism we call the UMC.

Are you having déjà vu yet? Once again, a missional movement that began in the United Kingdom has found a home in the United States. Fresh Expressions US has played a central role in the catalyzation and perpetuation of this movement. Through strategic partnerships with conferences, denominations, dioceses, and networks, institution and movement are for the moment learning to catch a wave of the Spirit together.[15]

The United Methodist Church (UMC) is the largest single mainline denomination. Mainline denominations declined from 18.1 to 14.7 percent from 2007 to 2014, and the UMC fell from 5.1 of US adults in 2007 to 3.6 percent in 2014.[16] The UMC has been declining in membership at a fairly consistent rate of around 1.6 percent (consecutively each year) since 2006, with worship attendance decreasing approximately 2.9 percent during that time frame.[17] Decline for the UMC is not a new phenomenon; it has been occurring for approximately forty years.[18] The current levels of decline are bringing it to a crisis point.

My primary mission field is the Florida Conference of the United Methodist Church (hereafter FLUMC). Michael Polanyi suggests obsession with one's problem is the "mainspring of all inventive power," waking with it, eating lunch with it, and sleeping with it.[19] This I have done as an ordained elder in the UMC throughout my ministry. For the past five years, I've been intentionally studying the decline of the FLUMC and the cultivation of fresh expressions as a possible vehicle of revitalization.

The Florida UMC measures vitality and decline by certain institutional markers:

1. Average Worship Attendance: The congregation's annual average of worship attendees.
2. Professions of Faith: New Christians, or first-time Methodists becoming members of a congregation.
3. Apportionments Paid: The percentage of a local church's giving that proportionally supports the church-wide budget of the denomination.
4. Expense vs. Giving Comparison: How much money is a local church receiving, compared to what it's spending (paying of bills, clergy compensation, health benefits, and so on).[20]

In 2017, the FLUMC was comprised of 625+ churches (+ correlates with multi-site scenarios). Of these, 472 churches were flat or declining in Average Worship Attendance (AWA) over the previous five years: 242 churches lost 20 percent of their membership, and 272 reported one or no baptisms. Of these churches, 304 who lost AWA are in areas where the population is growing. In 2018, these trends continued with 593 church entities reporting end-of-year statistics. Of those, 64 percent were flat or declined in membership, and 69 percent were flat or declined in AWA.[21]

The eighty-six churches in the North Central District (NCD) mirror the larger decline. The official data (executive summary) collected by the FLUMC for the NCD in the 2018 Imprint Report is revealing. Sixty-four of the 86 churches are plateaued or declining. Thirty-five of these churches are worshiping below 50 in attendance. Thirty-one congregations are in high-risk scenarios, showing three or more risk indicators like declining worship, decreasing finances, and no new members. Nineteen congregations had no baptisms or professions of faith in the last three years.[22] It could be argued that the handful of those that are growing are taking advantage of demographic trends, like retirement migrations or urbanization—already-Christians moving into an area.

Part of my role as cultivator of fresh expressions has been the creation of the Generative Pioneer Leadership Academy (GPLA), as well as the formation of District Fresh Expressions Teams in each of the eight FLUMC districts. The GPLA is the first prototype of what may become the training system for pioneer ministers. Also, in this role I have led dozens of local church workshops with congregations that want to explore the cultivation of fresh expressions in their community.

The NCD sprawls beyond Gainesville on the northern end, and well south of The Villages on the southern end, including portions of Marion, Alachua, Sumter, Lake Citrus, Hernando, Pasco, and Levy Counties. Most of my conference work has been trying to scale our local and district learnings, then spread them throughout the whole state. This is a method called the Positive Deviance Approach.

> **Positive Deviance**: Refers to an approach to social change based on "deviants" whose uncommon but successful strategies enable them to find better solutions to a problem than their peers, despite facing similar challenges and having no extra resources or knowledge.[23]

I mentioned early the reality of the NCD being a blended-ecology district of 86 inherited congregations and 80 fresh expressions. Currently, extraneous variables make a direct statistical correlation between fresh expressions activity and the revitalization of inherited congregations difficult. However, the NCD shows some very positive developments. Each of the congregations experimenting with fresh expressions has experienced forms of revitalization. Most notably is the growth in professions of faith and baptisms. This refers to an increase in reaching and forming new Christians, which places these congregations among a small percentage growing in this way.[24]

Wildwood, now a model of the blended-ecology way, has been one of the pioneering churches in the movement. The revitalization of the congregation can directly be attributed to the thirteen fresh expressions of church meeting throughout the week. There are hundreds of people who have been engaged in those microcommunities outside the relational sphere of the inherited church. You can see similar transformation taking place in the field stories following each chapter.

This is exciting news. Through fresh expressions, not only are people being offered Christ for the first time, but inherited congregations are being revitalized by this approach. Joining into the "movementum" of fresh expressions allows existing churches to catch a fresh breath of resurrection.

While some claim the Methodist movement traded in missional zeal for respectability, the Fresh Expressions movement is allowing us to make Methodism vile again. Institution and movement are beginning to operate together in a life-giving way. Can we learn to do so without once again exiling the very apostolic impulses that may give us life? Can we learn from our past mistakes to make possible a new future? Can we embrace both a neighborhood and network approach to mission?

## Church in the "Flows"

While many resources have contributed to a neighborhood theology, a theology of place (also known as the parish model),[25] I want to offer a network theology, a theology of the space of flows in a network society (if you will, a network model). Understanding and adapting to the emergent societal structure enables us to explore new avenues for mission. We need to always engage *people* and *places* missionally. Yet, fresh expressions allow us also to engage *practices*, as a viable way to engage unreached *people*, connected by *flows*, in the *places* where they do life, and *digital* as well as *analog* forms of church. Thus, we expand our missional vocabulary and tools to include *people, places, networks, flows*, and *practices*.

The Fresh Expressions movement is allowing us to be church in the flows of a network society I discussed in the previous chapter. We need to continue to harness the power of attraction and the neighborhood mission model, while also finding a way to plant churches in the hyper-connected Matrix world of the digital frontier, which Moynagh and Worsley describe as "a world above the world."[26]

To understand how church forms in the flows, let's take the London Underground as an example. London, a city of ancient and rich history, has just as much going on upon the surface as it does beneath. A complex subway network, the London Underground or, "the Tube," connects people across the city. By harnessing the power of this underground transit system, one can travel just beneath the surface of the vast urban space. There are other ways to travel around the city; however, if one knows the Tube, how it connects, and which line to change at which station (nodes of the network), one can travel affordably, efficaciously, and rapidly.

Foreigners should not travel the Tube alone! Even with a map, an app, and doing prior research, the Underground is a complex network that takes years to fully understand. You need a local guide, a "person of peace," who knows and can show you the way. The Tube is a manifestation of layered indigenous culture. Many people utilize it their whole lives, and to them it is just the normal means of travel. Beneath the surface of the city is a way of being and doing that may seem strange to a foreigner. There are customs, dos and don'ts of communication, indigenous language about "minding the

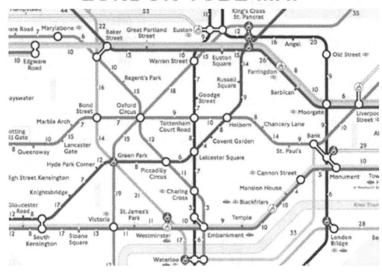

gap," and, of course, the buskers who perform for pocket change. To understand the Tube you need to get in, be an incarnational presence, and join the mobile flows of people and culture.

The Tube transports people, ideas, and culture across geographical boundaries to connect in physical places around shared practices, be it work, school, or play. This mobilization of people rapidly across time and space also causes geographical dislocation. One is no longer confined to a single neighborhood in the city, but can now travel great distances, exploring new places and leaving old ones behind.

## McGavran Remixed?

Martyn Percy offers a significant critique of the Fresh Expressions movement in an essay titled "Old Tricks for New Dogs?" Percy rightfully makes a connection between fresh expressions and Donald McGavran, particularly the highly criticized Homogeneous

Unit Principle. Percy finds it puzzling that there is no mention of McGavran's work in the Fresh Expressions literature, being that his "missiological DNA has deeply influenced the movement."[27]

Donald Anderson McGavran was a missiologist who was the founding dean and professor of mission, church growth, and South Asian studies at the School of World Mission at Fuller Theological Seminary in Pasadena, California. McGavran was the son of missionary parents and later followed in their footsteps. In 1955, after thirty-two years on the mission field in India, he wrote *The Bridges of God*, thus launching what would later be called the Church Growth Movement. McGavran spent much of his life trying to promote effective missional evangelism and Christian conversion.

Martyn Percy largely centers his critique of fresh expressions as "old tricks for new dogs," in that they are,

> primarily, contemporary versions of the homogeneous unit principle for church growth that was promoted over forty years ago, but was subsequently widely discredited by theologians, and also condemned by missiologists for its focus on pragmatism and its willingness to sanction narrowly constituted groups (on the basis of age, gender, race, class, wealth, etc.) as "church," which of course then legitimizes ageism, sexism, racism, classism and economic divisiveness.[28]

**The Homogenous Unit Principle:** At the simplest level describes subsections of society in which the members of those subsections have some characteristics in common and prefer to become Christians without crossing racial, linguistic, or class barriers.

Perhaps in his critique Percy throws the baby out with the bath water, so to speak. McGavran's church growth principles may offer incredible resources for the new missional frontier. The major criticisms of his missiological approach were as follows:

reliance on segregated homogenous units, separation of conversion from spiritual formation, reliance on numerical growth as primary criterion of growth, pragmatism, and overemphasis on the church.

Missiologist Ryan Bolger reminds us that these critiques were more reflective of McGavran's American "translators" than how church growth was originally conceived and practiced by McGavran. In the 1990s, the term "church growth" was hijacked and employed by church marketers in the growth of the suburban megachurches.[29]

Percy facetiously describes fresh expressions as a perfect fit for a post-institutional culture that avoids investment in complex organizations and infrastructures for the common good.[30] I would agree that he may be on to something; however, that critique does not take seriously the shifts that have occurred in the arising missional moment or the synergistic relational exchange of the blended ecology. If McGavran's principles are developed further, they provide powerful possibilities for the seeding of the gospel in our time, particularly when fresh expressions are held together in creative tension with the inherited church.

In *The Bridges of God*, McGavran asks the question "How do peoples become Christian?" rather than the Western approach of converting "individuals." Societies are made up of layers of social groups, and individuals are often limited to those circles in their own intimate strata.[31]

Vincent Donovan found McGavran's insights to be true in his own experience as a missionary to the Masai people in Tanzania for seventeen years. People are more than an aggregation of individuals. Donovan writes, "I noticed that every separate and homogenous group among the Masai had its own character, its own reactions, quite different from other groups. I began to think of each group as a kind of distinct personality, much as I had been accustomed to doing with individuals in America."[32]

Both Donovan and McGavran found that the highly individualized Western method of evangelizing people one by one, and bringing them back to the mission compound for Christianization, was an "extractional" and highly ineffective approach.[33] "In short, it is not possible or desirable to convert the Masai as individuals, but it is possible to evangelize them as groups," writes Donovan.[34]

Roland Allen also critiqued an extractional missional approach, in which evangelization was entirely dependent upon the construction of a building. He rejects "the prevalence of the idea that the stability of the church in some ways depends upon the permanence of its buildings."[35] Something certainly not part of the apostle Paul's missionary methods.

Allen highlights how this reduces Christianization to a financial operation. The mission becomes a transaction of foreign investment, followed by extraction of indigenous converts into the compound. Allen writes, "But it ought not properly to be a financial operation, and the moment it is allowed to appear as such, that moment very false and dangerous elements are introduced into our work."[36] He advocates that teaching, organization, finances, and so on must emerge from a healthy mutual responsibility among the people themselves in contextually appropriate ways to their social groups.[37]

People live in "social organisms"; they adopt changes as groups or not at all. McGavran employs the term "group mind" to describe how individuals don't understand themselves as a self-sufficient unit, but part of a group. Peoples are Christianized as this "group-mind is brought into a life-giving relationship to Jesus as Lord."[38] This social factor is often not considered in the Western missional posture. The inherited-only mode can be an extractional phenomenon.[39] In short, collectivistic cultures that prioritize group over self do not follow an individualized decision-making process. Peoples become Christian through a chain reaction of conversions, spreading through the group mind. McGavran calls this a "people movement." This is how "peoples" become Christians. Over time, each small group, a "workable community" can become a mass swell of new Christians.[40]

In *Understanding Church Growth*, McGavran defines peoples as tribes, castes, clans, or any tightly knit segment of society, and a movement consists of a series of several small groups coming to a decision. The joint decisions of a number of people in the group enable them to become Christian without social dislocation while remaining in full contact with their non-Christian relatives.[41] People-movement churches are a form of multi-individual, mutually interdependent conversions that are less dependent on the pastor/missionary. They quickly raise up indigenous leadership and worship not only on Sunday mornings but during the week as much as possible. McGavran warns against the premature expectation of immediate moral purity or demanding "the fruits of the Spirit" before an organic process of discipleship.[42]

McGavran acknowledged the complexity of North America, with its individualistic culture and many strata of society with varying degrees of dissatisfaction with themselves. He notes the possibility of many types of people movements and describes webs of relationships and friendships that are "bridges" of evangelization that should be found and used. Ideas, practices, foodstuffs, and convictions stream across these relational bridges. With profound prophetic insight, speaking of the US context, he notes how evangelism must be more than inviting people to church, but finding ways to be with non-Christians in daily life.[43]

In loosely knit societies like the US, relational bridges are less influential. However, Christians should utilize these bridges no matter how weak or narrow they may be. While McGavran admits to the possibility of segregation, he encourages building conglomerate congregations of mixed ethnic, linguistic, and educational backgrounds. For practical missional necessity, alongside those congregations, he advocates for the people-movement approach as well. Most congregations are already homogenous in nature and further divided by narrowly defined internal practice affiliations, choir, sowing circle, scout programs, and so on. Multiplying churches among one kind of people is necessary, for "there is no other way in which the multitudinous pieces of the human mosaic can become Christian."[44]

This insight does indeed inform the fresh expressions approach. The attractional-only mode of church, meeting in a particular place at a particular hour, has become inaccessible to many. A powerful way to reevangelize a post-Christendom culture is by creating new Christian communities among groups of people where they do life.

Ryan Bolger develops McGavran's thoughts further in a dynamic way by correlating McGavran's "mission stations" and "people movements" as the two primary modes of church today: mission stations (Gathered Colony Churches, attractional, modern; for our purposes, inherited mode congregations) and people movements (People Movement Churches, emerging, postmodern; for our purposes, fresh expressions of church). Bolger states that these two movements represent two different sociocultural systems: the first represents modernity and the second, postmodernity. He then discusses the implications for mission of a third sociocultural system, global information culture.[45]

Nineteenth-century mission stations in non-Western countries were spaces where gathered colonies of Christian believers would meet and live. Mission stations assumed a dominant view of Western culture. McGavran describes the "out of" dimension of conversion in the mission station approach, "mainly *out* of the tribe, *out* of the caste, and indeed *out* of the nation. Converts felt that they were joining not merely a new religion, but an entirely foreign way of life—proclaimed by foreigners, led by foreigners and ruled by foreigners. Converts came alone."[46] Thus the approach created broken marriages, severance of family ties, lone converts, in isolation, becoming dependent on the Western foreign missionaries.

Attractional churches in the postmodern society serve as a kind of mission station, where the approach is *to extract converts, and gather them at the compound*. The church functions as a modern organization, where ministers are compensated for their services in preserving the institution.[47] It is deeply attractional in nature and primarily static. Alan Hirsch warns that the *attractional* approach is also *extractional*, because it severs ties with the host culture and relational networks.[48] Thus, many people who have been participating in the inherited congregation for long periods of time find that their social network becomes isolated to only those in that church community and all social activities revolve around the church compound.

McGavran's people movements, on the other hand, respect the various cultures, do not operate from the Western superiority assumption, and enable people to become Christians without social dislocation. The focus is *to be church with the people where they are*. Since the goal is not extraction, but withness, people remain in full contact with their non-Christian relational networks. Indigenous, holistic, and reciprocal, these people movements reflect the missional, incarnational, and emerging approach of post-modernity.[49]

Within this current time of liminality and paradigm shift, Bolger recognizes that modernity and postmodernity both still exist today in different locales. Yet a nascent sociocultural dynamic has emerged that promises to overwhelm the previous two—global information culture. Bolger describes the mobile, networked, and movemental nature of culture. As he describes the movement of people, objects, and things from one node to another in social space, he discusses the emerging social structure in the language of Castell's "flows": the means through which these movements and connections occur.[50]

Borrowing from the work of Arjun Appadurai, Bolger cites the five flows as *ethnoscapes* (movement of peoples), *mediascapes* (movement of media), *technoscapes* (movement of technology), *finanscapes* (markets, movement of money), and *ideoscapes* (political, movement of ideas). These flows describe the fluidity and mobility of culture. They "begin and end, develop and disintegrate, connect and disconnect; they are fluid, dynamic hybrids, without any sense of cultural 'essence.'"[51]

Arjun Appadurai pioneered these terms in describing the global cultural economy as a complex, overlapping order where fundamental "disjunctures" between economy, culture, and politics exist. He sees these "scapes" as building blocks of imagined worlds and the relationship between them as way to understand *disjuncture* in a globalized society. Appadurai discusses how these "scapes" are the five essential constructs that overthrow the previous notions of separate economies and "pure capitalism" and cause a "disorganized capitalism."[52]

Thus, the very nature of a hyper-connected global community creates disjuncture by the loss of commitment to a particular locality. The separation caused by the emerging societal structure leads to *deterritorialization*.

**Deterritorialization** (De-territorial-ization): Refers to the disconnection between peoples, culture, and place. This term was first used in the English translation of the work by Deleuze and Guattari (1987). For our purposes, this refers to the distancing from one's locality made possible by these flows in virtual, cultural, and physical globalization.[53]

Physical globalization is "about people, things, and the rules governing them jumping physical boundaries."[54] Because of the compression of space and time, which simply means "things are getting faster and that you can jump great distances" with relative ease, people are no longer inhabiting a world that is "bound by territory."55 When people enabled by the space of flows jump to one geography, culture, government, they obviously leave another behind.

Bolger describes the concept of *deterritorialization* that pervades this new social dynamic as the severance of social, political, or cultural practices from their native places and populations. Hence, locally speaking, in the network society, cultures now consist of people connected by flows around practices. The performance of these dynamic practices cross geographic boundaries within uneven information flows. While people will continue to meet each other face-to-face in local places, because of the mobility and fluidity of flows, they will inevitably disconnect from other individuals and locations.56

As we live in the space of real virtuality, hyperconnected by the screens of our tech devices, we become dislocated from our neighborhoods. In the network society, the web as a global integrated communication system is a new communal place. While "virtual" implies presence on the online platform, which may be defined by the lack of materiality, this separation is not so clear in a coronavirus world. The web and wireless communications are more than traditional media, they are an extension of human presence (distanced contact). The COVID-19 pandemic caused us to consider a distributed form of church, connected across geography and time in the digital space of flows. Christians realized the World Wide Web is our parish and screens are our pulpits.

This does not mean we should settle for a digitally distributed church only. This would be just as fragmented as a physically collected—only church. In fact, we are seeing three important trends:

1. Young folks are learning the value of old-school acts of love: phone trees, care packages, or sending a letter by snail mail.

2. Older folks are learning the value of love through digital technology: virtual is real, social media provides connection, church doesn't need a building.
3. Placefulness: Jenny Odell employs this term to describe sensitivity and responsibility to the historical (what happened here) and ecological (who and what lives or lived here). Odell holds up bioregionalism (this involves the interrelation of human activity with ecological and geographical features) as a model for how we might be able to think about our place again.[57]

Incarnation is all about "placefulness."

We need collected *and* distributed, digital *and* analog, forms of church living together.

People now journey daily with and among many tribes in networks centered on shared practices. As this new social reality develops, mission strategies focused solely on people or locations are incapable of reaching the growing share of the population (the blue oceans, if you will). To engage this emerging reality, we will need to find ways to incarnate the gospel in the space of flows. Bolger suggests the following equation: holistic people movement + deterritorialization = practice movement.

**Practice Movements:** A missional approach appropriate for a globalized network society that focuses on the activities that bind people to each other in time and space (i.e., practices). Place becomes secondary to the social space of connections enabled by microelectronics-based information and communications technologies. Diverse peoples flow in and out of practice-centered communities. These movements involve pioneering Christ-followers who engage these practices through establishing an incarnational presence within the common community.[58]

In *Emerging Churches: Creating Christian Community in Postmodern Cultures*, Eddie Gibbs and Ryan Bolger use the word *practice* in a more particular way than only the activities themselves, rather "similar to the way it is used for a medical or legal practice or the business concept of 'communities of practice.'" So, this is a group of people who display a growing competence in a particular domain, perfecting the practice over the course of a lifetime through consistent contact with others. Gibbs and Bolger highlight a system of apprenticeship in which more accomplished practitioners "mentor their young apprentices, most often implicitly, in the ways of the craft. Much of this accomplished by spending time together as they participate in an embodied set of skills."[59]

Gibbs and Bolger define emerging churches as "communities that practice the way of Jesus within postmodern cultures." They identify three core practices of emerging churches that combine to generate further practices: (1) identifying with the life of Jesus, (2) transforming secular space, and (3) living as community.[60] These are essential to the life of fresh expressions of church.

For our purposes, communities of practice are groups of people who share a common passion for an activity and grow in the performance of that practice as they interact regularly over time. Followers of Jesus embody the three core practices within those communities gathering around a multitude of possible activities. Within those practices, "through shared actions and words, [they] point to the kingdom in such a way that the practice itself moves towards God."[61]

The practice itself will be transformed as the disciple seeks to live under the reign of Christ. Other participants in that practice are invited into that transformation through authentic relationship. Conversion occurs organically through the messy relational process around the shared practice as isolation is healed. A contextual form of church is forming, native to that practice, as faith and non-faith exist together. The Holy Spirit is transforming the dispositions of the participants as they enter more fully into the kingdom reign.[62]

These emerging communities operate in a "centered-set" way, rather than a "bounded-set." They are communities that primarily follow a "belonging before believing" journey.[63] As I will show in the grafting process later, both bounded and centered sets are valuable. The blended-ecology ecosystem harnesses the power of both.

**Bounded-set:** Communities that have clear boundaries, established around beliefs and behaviors, which are patrolled and enforced. One is included or excluded based on adherence.

**Centered-set:** Communities compromised of non-negotiable core convictions that are enthusiastically supported and maintained. While an inclusive community, the core convictions shape behavior. One is free to explore moving toward the center, regardless of where in proximity they may be to those beliefs and behaviors.[64]

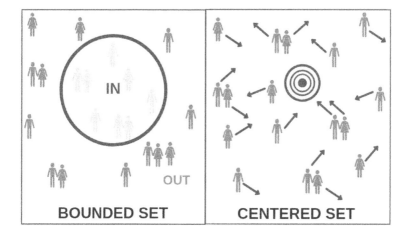

In fresh expressions, the questions are centered around how God is already at work here. How might this practice be transformed to point to Jesus? How do we find healing from isolation together through authentic witness? Christ-followers move between the practices, inhabiting different relational spheres, planting the kingdom seeds, searching for the already existing life-affirming tendencies, transforming the activities within the practice. This is church among the social space of connections. Micro-community churches gather and disperse, connecting relationally around the practices in endless contextual variations.[65]

The critiques of Percy, Davison, Milbank, and others don't take seriously these fundamental shifts in societal structure.[66] No amount of tinkering in the neighborhood parish that operates primarily in the attractional-only mode will engage a vast majority of the population in a network society.

Homogenous units take on a different reality in these global flows. Fresh expressions form among groups of people who are a "workable community," often connected by some ritual, place, or hobby. These are living social organisms distinct from other social groups. The focus is not to extract people from their indigenous communities and bring them back to the church compound for proper Christianization, but to help those communities form church where they are. This enables the church, largely inaccessible to many, to manifest in every nook and cranny of everyday life.

The people in these groups can be as diverse, or homogeneous, as the bundled practices call for, or the neutral places where they take place. "Practice movements" feature an incredible array of age, gender, race, class, and wealth, while others are more appealing to certain demographics. They are a contextual manifestation of the people and places connected by flows in which they exist, so in that sense they can be homogeneous but often reflect diversity. Diversity, or lack thereof, is a reflection of the practitioners of the practices in the context itself, which are *fundamentally more diverse* than inherited congregations across the board.

Percy concedes "that fresh expressions can make a modest and positive contribution to the mixed economy of church life."[67] While this understated concession cracks open the window to allow a fresh draft of understanding toward how the Spirit is working to blend inherited and emerging forms in a life-giving exchange, it only takes a single breath of fresh air to transform an ecosystem.

## Fresh Expressions—A Breath of Fresh Air
*John 20:19–23*

Sometimes you need a breath of fresh air. The first disciples certainly did. Once, they were holed together in a little room with the doors locked and the windows barred. The room was heavy with the stench of fear—suffocating, even. Can you imagine the headlines in *The Jerusalem Times*?: "Another Rebel Rouser Crucified"; "Obscure Nazarene Who Claimed to Be God Put to Death; Disciples Scatter Like Roaches!"; "Another Political Seditionist Executed."

There they were, trembling, holed up in a little room, terrified that they would find the same fate as their leader. Can't really blame them; this is scary stuff. The whole place stunk to high heaven with the body odor of a bunch of grown-ups cowering in fear. The air in that room was poisoned with terror.

Then Jesus entered the room, and what an awesome entrance it was; he just materialized right there in their presence! The room was full of chaos, but Jesus spoke peace. And when he spoke, with the familiar voice that they knew so well, the fear in the air began to dissipate. Then he showed them his hands and side; his resurrected body is transformed at a molecular level, but still bares the wounds. The wounds served to validate who he was and what he promised.

Then he breathes on them . . . a breath of fresh air. The breath is disruptive to their suffocation. Jesus turns the scent of death into the fragrance of joy. Then he says, "Just as I am sent, I am sending you." If it all ended in that little room, if all the time he invested in them and loved them, stopped there in that place, it would all be for nothing. You see, he was counting on them: he was sent, so that they could be sent. When he breathes, he says, "Receive now the Holy Spirit." Notice how all three persons of the Trinity are present, all the Christology and pneumatology of this gospel is fulfilled. Missiology and ecclesiology are all mixed together in one community of sent-ness. It's the resurrection, Pentecost, and Great Commission all wrapped up in one moment (John 20:19–23)!

They, in turn, filled with the Holy Spirit, breathed that new life into others. The breath of fresh air is the turning point, an encounter with the resurrected Jesus. Empowered by the Holy Spirit, they went forth and brought the gospel to the entire world. Something about a breath of fresh air can change everything. The church is sent with a breath of fresh air.

*Jesus disrupts the suffocation of decline by awakening us to our sentness.*

If there is one fitting image for the church today, it's here in John 20. How many congregations are stuck between the walls of their facilities, choking on fear and incertitude? What rational person has not at times wondered if Christianity in the US has ended, train wrecked on a lonely cross? Throughout history, there are times when Jesus breathes his sending breath afresh on the church. There are times when we are called to move outside the walls of our familiar institutions. We are living in one of those times.

## Fresh Expressions as Disruptive Innovation

How can suffocating institutions find a breath of fresh air that may let them live again? Fresh Expressions is one way that Jesus is breathing afresh on the church. Let's return to the concept of how institutions can harness the power of disruptive innovation—traditioned innovation.

The disruptive innovation process typically harnesses a technology that circumvents the current structures and bureaucracies. When this occurs, it changes the market, and the entire system has to respond to the innovation. Forward-looking, proactive organizations can harness the energy, ride the shift, and capitalize on the new emerging scenario through the power of dual transformation. Rigid institutions that misunderstand their own purpose, who base their identity in how they have been successful in the previous market, will ultimately fail.

I spoke earlier of the shift from neighborhoods to networks. These networks encompass tens of thousands of micro-communities (McGavran's tribes) and billions of people who have no connection with a church. The likelihood of them suddenly having an overwhelming desire to show up some Sunday morning to experience something that many see as an obsolete relic of a past age is unlikely. When they do, chances of connecting deeply in the life of a congregation stuck in a 1990's time capsule is equally unlikely. A fitting analogy would be visiting a museum. I may visit a museum, but the likelihood that I will try and set up residence there is extremely slim.

Let's look again at the analogy of the Tube as an illustration for the new missional frontier.

In the Fresh Expressions movement, we call the missionary teams cultivating communities of Jesus throughout the space of flows in a network society "pioneers." While in some sense all people have the capacity to start something new, we describe three essential roles for the Fresh Expressions movement to thrive: pioneers, supporters, and permission givers.

**Pioneers**: Are passionate about mission on the edges.

**Supporters**: Are passionate about supporting and releasing pioneers.

**Permission Givers**: Are passionate about using their role to foster the release of pioneers and to influence the system to be more willing to experiment.

The Church of England defines pioneers as "people called by God who are the first to see and creatively respond to the Holy Spirit's initiatives with those outside the church; gathering others around them as they seek to establish a new contextual Christian community."[68]

The places where pioneer teams engage not-yet-Christians around shared practices are the first, second, and third places of our larger communal ecosystems.

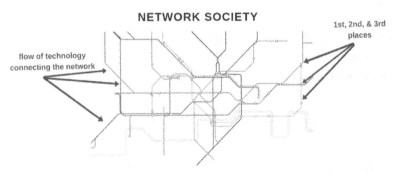

## Google It

**First Place:** The home or primary place of residence.

**Second Place:** The workplace or school place.

**Third Place:** The public places separate from the two usual social environments of home and workplace that "host the regular, voluntary, informal, and happily anticipated gatherings of individuals." Examples are environments such as cafes, pubs, clubs, parks, and so on.[69]

The fresh expressions approach is a form of "practice movement." While it is ultimately about reaching people, it focuses on the activities that people gather around for communal life. Pioneers establish relationships and share the gospel with diverse peoples who flow in and out of the practice-centered communities. "Workable communities" are evangelized in groups in the normal spaces, rhythms, and practices of their everyday lives.

Let me offer some examples to flesh out what this looks like in real practice. Did you know people love their dogs? There is an entire subculture of people who find that their fur babies add meaning and fulfillment to their lives. They take their dogs to the dog park religiously, thus Paws of Praise is church in the dog park. How about fit culture? Runners run . . . religiously! They gather in community around the practice of running together. So, Church 3.1 is church with a group of runners as they meet for their weekly 5k.

In the UK, how about the fresh expression in Essex for skateboarding and BMX culture? Or how about the church of surfers in Cornwall? Or perhaps SoundCafe, a fresh expression with those experiencing homelessness in Leicester?

What about Tex-Mex? There is an entire tribe built up around a deep love for a good blend of Mexican/Southern American food characteristic of the border regions of Texas and Mexico. More specifically, there are even communities of folks who love Moe's Southwest Grill and dislike the community of folks who prefer Chipotle, and vice versa.

When you arrive at Burritos and Bibles, a church emerging among a community of burrito connoisseurs, you are not greeted by an usher with a bulletin. Rather the staff yells excitedly, "Welcome to Moe's!" You don't sign an attendance pad, rather you check in on the various social media platforms. The Bible is on your iPhone and the sermon is a conversation. I've watched with great joy as people entered a relationship with Jesus by the ice machine or received Holy Communion (unleavened tortilla and Hi-C) for the first time.

How about gaming? Gamer.Church is a fresh expression of church among people who are immersed in the video gaming community in Huntsville, Alabama. How about kayaking? You can join a fresh expression in Jacksonville, Florida, called Kayaking with Jeff, having church together while paddling down the river.

How about tattooing? This is a huge practice in our society.[70] Tattoo Parlor Church is a fresh expression worshiping Jesus in Fat Kats Artistry in downtown Ocala, Florida.

Let me tell you about my friend Nick. Nick was one of the artists at Tattoo Parlor Church. While we "be the church" in the front room of the parlor, he is in the back freshening up living canvases with colorful faith-based symbols. We noticed Nick would often linger and hang out, listening to the conversations we were having about Jesus, even politely bowing his head when we prayed, but never engaging. One day when we were having the Lord's Supper, Nick finally popped the question, "So, what is the Communion thing all about?" That opened the door for us to share about God's incredible love in Jesus, who invited ex-cons, prostitutes, church folks, and tax collectors to his table. After an extensive conversation about what all this meant, Nick responded with, "Okay, I'm in, I need some Jesus in my life." Then he accepted Christ and took Communion for the first time.

One of the questions I often raise across the US is, "Is there any way we would have reached Nick with our Sunday morning attractional-only model?" The answer is no, because he is one of the 60 percent of the population who work on Sundays or would never come. The next question is, "How would many churches receive Nick, with his head, face, and neck covered in tattoos?" Most would not receive him very well.

When COVID-19 struck, we lost our second and third places. Our church was forced to move into an entirely distributed form. This caused us to harness the only spaces we had left, the home space and the digital space. Our approach with worship was not to do the stage production in an empty sanctuary bit, but to return to the church we see in the book of Acts, who met primarily in their homes. We call this "Living Room Church." Using various technologies, we have sermonic conversations, pray, sing, have Communion, and interact together. Some of our fresh expressions died; others, like Digital Yoga Church (practicing yoga together through Facebook Live and YouTube), Supper Table Church (families eating meals together in quarantine connected by screens), and Underground Seminary (a gathering of lay and clergy learning together through Zoom) began to thrive like never before.

This is happening in endless contextual variations on social media and in gyms, movie theaters, pool halls, pubs, community centers, karate dojos, dog parks, yoga studios, hair salons, and so on, all over the US. Many of the emerging forms of church are interacting synergistically with inherited congregations. This is traditioned innovation in the deepest sense of the word.

As you can see, the Fresh Expressions movement allows an adaptability and responsiveness that the larger church has lacked for quite some time. It also allows us to harness the latest technologies in profound ways, for instance, using social media to gather people in physical places across geographies. We can do this without abandoning the inherited church that gave us life.

In the blended ecology, with the breath of Jesus' Spirit in our lungs, we can harness the power of flows, transfigure the common practices in the first, second, third places, while cultivating growth in the inherited congregation.

## FIELD INTERVIEW
# Luke Edwards

Fresh Expression Pioneer,
Pastor of King Street Church

Luke Edwards is the associate director of church development for the Western North Carolina Conference of the United Methodist Church and a trainer for Fresh Expressions US. He was the founding pastor of King Street Church, a network of fresh expressions in Boone, North Carolina. Participating in local, regional, and national levels of the Fresh Expressions movement has given Luke a unique perspective into the future of the mainline church in a post-Christian society.

### Can you briefly describe the fresh expression(s) of your church?

King Street Church is a network of fresh expressions. We have fresh expressions that meet in a downtown storefront, a homeless shelter, and the county jail. We've prioritized folks who are not yet connected to a church, particularly those who have been discarded by society.

Many of our church members have criminal records or struggle with mental illness, addiction, and traumatic pasts. We come together in chaotic little fresh expressions of church to read Scripture, apply it to our lives, and reflect on where God is moving among us.

## Explain the blended ecology dynamics between the inherited church and your fresh expressions. What kind of tension, if any, goes on between the two?

King Street Church has a really beautiful relationship with our inherited church. We are a campus of Boone UMC. King Street Church is not its own entity. We are not chartered. We are fully under the umbrella of Boone UMC. This allows KSC to focus fully on creative ministry. The administrative staff of Boone UMC handles our finances and statistical reporting. In addition, as the KSC pastor I am held accountable by the traditional systems in place at Boone UMC (i.e., staff parish committee). In exchange, Boone UMC is able to extend its reach to folks they were not able to connect with. Folks at Boone UMC take great pride in the impact that King Street Church is making in our community.

## How have you seen the fresh expressions have a positive impact on the existing congregation? In what ways?

King Street Church has widened the church family of Boone UMC. Because of King Street Church, Boone UMC now has family members who are incarcerated, folks who are experiencing homelessness, folks that would not set foot in the church building. In addition, KSC has given Boone UMC members a refreshed sense of mission and reminder of why the church exists. Once or twice a year a formerly incarcerated member of King Street Church shares their story in Sunday morning worship at Boone UMC. They're always greeted with applause, hugs, and warm encouragement.

**Knowing that launching fresh expressions in your congregation involves time, sacrifice, resources, and people power, why do you believe it's worthy to pursue?**

Starting new congregations remains one of the most effective ways of making new disciples. Starting an inherited church is expensive, and our resources continue to dry up. Starting a fresh expression is an excellent way to make new disciples that costs little to no money. The sacrifices of time and people power quickly feel worth it when children of God who have been outcasts find a family. There's nothing like looking around the table at King Street Church, seeing my friends laugh and cry together, some of them finding a sense of belonging for the first time in years, others for the first time in their life. There's nothing more worthwhile than that.

CHAPTER 5

# Deep Roots—
# The Blended Ecology

Then the angel showed me the river of the water of life, bright as crystal, flowing from the throne of God and of the Lamb through the middle of the street of the city. On either side of the river is the tree of life with its twelve kinds of fruit, producing its fruit each month; and the leaves of the tree are for the healing of the nations. (Rev. 22:1–2)

The books or the music in which we thought the beauty was located will betray us if we trust to them; it was not in them, it only came through them, and what came through them was longing. . . . For they are not the thing itself; they are only the scent of a flower we have not found, the echo of a tune we have not heard, news from a country we have never yet visited.
—C. S. Lewis

The blended ecology is deeply rooted in a scriptural vision of the church. It is, in fact, the deepest story of our communal life, springing forth from our legitimating narrative. The Bible never explicitly defines what the church *is*. It offers us a kaleidoscope of images of what the church is *like*. Where we want a definition, Scripture sings a story.

The story a person or community inhabits shapes their behavior and health. For instance, as an abused and abandoned child, I defined myself as someone who was defective, unworthy, and broken for most of my young life. I engaged in all kinds of unhealthy behaviors to numb my shame. I accepted a false legitimating narrative that said, "I am not enough." When I heard Jesus call me "beloved" and accepted an invitation into a relationship with him, I exchanged that death-dealing narrative for a new story. If you change your metaphor, you can change your life. This is not only true of individuals, but of communities, and, most particularly, the church.

Paul Minear speaks about the power of a derived self-understanding flowing from a dominant image. He warns that if an inauthentic image dominates the church's consciousness, there will be decline and communal deterioration. He writes,

> If an authentic image is recognized at the verbal level but denied in practice, there will also follow sure disintegration of the ligaments of corporate life. The process of discovering and rediscovering an authentic self-image will involve the whole community not only in clearheaded conceptual thinking and disciplined speech, but also in a rebirth of its images and its imagination, and in the absorption of these images into the interstices of communal activities of every sort."[1]

Quite simply, the church is stuck in a bad metaphor. We need to get out. The wrong self-image causes deterioration and decline. This is part of the identity crisis contributing to the decline of the church in the US. We have lost our legitimating narrative and imported the images/structures/practices of the American corporation into the church to the degree we have corrupted her at a fundamental level. We need to change the metaphors to have new life. We need to draw our life from the Holy Trinity and root our identity in the incredible tapestry of biblical images: bride, body, tree, vineyard, family, field, urban garden, and many more. Revitalization starts with finding the right image again: a mission metaphor.

Paul Avis writes, "As the mystical body of Christ, the nature of the church cannot be plumbed by our puny human intellectual efforts."[2] Indeed, trying to discern the nature of the church is a comical endeavor, although a necessary one. While the church is a significantly complex living organism, we should not need an advanced degree to understand and talk about her. While much energy in thinking about the church is focused on the nature, structure, mission, and the various identities and polities of her many denominations, I want to explore a simpler question: What are the primary ways God has been with us throughout time?

Perhaps the most fruitful endeavor toward recovering a healthy self-image for the church's revitalization is simply journeying through the scriptural witness to discern what is the history of the *dominant modes of God's presence with humankind.*

We spend so much time deconstructing the biblical images individually like machine parts, trying to understand the pieces, then putting them back together.

All the scriptural images taken together highlight a simple key in understanding the mystery of the church—the church is a community inhabited by the birthing, sustaining, transforming *presence* of God. Without the Spirit, the body of Christ is merely a corpse. What the church is or isn't is derived from the very life of God. No God; no church. No matter how many parlor tricks one may attempt to make it seem otherwise.

In a hyper-connected world, yet trapped in the individualism of the modern condition, we are alone,[3] longing for real community and connection in a network society typified by deterritorialization—the disconnection from one's locality. The deepest pain of our human condition is isolation.

It is in this condition that the church has a gift to offer, what Michael Moynagh calls "communal life with Jesus."[4] In fact, this is the only gift that the church alone can give. For instance, many organizations can feed the hungry, clothe the naked, work for social justice reform, care for the elderly, and so on. The church should certainly be doing those things under the direction and power of the Spirit. But the church alone can give the greatest gift of all—communal life with Jesus—a gift the world desperately needs.

The church is the primary way that God offers Godself in the earth, healing the isolation of our sin-fragmented condition—the body of Christ, broken and given to the world.

So, what are the primary ways God's withness manifests with God's people? God's presence fills the whole universe; there is nowhere one can go where God is not (Jer. 23:24).

However, there are primarily two *modes* of how God has gathered people around his presence throughout history:

**Stationary mode:** A fixed place where God dwells—attractional—God invites us into God's holy space.

**Mobile mode:** God dwells with us on the move—incarnational—God moves into our space.

I use the word *mode*, not simply to denote a way something is experienced or expressed, but in the musical denotation, as a set of musical notes forming a scale and from which melodies and harmonies are arranged from pitches in intervals.

In the movie *Australia*, Nullah, a brave, half-Aboriginal, orphaned child uses the deep magic of the Aborigine people to sing "Mrs. Boss" (Lady Ashley) to him. Nullah's ancestors believed that the Creator sang the universe into existence. In a very emotional scene in the film, when Nullah is being taken away, this is their exchange:

**Lady Ashley:** I will come and find you; whatever it takes, we'll be together again.
**Nullah:** I believe you, Mrs. Boss.
**Nullah (whispers):** Mrs. Boss, I sing you to me.
**Lady Ashley:** And I will hear you, my darling.[5]

When speaking of the modes of God's presence, I'm simply saying there are primarily two ways that "God sings us to him."

I'm completely aware of what an oversimplification this is; however, what I will show is the great value of local churches understanding that witness manifests in primarily these two ways from cover to cover in the Bible: as a stable, centered presence deeply rooted in a place, that draws everyone in orbit into worship, and as a mobile, dispersed, scattered presence, running wild in the earth.

Most churches operate primarily in one of those modes, but what are the implications if a local church can embody both?

Michael Moynagh highlights the absurdity of the attractional-only model with the question "Gathered for worship, scattered for life?" He points to the deficient nature of the current model as Christians gather for worship on Sunday mornings, then enter the world as individuals. He highlights the potential of fresh expressions to allow Christians to both *gather* on Sunday mornings and then create *scattered gatherings* throughout the week.[6] One can also see the absurdity of the emerging mode operating in isolation as well when the deep roots and stability of local congregations are available to offer centering for these fragile communities.

Moynagh discusses the tensions of the mixed economy, some being that there are those who are using the emerging mode to function apart from the inherited church. Also, inherited churches can stifle the creative innovation of the emerging modes, and despite the potential of the blended way, denominations have yet to fully embrace and fund it.[7]

Moynagh sees the "mixed economy" as "pockets in the same pair of trousers." He offers five lenses as a theological base for structuring the church missionally in the blended-ecology way: (1) Trinitarian perspective: This mixed mode reflects the relational personhood of God. (2) Creation perspective: God creates male and female in God's image; this diversity reflects the divine image. (3) New Testament perspective: Jerusalem and Antioch function together. (4) Sacramental perspective: Baptism and Holy Communion reflect unity and diversity to the world, thus the unique individual is given a new communal identity and the diverse community centers around the one table. (5) Prophetic perspective: Prophets standing in the wilderness can confront the community with a call to fidelity. Healthy conflict is often part of the healing process.[8]

This is a solid theological base from which to build our understanding. Let's explore some of these themes more deeply.

## Holy Trinity—A Community of Withness

The study of how God dwells among us must begin with God. The church finds the legitimating narrative from which our structure flows in the very being of the pioneer God. Lincoln Harvey in reference to the mixed economy says,

> God's own economy—his handiwork, so to speak—"reflects" his eternal nature. If this assumption is allowed, it enables us to reimagine the mixed economy and see it as a lively reality, appropriately reflecting the dynamic and loving interrelationship that is God the Father, Son and Holy Spirit . . . celebrating the positive interplay of innovation and stability, continuity and change that the current situation demonstrates.[9]

The linking of mission with the Trinity was a revolutionary innovation in missiology. No longer is mission understood as a secondary subject of ecclesiology or soteriology, but is now understood as derived from the very nature of God. David Bosch writes, "The classical doctrine on the *missio Dei* as God the Father sending the Son, and God the Father and the Son sending the Spirit was expanded to include yet another 'movement': Father, Son, and Holy Spirit sending the church into the world."[10]

What are the implications if we follow this understanding through the lens of ecclesiology to the very structure of the church? What if we were to understand the *perichoresis*—the Greek term that expresses "interpenetration" as the true potential form of the church? Or what if how the persons of the Trinity relate as a "community of being" is the very form the church can take? What would that look like?

Martyn Atkins writes of the essence of the church being a "derived nature" from the triune Godhead. The church as a "chosen partner" in God's mission, has no essence "in itself," but rather the "essence necessarily derives from the Christian Godhead, and therefore the nature and life of the Church is created and configured by the life and character of the Christian Godhead." Atkins writes that the "meta-story, the overarching thrust of Scripture can be discerned, is deeply significant, and bears witness to the fundamental character of God, who can legitimately be understood as supreme missionary and evangelist."[11]

*The form of the church also is derived from the missionary Trinity.* Quite literally, the shape of the church emerges from the person of God—that form is a blended ecology.

While all images that seek to embody and explain the mystery of the Trinity break down, I want to offer up one to help us think about the relational being of God and how that structure is enfleshed as church. The structural image is the double helix of DNA, the trunk

# The Blended Ecology

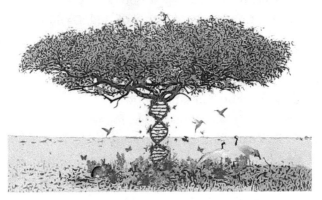

of our tree of life, if you will. Take a closer look at this image of the tree of life.

Notice the triality of the DNA structure of the trunk. One can say that DNA is the basic building block of life in its simplest form. That form manifests in the three-in-one structure of the double helix. I find it intriguing that the double helix offers us a tangible model of the relational matrix of our Trinitarian God.

> **DNA:** Deoxyribonucleic acid, a self-replicating material present in nearly all living organisms as the main constituent of chromosomes. It is the carrier of genetic information. Most DNA molecules consist of two biopolymer strands coiled around each other to form a double helix.

As you can see in the diagram, DNA resembles a spiral ladder. Structurally speaking, if you observe the two sugar phosphate strands as the backbone of the double helix, the four nitrogenous bases are the ladder rungs that bond them together. Without an

extensive biological lesson on the wonderful world of molecular genetics, for our purposes, let's simply note the actual structure. Elegance describes this form—pleasingly ingenious and simple.

One can easily envision the two "backbone" strands of the double helix as God the Father and God the Son; the "rungs" that bind the structure together could be considered God the Holy Spirit. If you prefer, you could replace each person of the Godhead in this corresponding three-part form, and it would still be theologically accurate! (For instance, God the Father as bonding rungs, Son and Spirit as backbone, etc.)

So, at one level, we could say the Trinitarian form of God is the essence of all creation. At the molecular level, three-in-oneness is the basic building block of all life. Now, that's a new look at humanity being created in the image of God. At another level, the image demonstrates the relational nature of God's own being; if you take away any component, or in our case, person, you don't have the Christian God anymore, you have something else. For our purposes, I want to use this framework of the very relationality and personhood of God to propose a structural design for the church that bears God's image.

The church as an institution, structurally speaking, should be based in God's own being, not McDonaldized corporate business models of the twentieth century. Before you shrink back from the words *structure* and *institution*, consider that institutions in and of themselves are a gift from God that shape the *habitus* of human beings. Alan Roxburgh says, "Structures, then, are how legitimating narratives are given material expressions in organizations, groups and societies. We are embodied, meaning-making social beings who create structures to carry the stories that mold and define our lives."[12]

**Habitus:** A system of dispositions, a corporeal knowledge that we carry in our bodies. A kind of second nature, or hardwiring, formed by story, parents, peers, and the repeated physicality of doing things again and again. Repeated behaviors become habitual, reflexive, and borne in our bodies. Learning habitus involves both bodily movement—kinesthetics—and engagement of the imagination—poetics.[13]

Furthermore, whether we like it or not, we inhabit a world of institutions. Institutions themselves are not easily changed, but they can be futurefitted. To release revitalization of existing congregations, we must not only reclaim our formative story (legitimating narrative) and remix it in a culturally compelling way, we must also reconfigure the local church in ways that reflect that formative story. Anarchical language of throwing down Jurassic institutions is not helpful for our task. Niall Ferguson reminds us, "Institutions are, of course, in some sense the products of culture.... Because they formalize a set of norms, institutions are often the things that keep us honest."[14]

As the church, for better or worse, is the most formative institution in Western history, it is more helpful to deal with that reality honestly. However, my concern is not the reformation of the institutional church from some top-down model. The structural remix I propose, while not anarchical, is in some sense subversively revolutionary. My approach is a bottom-up, grassroots, futurefitting proposal. I am speaking to (re)missioning local congregations to catalyze renewal. That kind of grassroots revolution and bottom-up innovation is, in fact, a part of the legitimating narrative of the church.

## Blended Ecology—The Deepest Story

A church stuck in one mode is not singing the whole God song. We looked briefly at some of the renewal movements in history, particularly early Methodism as an example. The times when the church has reflected these two primary modes of God's presence in her life simultaneously are the times of her greatest vitality. Let's now search the Scriptures together to recover this narrative, the most pronounced being that of Jerusalem and Antioch in the book of Acts.

Depending on your theological tradition, you may find it helpful to understand the rungs of this proposed structure as Scripture, tradition, reason, and experience. The Spirit working through Scripture is one of the rungs that holds this double helix together. This anchors us in the Spirit's work of the past as we dance the edge of chaos, reaching for the rope of hope the Spirit is throwing from the future.

Among the plethora of scriptural images for the church: body of Christ, people of God, bride, new creation, fellowship of faith, temple of living stones, family, and so on, or the many that are agrarian in nature—vineyard, loaf, olive tree, fig tree, field, and urban garden.

While the tree of life itself is not implicitly an image of the church, it is a profound symbol of the consistency of God's presence with humanity. Our story begins at the tree (Gen. 2:9), goes horribly wrong at the tree (Gen. 3:22), begins again at the tree (Gal. 3:13), and continues indefinitely at the tree (Rev. 22:2). The tree is present at creation, fall, redemption, and new creation. It qualifies the community that gathers around it, for if Jesus is the "way, truth, and life" (John 14:6), then the life of this tree is the life Jesus gives.

Further, trees play a prominent role in the scriptural narrative. In the Old Testament, the major symbol of Israel's life was the fig tree (Hosea 9:10). The prophets used the tree as a symbol of the coming kingdom where even the birds (Gentiles) would find shelter (Dan. 4:1–12). Ezekiel used the symbol of the tree to describe the vitality of the people's relationship with God as "dry or green" (Ezek. 17:24). Jesus frequently used trees as prominent images in his teaching: small mustard-seed beginnings that bring that kingdom tree into being (Matt. 13:31–32), vineyard and branches (John 15), barren trees that needs revitalization (Luke 13:6–9), cursing a fig tree as a figuration for a fruitless people (Mark 11:12–14), trees not planted by the Father will be uprooted (Matt. 15:13), and so on.

It is often overlooked that the menorah—the lampstand in the tabernacle—itself was constructed and ornamented in the treelike form (Ex. 25:31–37). The menorah not only symbolized the tree of life but also the burning bush, both which were symbolic of God's presence. Earlier we saw how this tree of life, stylized in the lampstand, was mobile in the tabernacle: the microcosm of a traveling Eden, where the wild God moved along with the people, again "walking in the garden in the cool of the day" (Gen. 3:8 NIV). The fiery tree-of-life lampstand, ark, and other tabernacle items were relocated into the temple (1 Kings 8:1–4; 2 Chron. 5:2–5), now as an Edenic place of God's stationary presence on Mt. Zion.[15] Later, the menorah became a central image of the synagogue, the remixed burning bush, tree of life, now shedding light on the Torah.

The deepest structural narrative of the community of faith in the Bible is not tabernacle, synagogue, *or* temple, Jerusalem *or* Antioch, the gathered *or* the scattered, the inherited *or* the emerging, the attractional *or* the missional; it's the *blended ecology*. God sings us into his presence in both these modes.

## Tabernacle, Synagogue, and Temple

One of the first post-fall images the Old Testament reveals for God's withness as the communal center of humanity is the *tabernacle mode*. Following the exodus from Egypt, after a period of wandering, the story is institutionalized in the ritual practices taking place in the tabernacle. The formative story, the legitimating narrative, is one of liberation from an enslaved condition. YHWH is the agent of the intervening action of that redemption, whose presence is now the rightful center of this wandering, mobile community.

The Scriptures describe the tabernacle as designed by God himself (Ex. 26). The tabernacle is an incredible testament to the creativity of God; the meticulous detail of every facet of the construction results in a beautiful mobile dwelling. Certain individuals are recruited into the construction and maintenance of this splendid but mobile edifice.

Beside Moses, Aaron and his bloodline become the professionalized class now tasked with maintaining the tabernacle and conducting the various ritualizations of the formative stories (Ex. 28:1). They become middle men between YHWH and the people, representing God to the community, and the community to God. The space of their activities is the tabernacle, the religious center of the community. God also sends prophets in the wilderness, outside the religious system, to speak a word to, for, or against the priestly system (see Amos or Jeremiah, for instance).

There is a clear and compelling missional imperative of both God and the people who reflect God. We discover God's promise to Abraham to make his descendants as numerous "as the stars in the sky and as the sand on the seashore" (Gen. 22:17 NIV) will be fulfilled by this new relational arrangement. YHWH gifts the covenant to the people to offer protective boundaries for their own well-being and so that they might reflect the actual character of YHWH to all the nations. As covenant people, a kingdom of priests, and a holy nation, their habitus, the very rhythms of their being, will be a "light" to which all the "nations" of the earth will stream (Isa. 60:3).

The locus of YHWH's presence with these redeemed ones is embodied in the tabernacle. In the liminality between liberation and promised land the wild God is a mobile force amid the people, a God on the go, leading, guiding, and sustaining the people throughout their wilderness wandering. The new normal of this community is a shining visitation of YHWH in the tabernacle, a burning presence of fire and smoke (Ex. 40:34–38).

The tabernacle is designed in such a way that it can be packed up and moved to the next location whenever necessary. Just as God is not stationary but moving, so is the tent that houses God's presence. The mobile community is responsive to the environment, flexible, able to change course at the will of God. The tabernacle mode, while susceptible to the forces of nature, can read the climate and move whenever necessary. There is an idea that the tabernacle is a form of God's withness, God's home address, primary residence, *and* God is simultaneously everywhere else in the entire universe.

Once the people cross over into the promised land, eventually the *tabernacle mode* is replaced with the *temple mode*. When Solomon completes the temple, the tabernacle itself, with all the consecrated items, are moved into the temple (1 Kings 8:1–4; 2 Chron. 5:2–5). The temple, now illuminated with the tree-of-life, burning bush lamp-stand, is a kind of remixed version of the Edenic tabernacle, only now stationary. The wild, mobile God settles down in a stationary place, saying to Solomon, "I have consecrated this temple . . . by putting my Name there forever. My eyes and my heart will always be there" (1 Kings 9:3 NIV).

Note that several compromises are made along the way, including that the people decide they would rather have a human king than a living God ruling over them (1 Sam. 8:6). There is an almost bipolar discussion of the temple in the Old Testament. On one level, the concept is almost absurd: "Are you going to build me a house?" (2 Sam. 7:5, author's paraphrase); "But who is able to build a temple for him, since the heavens, even the highest heavens, cannot contain him?" (2 Chron. 2:6 NIV). On another level, God gives precise instructions about its construction handed down from David to Solomon (1 Chron. 28)—down to the measurements, materials, and color schemes (1 Kings 6). God seems to have quite the flare for fashion and interior design, as priestly garments and both tabernacle and temple décor are incredibly elaborate (Ex. 36–39).

In this new temple-centered mode, the legitimating narrative is now institutionalized in a stationary place, where the formative stories are reenacted by the professionalized priesthood. The locus of God's power is now centered on a dwelling of magnificent scope and breathtaking architecture. Solomon's temple was considered to be one of the ancient wonders of the world. The edifice itself would have inspired anyone who beheld it. This is the attractional model extraordinaire!

Zion becomes the throne of YHWH, the holy hill where God dwells (Ps. 135:21). The locus of God's power is now stationary, fixed in one location as the center of the universe. The ritualistic center of the community is now localized on this mountain. The formative stories are now sacralized in the religious routines of the professional priesthood. Again, they serve the function as mediator between YHWH and people.

God draws people into the orbit of his presence to worship. God sings humanity to the holy hill. This shift to a centralized location as the home of YHWH is foundational to an understanding of the attractional model. Faithful adherents to Judaism must now make the journey to Jerusalem to reenact ritually the legitimating narratives.

Next, we shall briefly explore the *synagogue mode*. While some scholars argue for pre-exilic roots to the synagogue, most regard it as a postexilic development. The Babylonian captivity necessitated the emergence of the synagogue, a term synonymous with both a gathering of *people* and a *place* where they gathered (synagōg).[16]

The synagogue is a both/and kind of mode. The synagogues resemble the concept of the tabernacle as a more localized, contextual, religious center but did not replace the expectation of pilgrimage to the temple. The annual temple pilgrimages grew more complex as various empires subjugated Israel and injected communal life with foreign powers, deities, and philosophical systems.

The New Testament gives us a window into how both temple and synagogue were functioning fully together in the blended-ecology way. The temple was the epicenter of the attractional mode; the synagogues emerged contextually as communities formed and grew large enough to support the requirements to plant a synagogue (a quorum of ten Jewish men).[17] People typically made the temple pilgrimage one to three times each year for the three major feasts—Feast of Unleavened Bread, Feast of Weeks, and Feast of Booths—but they worshiped at the synagogue each Sabbath.

Even under conditions of subjugation and diaspora, the innovation of the synagogue coupled with the temple allowed the Israelites to thrive and multiply in an unprecedented way. Julius Caesar first granted Judaism the status of a *religio licita* (permitted religion). Some scholars estimate a Jewish population of 7 to 8 million, or perhaps as much as 10 percent of the empire's entire population.[18] Through harnessing both the attractional and emerging modes of gathering in God's presence, their faith spread throughout the ancient world, and they proliferated. After the destruction of the temple in Jerusalem in AD 70, the synagogues alone became the dispersed, polycentric mode of God's presence, the centers of religious and communal life.[19]

We see clear parallels of the gathered and scattered mode of community throughout the Old Testament. Perhaps there is a case for the blended ecology, particularly in times of exile and liminality. Moreover, there is theological validation for both the stationary and mobile, attractional and contextual, for both the inherited and the emerging forms. Thus, this way is not only a structure firmly rooted in the triune person of God, it is firmly rooted in the history of God's presence with humanity. In all times, spaces, and cultures, the need for the blended ecology will inevitably emerge.

Now let's move to the New Testament to see where the blended ecology is powerfully present in the primitive church.

## Jesus as Enfleshment of the Blended Ecology

The tree of life, one of the most persistent images of God's presence throughout Scripture, is enfleshed in the person of Jesus. Leonard Sweet says, "The grave turned into a garden. And we're back to Genesis 2. Jesus is the Tree of Life returned to earth again."[20] It's unfortunate that Christians have not more effectively harnessed the symbolic power of the tree imagery or the fiery tree-of-life lampstand. In the church of Jesus, for the most part, the tree of life becomes the cross (Gal. 3:13). The "cursed one" hanging from the bloodstained "tree" makes it possible for us all to fully enter a relationship with God.

It's noteworthy to mention the blended ecology of Jesus' own life and ministry—synagogue and temple—coexisting together. Jesus worked in the fields and he visited the temple. He preached sermons on the mountains and he preached in the synagogues. He spent time at the tables of sinners and tax collectors and religious leaders. He is the embodiment of both attractional and emerging: he was the most attractive force of a human being that ever was *and* he was completely dedicated to incarnationally entering the lives of people where they were.

The incarnation itself is the enfleshment of this, as Jesus descends, to come and move into the neighborhood of our space. Jesus literally is the new (*skēnoō*) "tabernacle" among us (John 1:14). God descends, empties, and enters our sin-broken lives to reshape us through loving relationship (Phil. 2). Jesus is the new temple, but "greater" (Matt. 12:6). On the cross, the temple veil is torn (Matt. 27:51), and the fragmented religious system is now fulfilled, making access for all people to fully reenter the Edenic God space around the tree, walking in the presence in the "cool of the day" (Gen. 3:8 NIV).

Thus, Jesus is the fulfilled embodiment of temple, tabernacle, and Torah. His flesh and blood become the new temple/tabernacle that all the Old Testament pointed toward (Luke 22:19; John 2:19). Jesus blends together all the forms of God's withness into one incarnate life.

All the modes of God's presence are synthesized into one megamodel: a stationary, mobile, enfleshed, incarnational, attractional, emerging, flesh-and-blood tabernacle, temple, synagogue—fully human, fully God, man!

Jesus is a blended ecology, the life of heaven *and* mud-stuff. He is the two modes of God's withness weaved into one orchestra—the fullness of God's song—singing all humanity to him.

Now that Jesus sits on the throne of the cosmos, in all his enfleshed, beautiful, Palestinian, death-conquering self, *and* through the sending of the Holy Spirit, he is "with us always" (Matt. 28:20). The church should be the literal embodiment of everything that Jesus was and is. We are now "the body of Christ" (1 Cor. 12:27) and "temple of the Holy Spirit" (1 Cor. 6:19). We are the new temple, "living stones" built upon the one who is the rejected cornerstone (1 Peter 2:4–5). Mobile and stationary, attractional and emerging. Every community of Jesus' followers, gathered and scattered, offer the very life that is the tree of life. Little oases of new creation, the green spaces, giving the fresh breath of resurrection in polluted urban ecosystems.

The church is a blended ecology, a colony of heaven, in, for, and among a sin-marred valley.

## Jerusalem and Antioch

Obviously, the strongest example of the blended-ecology pattern emerged very early in the life of the church in Jerusalem and Antioch.

Jesus, just prior to the ascension, lays out the missional plan, "But you will receive power when the Holy Spirit comes on you; and you will be my witnesses in Jerusalem, and in all Judea and Samaria, and to the ends of the earth" (Acts 1:8 NIV). We see that very pattern of the churches' growth occur throughout the book of Acts. Pentecost is a remix that enables Jesus' instructions to develop. There is a clear parallel between the tower of Babel, with God confusing the languages of humanity, and Pentecost, with God enabling the gospel to be proclaimed in all the native languages of the earth.

Furthermore, what happens at Pentecost is a remix of the legitimating narrative. Pentecost, which means "fiftieth," is a Jewish festival that celebrates the giving of the law fifty days after the Passover. The remixed Christian mash-up is the giving of the Holy Spirit fifty days after Jesus' resurrection.

The shining presence of the old wild-God of the tabernacle shows up as the wild-child of the Trinity in flaming tongues, creating a new tabernacle out of a flesh-and-blood people called the church. The Holy Spirit enables the disciples to go native, so the bystanders witness "them speaking in the *native* language of each" (Acts 2:6, italics mine). This is more than a firework show—the Spirit is thrusting out the newly born church from the womb of Pentecost.

The church, the body of Christ, is now the way God will sing all peoples to his presence. The church is God's song—it's a song of two modes.

The very genesis of the Christian movement is a remix, and a blended-ecology structure is evident right from the start. In Jerusalem, the movement flourished in this way for a period. Notice the *andness* captured in the earliest portrait of newly birthed churches' life. "Day by day, as they spent much time together in the temple, they broke bread at home and ate their food with glad and generous hearts, praising God and having the goodwill of all the people. And day by day the Lord added to their number those who were being saved" (Acts 2:46–47).

So, the two major places of their activity were the *temple* and the dinner tables of their *homes*. It was not one or the other, but *both* that allowed the movement to explode with growth. Their life together consisted of the church compound *and* the first place, a larger gathering of the fledgling church, and smaller intimate gatherings around a meal. This created a thriving scenario and the exponential growth of the church: "And day by day the Lord added to their number those who were being saved" (Acts 2:47).

This creates tension with the inherited religious system, but just as we saw with the temple/synagogue scenario, even in adverse circumstances, the attractional and emerging modes operating together create a thriving missional ecosystem.

Furthermore, very early in the primitive church, right in the genesis, two distinct brands of the faith begin to emerge (Hellenist and Jewish, Acts 6). The church restructures itself to deal with those emerging distinctions. So, a group filled with the Spirit are chosen as deacons (*diakonia*) for the servant ministry of the church, so the apostles can dedicate themselves to prayer and the Word (Acts 6:2–6). Also, it's significant that these two modes operating together result in the "number of the disciples increased greatly in Jerusalem, and a great many of the priests became obedient to the faith" (Acts 6:7).

Indeed, "Mission is the mother of theology" and, more specifically, mission is the mother of ecclesiology. The structures of the church emerge as they bend and respond to the emerging missional opportunities, thus the Möbius strip song of ecclesiomissiology. The apostles widely structure around the needs that arise within the community rather than put forth one rigid model that must be followed to belong. The structures are born improvisationally as new needs arise among new groups.

The movement begins expanding out from "Jerusalem, Judea, Samaria, and all the ends of the earth." While the initial activity is centered in the temple where the disciples gathered daily, it was also moving out to the edge on the road to Ethiopia (Acts 8:26–27). Very early, a beachhead of the church is established in Jerusalem, and contrary to popular belief, it has never left. The first wave of persecution does force the disciples to move out and essentially denies access to the temple (Acts 8:1), yet they continue to gather and have a presence in Jerusalem, at the tables. Even during the subsequent outbreaks of Roman imperial persecution, the Jerusalem church moves underground but continues to exist there as evidenced by the letters of Paul.

As the movement spreads out to the edges just as Jesus prophetically commanded, different contextual expressions of the faith begin to emerge. The first Jerusalem council offers us a model for how the blended ecology can work together in a synergistic way. The early church faced its first huge life-threatening issue and was forced to restructure according to the missional need. The bigwigs in Jerusalem (the gathered church) heard that a group of missional renegades were experiencing tremendous growth among the Gentile converts (the scattered church). However, this was a very different church with very different people. Word on the streets was that they weren't even being circumcised or following the law!

This threatened to tear the whole church apart and destroy the entire movement.

So, what did they do? They formed a committee, scheduled a meeting for next month, and tabled the issue so they could think about it. This is the story we read in the book of Acts, right? No, not exactly! Yes, they did have the first committee meeting, and yes, it did turn into something of a beer bottle fight like many of the committee meetings you may have experienced, but they acted quickly, decisively, and in unity.

They also made some huge adjustments. The Gentiles were not willing to put that kind of skin in the game . . . literally! For Jews, circumcision was the mark of a faithful Hebrew male going back to Abraham. You can see this is no small matter, but the early church didn't bat an eye. They responded in a flexible way and moved on.

The missional need shaped their decisive action. They had a focused vision on the thing that mattered the most . . . introducing people to Jesus Christ. One could argue that they reduced the circumcision mandate and obedience to the 613 laws to three that were quite contextually specific (Acts 15:29). Essentially, Paul's letters are aimed at institutionalizing what happened at the Jerusalem council in a robust theological system that would guide the life of those emerging communities.

Paul's ministry in Acts offers an incredible plethora of examples of how the blended ecology worked in the early church. In his letters we find a solid theological base, as well as a treasure trove of examples and resources to undergird recovering this way for the church today.

As Paul planted emerging communities throughout the Roman Empire, he sustained the relationship with Jerusalem. He reveals in his letter to the Corinthians his intent to nurture good relationships between themselves and the believers in Jerusalem, even laboring to collect an offering on Jerusalem's behalf (1 Cor. 16:1–4). The Jerusalem church seems to have been struggling and overwhelmed with people experiencing poverty, and Paul was accessing his relational networks for funding to help. Some denominations are familiar with a system of apportionments, in which a percentage of the offering goes to the central governing body of the denomination. This institutional phenomenon has its basis in the blended-ecology way.

One can see through Paul's exchanges with Peter and other church leaders that the influencing is not a one-way street. Paul sometimes calls the inherited leaders out, and they in turn at times tried to reign Paul in. Jerusalem is influencing Antioch and vice versa (Gal. 2). The two are operating in a mutual exchange of life that is illustrated with the Möbius strip. The blended ecology is not healthy if both inherited and emerging forms do not have some influence on the other. As both grow and influence each other, the whole church is strengthened.

In Acts 16, we see a scriptural example of how fresh expressions of church can emerge in a networked system with little to no Judeo-Christian influence. We can see up until this point in the narrative that Paul's missional strategy is to start in the synagogue. He would use the Scriptures to demonstrate that Jesus was the Messiah.

The response of the synagogues was predominantly negative; as an apostle of Jesus, he sees his struggles as building an impressive list of credentials,

> far more imprisonments, with countless floggings, and often near death. Five times I have received from the Jews the forty lashes minus one. Three times I was beaten with rods. Once I received a stoning. Three times I was shipwrecked; for a night and a day I was adrift at sea; on frequent journeys, in danger from rivers, danger from bandits, danger from my own people, danger from Gentiles, danger in the city, danger in the wilderness, danger at sea, danger from false brothers and sisters. (2 Cor. 11:23–26)

Often those who are wired for pioneering ministry unfortunately report having a similar experience as Paul in the inherited church.

In Philippi, he must adapt his missional approach, as there seems to be no synagogue to work from. The text clearly demonstrates that the Holy Spirit, used interchangeably with the Spirit of Jesus, is leading Paul and his team. When the team can find no inherited framework from which to work, they discover on the Sabbath a place of prayer down by the river. Paul connects with Lydia, a "person of peace" with whom a fresh expression of church is born in her home (Acts 16:40). These little emerging communities are forming all over the missional landscape, while Jerusalem continues to function as a central hub.

We see here in Acts the blended ecology at work. There are also multiple places in Paul's letters where we see the inherited and emerging church working together. Paul describes occasions when he went back to Jerusalem to conference with the leaders there. Those encounters are not always without contention (Acts 15; Gal. 2:11–13). There still today exists a very real tension between inherited and emerging forms of church. However, we see the Jerusalem and Antioch modes, gathered and scattered, tethered together throughout. There is a life-giving exchange happening as the Jerusalem church hears the stories of Gentiles coming to Christ, and the Antioch mode gets its authorization and centering from the Jerusalem church (Acts 15).

Using Acts 15 as our model, this diagram shows the modern iteration of the blended ecology:

Paul uses the accepted societal realities, remixing and adapting them for the greater missional purpose, in collaboration with Jerusalem and the larger emerging church. In *The First Urban Christians: The Social World of Paul the Apostle*, Wayne Meeks provides insight into the complexity of the Christian movement in urban centers. While in some ways Christian communities were

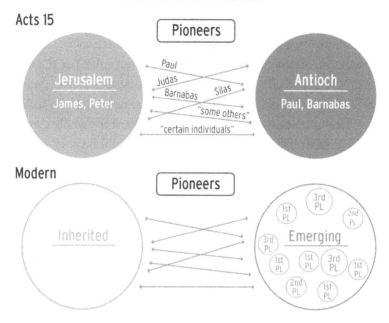

exclusive (for instance, baptism and participation in the Lord's Supper required extensive catechesis), in other ways they were radically inclusive, mixed communities that did not follow established societal, hierarchal rules, consisting of wealthy, poor, women, slave, and freeborn persons.[21]

Meeks shows that Paul and the first urban churches followed an approach similar to the one I'm suggesting here for a network society. They used the household, voluntary association, synagogue, and philosophic or rhetorical school, these "workable communities" as smaller scattered cells of the whole gathered church.[22]

The household was the basic cell of the movement, but the members participated in a larger gathering of the whole church. They also used the clubs, guilds, and associations of the Roman world, which could be formed around practices, common trades, or crafts. We already saw how Paul engaged the synagogue as a kind of starting point. Also, some Christian gatherings resembled the scholastic communities of the philosophic/rhetorical school.[23]

Meeks identifies the gathered-and-scattered nature of the early church, which consisted of many cells with local identities, and a high level of cohesion with the larger movement. So, the *ecclesia* (called assembly) consisted of the larger reality of the whole church, plus the smaller local realities. "In time they would invent a unique network of institutions to embody and protect this connection, and the resultant combination of intimate, disciplined local communities with a supralocal organization was a major factor in the social and political success of Christianity in the age of Constantine."[24]

This gathered-*and*-scattered form, expressing both the stationary and mobile modes of God's presence, are indeed a *blended ecology*. Once Constantine legitimated Christianity as the state religion, the two modes largely collapsed into a single attractional model, dominated by a single form of worship.

In a post-Christendom network society, a single attractional mode cannot reach most of the population. In times of liminality, even persecution and subjugation, the church has thrived through reorganizing to embody both the attractional and emerging modes: Tabernacle and temple, Jerusalem and Antioch, deep roots and wild branches. Just as Paul sustained the relationship with the inherited church, while utilizing local synagogues, households, clubs, networks, and so on. So, can every local church utilize the first, second, third places and shared practices of the larger community?

Just as the early church adapted and improvised, so will inherited congregations need to do so to experience revitalization. Every church can have a Jerusalem and an Antioch—to sing the world to God in both modes. This will require a remix.

FIELD INTERVIEW
# Mia Chang

Church Planter,
Fresh Expression Pioneer,
NextGen Church

Mia Chang is a church planter, lead pastor of NextGen Church, wife to Steven Ku, and mother to two young adult children. Born in Korea but immigrated to the US at the age of nine, she considers herself a 1.5 generation Korean American. Mia grew up in Jersey City, New Jersey, and studied early childhood education in college. She worked as a public school teacher in New York City and New Jersey for nearly ten years before stepping into a full-time pastorate role.

NextGen Church is a growing, multicultural community of faith in Princeton Junction, New Jersey. The church is located in an affluent New Jersey suburb where the average household income is one of the highest in the nation. Having a train station to New York City and Philadelphia, many of the residents are commuters working in either of the two cities. Princeton University is the focal point of the community and draws many young families with children to the area. In this milieu, NextGen Church seeks to reach the unchurched members of Princeton and its neighboring communities. The church celebrated its tenth anniversary Sunday, December 12, 2018.

## Can you briefly describe the fresh expression(s) of your church?

NextGen Church was planted in an organic way, where I did not intentionally and strategically set out to establish a church. It began with three families coming together to share a meal and explore the Bible together. The weekly gatherings led to worship, then community outreach events, and prayer gatherings. Discipleship occurred naturally out of our time together. At the time, I was unaware of the Fresh Expressions movement, but NextGen's birth and growth reflected the formation of the Christian communities in the book of Acts.

When I first came to learn about Fresh Expressions, it was as if NextGen was not alone but part of a greater community of fellow risk takers and pioneers for the kingdom of God.

Currently, we are engaged in two fresh expressions: Capital City Academy and Epostlenaut Media.

Capital City Academy is an afterschool ministry in Trenton, New Jersey. It operates daily from 3 p.m. to 6 p.m. in one of the public schools in the city. This ministry came about when one of our members became a teacher at the school. Upon visiting her classroom, we learned that the school was one of the lowest performing schools in the state, and its needs were vast. With the purpose of being a good neighbor and witness for Christ, we became an active supporter. Working closely with the school's administration, we provided various needs of the school. For example, we collected wish lists from the classroom teachers and provided resources for their classrooms: we provided six air-conditioning units for classrooms, a water cooler for a faculty lounge, and luncheons for teachers' appreciation month. In addition, we provided academic tutorial services on Saturdays to struggling students. We were engaged in the life of the school in their graduation ceremonies, PTA events, and school festivals.

After three years, we were asked by the administration to take over an after-school program when a prominent youth organization moved out of the area. We are now three years into leading the after-school program. The challenges of operating an after-school program are great; however, we hope that it will provide the opportunities to one day begin a worshiping community. We have partnered with a neighboring First Baptist Church of Trenton and are working toward building deeper relationships with the families of the after-school students.

Our second fresh expression is Epostlenaut Media. It is an attempt to reach the post-millennial generation, specifically those on the autism spectrum. One of NextGen's members, Randa Yee, is a parent of an autistic teen. Her heart for the autistic community and passion for anime and manga led to the birth of this fresh expression. Autistic young adults seem to possess a natural proclivity to media; therefore, using media as the forum, we are meeting to create stories and publish them online. Currently, the members are meeting at Randa's home to develop the stories for publication. As God's nod of approval and provision for our fresh expression, we have just received a $10,000 grant from the Palmer Foundation to purchase more software and computers. We are in the process of building a studio in our church space so we can host more young adults and deepen relationships with one another.

## Explain the blended ecology dynamics between the inherited church and your fresh expressions. What kind of tension, if any, goes on between the two?

I would not consider NextGen an inherited church since we are still young in our developmental stages; however, tension is natural and is a helpful component for growth. For example, approximately five years ago, we began a weekly after-school program for the children of Hightstown, a neighboring town about fifteen minutes away. We attempted to address the concerns of the Spanish-speaking immigrants who needed after-school care for their children. NextGen, in partnership with a local pastor, Oscar Guerrero, led a program that provided academic support and enrichment activities in the areas of art and music. NextGen members served as teachers and drivers to these children. We transported students from their apartment complex in Hightstown to Princeton Junction for their activities. The tension arose when the ministry grew; it was becoming more difficult for NextGen to care for the children and families in ways that would lead to further growth. The work was becoming more taxing and financially draining. It was not feasible to transport the children from their home to NextGen. This tension was an indication that God was leading us to the next step. At this critical time, the First Baptist Church of Hightstown opened its doors and invited us into their space. They wanted to partner with us and work together in planting a church. At that point, the FBC of Hightstown, a historic, inherited church of more than two hundred years, came alongside the fledgling fresh expression of church to share God's vision. In 2016, New Hights Christian Church was birthed, and it is continuing to reach and serve the Spanish-speaking families of Hightstown. The church is fully independent from NextGen, although we are good friends who continue to inspire one another in the work of the kingdom. (For more information about the relationship between FBC of Hightstown and New Hights, please contact Oscar and Bruce Wood.)

## How have you seen the fresh expressions have a positive impact on the existing congregation? In what ways?

Fresh Expression gives the church vitality and new life. Led by the Holy Spirit, the church continues to look outside its walls and consider the needs of their greater community. This leads to prayer for others and the courage to take risks for the kingdom of God. The church then becomes actively engaged with their world and witness the power of the Holy Spirit, since it is the Spirit who plants and raises the fresh expressions.

**Knowing that launching fresh expressions in your congregation involves time, sacrifice, resources, and people power, why do you believe it's worthy to pursue?**

Yes! Fresh expressions are not easy, and it is not for those who do not rely on the power of the Holy Spirit. Fresh expressions can be messy, frustrating, and downright painful, but when the Holy Spirit is at work, we are able to persevere and witness the transformation in our own hearts and in the hearts of others. Being part of Fresh Expressions is a privilege because we get to partner with the Spirit who is alive and active in our world; this makes our Christian journey all the more thrilling!

CHAPTER 6
# (Re)missioning— Time for a Remix

"No one sews a piece of unshrunk cloth on an old cloak, for the patch pulls away from the cloak, and a worse tear is made. Neither is new wine put into old wineskins; otherwise, the skins burst, and the wine is spilled, and the skins are destroyed; but new wine is put into fresh wineskins, and *so both are preserved.*" (Matt. 9:16–17, emphasis mine)

I play the notes as they are written, but it is God who makes the music.
—Johann Sebastian Bach

The forgotten Beatitude, "Blessed are the flexible, for they shall not get bent out of shape."
—Jesus (he said this somewhere, but no one thought to write it down)

God is a God of the remix. Humanity is a mud pie mash-up of dust and God-breath. Resurrection is a form of remix, the dubstep of transfiguring grace. God making us a new creation *now* is not about scrapping the project and starting over with new material. It's taking what is, infusing it with new life, and from that amalgamation forming something new from who and what we already are. God's making us a new creation in the *future* is about taking the DNA that makes us who we are and reconfiguring it in a splendid new resurrected form of which Jesus is the firstfruits. Again, that is God's plan for the whole cosmos, a massive force of recycling that brings forth a "new heavens and a new earth," not a galactic dumpster.

*For local churches to experience resurrection, we need to do some (re)missioning.* (Re)missioning is not about abandoning the church as we know it; rather, it's a remix. The church is the originator of the remix. A community that sings the world to God through two modes—stationary and mobile, inherited and emerging, digital and analog, attractional and incarnational.

We reflect our God and master remixer, Jesus. Godself is, structurally speaking, an interconnected matrix of relationship we call Trinity. A blending of diversity and oneness. God is a mind-bending community of *I Am*-ness, the diverse singularity of the three-yet-one. This relational perichoretic matrix is the genesis of our story. This God-story gives birth to us as humanity made "in the image of God male and female," diverse but one, created for relationship. This deeper narrative is the *content* that gives birth to the *form* of the people God has called "temple of the Holy Spirit" and "body of Christ" in the world.

---

**Remix:** To mix again, or to create a new version by recombining and reediting the elements of the existing.

If we make the story of God's Trinitarian personhood the structural design for the local church, exciting new possibilities appear for the current Western context. The first implication is that the presence and activity of God is assumed equally both in the church and in the world. The institutional church is not in an *Ichabod* scenario ("no glory"; 1 Sam. 4:21); the glory of God has not left the building as some emerging church advocates propose. Conjunctively, God is not only at work in the church, but is very much active in the world. The Trinity is inviting us to join in what that divine life is up to in all spheres of existence. Both the inherited and emerging modes of church are tools in the hands of the missionary God.

Just as God's own life is a communion in which oneness and diversity are shared in a divine dance, so inherited congregations planting fresh expressions allow the larger community to join into that life. The perichoretic nature of the Trinity demonstrates how in God's own eternal being there is a movement of giving and receiving love, in which God makes room. This mutual indwelling is the sharing of intimate relationship, in which Father, Son, and Spirit are differentiated by their relationships with each other.[1]

The blended ecology is a demonstration of this flow of mutual giving between the inherited and emerging modes of the church. It creates a dynamic otherness, which "makes room." The Holy Spirit dances between these modes, weaving together the emergence of a new communal ecosystem through pioneering teams of Jesus' followers. The God whose eternal life is a phenomenon of shared love, not self-contained individuals, draws the community into that life. As Migliore writes, "Just as the life of the triune persons is life with, for, and in each other, so the church is called to life in communion in which persons flourish in mutually supportive relationships with others. In such communion the church becomes *imago Trinitatis*, an analogy of, and partial participation in, the triune life of God."[2]

Perhaps just as unitarianism is a distortion of the Trinity, so is the attractional-only form a distortion of the church. In this scenario, the church becomes a bounded-set only, a closed system. There is no divine flow of mutual indwelling, no generation of otherness, no making room, except in a static and overly fixed sense. The pioneer teams, connecting in the first, second, and third places, release the movement of dance again; as communal life in the Trinity is offered, a new sequence of exchange is released. The inherited and emerging modes interpenetrate each other, creating a mutual indwelling, a being-in-one-another that manifests a greater level of communion throughout the relational ecosystem.

Thus, the relational story of the diverse singularity of the communal life of the Trinity also supplies the church her form, not a fixed structure but a fluid cascade of relational dance. When the church has forgotten that primary story, the synergy and relational movement collapses. We resort to a single fixed structure to weather the storms of change. It's like a skipping record, where a single beat of the lone stanza is played over and over again. The song is not complete, it cannot be, until it is bumped to play all the way through. Suddenly a symphony of orchestral jazz is released; both new and forgotten dimensions of the song burst forth. Then there can be movement and dance again. The song can be reversed, sped up; new elements from engaging the community are being introduced all the time. It is an emerging masterpiece that is never completed, for it is always being remixed by the Spirit.

In fact, James Womack describes *perichoresis* as being originally derived from a Stoic term for "mixture," which translates literally to mean "a mutual coextension of dissimilar parts entering into one another at all points."[3]

So how can a declining congregation practically open ourselves to the possibility of joining into the Trinity's perichoretic work of remixing communities with the circle dance of divine communion? By harnessing the process of remix, we can unleash the power of resurrection. This is one of the three forms of creativity I mentioned where we started: *blending* (the merging of two or more sources).[4]

Let's do some double listening to God and the cultural phenomena of music and film for lessons.

## Lessons from Music and Film

While fresh expressions require vision, they don't start with a vision statement; they start with a soundtrack. Vision is overrated (2 Cor. 5:7). We need to learn to listen again. Fresh expressions start with the ear, an act of surround-sound listening. We hear the soundtrack the Spirit is creating with a group of people, and we join into the rhythms of their life dance. This is not about sitting in a room wordsmithing a statement; it's about getting on the floor and improvising movement in community with others, seeing what emerges. Elements of the song are familiar; it's a beat we've heard before, but new elements are being added all the time.

Oh, the power of a good remix! Think about it; at a celebratory gathering of dancing and festivities, a wedding or birthday party that has gone dull, how does the deejay get people on the dance floor again? Just shout the word *remix* and go heavy on the air horn—now the party can get started! Some of the most popular songs in our day and time are remixes. Daft Punk's "One More Time" has been viewed on YouTube hundreds of millions of times all over the world and has been named by *Mixmag* as the number-one dance hit of all time. It's a remix![5]

Phil Collins 1981 hit "In the Air Tonight" was already a classic, but when it was remixed as Tupac's posthumous 2003 "Starin' through My Rear View," it was downloaded millions of more times than it was ever purchased in its original form. It became accessible to an entirely different generational wave.

The Police's 1983 chart-topping smash hit "Every Breath You Take" was resurrected and immortalized when Puff Daddy, Faith Evans, and 112 remixed it into a tribute to the legendary slain rapper Biggy Smalls in 1997. Remixes not only blend the best of generations together, but they can blend genres as well. An instant classic was created with "Numb/Encore," when the lyrics of Jay-Z were mixed with the music of Linkin Park. Just one week after its release, it topped the Billboard 200.

I am part of a network of fresh expressions in the fit culture that believe in being good stewards of our bodies by finding ways to stink and sweat six days a week. Most of us engage those practices to soundtracks. Music helps us move, flow, and stay in the rhythm of life. However, what exercise song is not made better by remixing a little electronic house beat, dubstep, or mash-up?

**Dubstep:** A form of dance music, typically instrumental, characterized by a sparse, syncopated rhythm and a strong bassline.

**Mash-up:** A recording created by digitally combining and synchronizing instrumental tracks with vocal tracks from two or more different songs.

In fact, the mash-up, which once began as a subversive disruption in the music industry, has now been harnessed to become a highly profitable endeavor for major corporations.

David J. Gunkel, presidential teaching professor of communication studies at Northern Illinois University says, "Mash-ups—a bastard art form created by the illegitimate appropriation and fusion of two or more audio recordings—were patently illegal, deliberate subversions of authority in the culture industry and critical interventions in the very material of popular music."[6]

The backstory behind Jay-Z and Linkin Park's collaboration that you might not know began with the subversive activity of DJ Danger Mouse (a.k.a. Brian Burton). Gunkel references the apex of "the mash-up revolution" as DJ Danger Mouse's extraction of rap lyrics from Jay-Z's *The Black Album* (2003) and the Beatles' 1968 *The White Album* to create the revolutionary *The Grey Album* (2004). Major record label EMI responded by summoning intellectual property law and issued a cease-and-desist letter, leading to 170 websites participating in the coordinated online protest now called "Grey Tuesday," distributing .mp3 copies of the mash-up over the Internet for free.

The result was the institutionalization of a disruptive innovation by the corporations who stood to make a profit. Gunkel says, "In the process, a 'revolutionary art form' such as the mash-up becomes domesticated and reinvested. Whatever critical interventions it might have deployed are now made to serve the system it was to have subverted, and what had been an outlaw underground movement is repackaged, repurposed, and retailed as a legitimate corporate product."[7] Some find this an apt description for the current state of the church in the West. What can we learn here? How can we appropriate the power of remix without institutionalizing it? How can inherited congregations harness the energy of emerging forms of church without domesticating them?

Perhaps the greatest remixes in human history may be the ones that have the most longevity. A good remix can withstand the test of time. If that is the case, then the greatest master of remix in human history is Methodism's very own Charles Wesley! In fact, don't tell the Methodists, but maybe the most popular remixes in human history were the ones Charles (prolific creator of more than six thousand hymns) produced when he took the bar tunes of his day and wrote the lyrics of Christian hymns to them.

Unfortunately, there is quite a bit of confusion around the phrase "bar tunes." The urban myth that Wesley and Luther used the common saloon songs of their day stems from the misconception of this musical term. Dean McIntyre reveals, "In German literature and music of the Middle Ages, 'Bar' was a poem consisting of three or more stanzas. Each stanza was divided into two Stollen (section a) and one Abgesang (section b), which yielded a form of AAB."[8] Not as exciting as remixing tavern songs, but remixes nonetheless!

So, Methodists across the world are singing remixes to those "bar songs" in the current *United Methodist Hymnal* every week. While the Wesleys may have been a bit too sanctified to hang out in actual bars, they did indeed use secular music as hymn tunes (for instance, the original composition by the great composer Handel as a tune for "Rejoice, the Lord Is King").[9] If longevity is any indication of greatness, this may be one of the greatest remixes of all time!

Also, at the time of the initial research in 2017, there were multiple movies in the theaters that are essentially remixes of classic films (classic for an '80's baby that is). *Flatliners, Blade Runner, IT, Tomb Raider, Overboard, Robin Hood, The Grinch*, and the most epic of them all . . . *Star Wars*. Filmmakers have discovered the power of a good remix. They have learned to take the movies held in the hearts and memories of generations past, blending and reconfiguring the classic imagery of the storylines with current signs of meaning.

Perhaps filmmakers are the greatest semioticians and (re)signers of our time. Film remixes generate billions of dollars and are experienced by hundreds of millions of people every year. They become foundational stories (even legitimating narratives for some) that shape our thinking and behaviors.

What would it look like for the church to remix our image stories afresh in the network society? What would it mean for the church to reappropriate the two modes of God's song, remixing them in endless contextual variations, to sing the world to Jesus?

## Sharing and Remixing Revolutionary Forces Changing the World

Let's come back to the digital revolution that is moving us forward from stone wheels to spaceships every couple of years. Modern prophet of technological innovation, Kevin Kelly, in his *New York Times* bestseller *The Inevitable: Understanding the 12 Technological Forces That Will Shape Our Future,* identifies two of those forces as "sharing" and "remixing." These are forces the church must learn to harness now if we are to experience renewal.

Sharing, along with cooperation, collaboration, and collectivism, are rapidly changing the reality of human community in a globalized network society. Kelly says, "The frantic global rush to connect everyone to everyone all the time is quietly giving rise to a revised technological version of socialism."[10] He goes on to discuss how this new brand of socialism is different than anything we've ever seen before, it's "digital socialism." This new American innovation is not the old-school political variety, but exists currently outside the reach of the arm of the state. In the realm of culture and economics, this form of collaboration disrupts business as usual in the world of capitalism.[11]

In the network society, technology is enabling the convergence of these forces to redefine our values in a consumeristic culture. The very concept of ownership is being challenged. The emerging generation is less concerned with owning something and more concerned with sharing in common experiences in the flows. In a networked world, communal engagement itself has been redefined. Through networking, tagging, archiving, and rating, humanity is working collaboratively together to create a collective super-intelligence. You contribute to it every time you Google something.

Oddly enough, a rapidly secularized society, harnessing the power of the technological revolution, is bringing us toward a more biblical concept of the kind of human community God designed from the beginning. The kind of collaboration taking place is making capitalism irrelevant. We are inevitably moving back into a stewardship concept of communal living that shares with one's neighbor rather than seeks to possess. The expectation of enjoying products for free that result from this technologically enabled collaboration is becoming the new normal.

COVID-19 gave the church a taste of harnessing this force. In the early stages of the outbreak, just think of how local churches worked together, sharing resources and using cheap or even free technologies to share the gospel across the digital frontier. Technology-enabled sharing became a lifeline of survival.

The cooperative networking of social media is replacing newspaper and TV networks. An alternative to state-based and market-based systems is emerging right before our very eyes. Referring back to Bitcoin, this means that currency will be made irrelevant, as we are seeing the first emergence of decentralized currency systems like it. Kelly reminds us that three of the most successful creators of commercial wealth in the past ten years, Google, Facebook, and Twitter, "derive their value from unappreciated sharing in unexpected ways."[12]

In this new network world of global collaboration, endless niches are being created that innovators are already finding creative ways to engage. Interconnected webs of micro-communities are transforming the meaning of community. People are gathering around common interests, passions, hobbies, and creative projects in the flows. Disruptive innovation is prevalent in most fields. Again, this is leading some large forward-thinking corporations to create new departments focused solely on disruptive innovation. The local church can restructure in this way and harvest the power of dual transformation.

Another technological force that is changing the landscape is the remix. It is the rearrangement of existing resources that ultimately creates value. Innovators are combining simpler creations to create new complex forms.

Most of the technological advances that are changing the world today are simply remixes of older technologies. This rearrangement and reuse of existing materials, coupled with sharing, is dismantling traditional understandings of property and ownership. Any creation that has value will ultimately be modified and reused. Innovators who harness that potential and create the most replicable remixes can create tremendous wealth. This forces us to see products in a different way, for nothing is really fixed. Everything is in a transformative process of becoming. These technological forces may bring us back to the future of the kind of human community envisioned in Scripture.

## Church (Re)mixed

So, what does all this have to do with the church and revitalization? In the eyes of emerging generations, the church's dance floor has gotten way dull. If you can imagine attending a gathering where people were stuck listening to a skipping record, desperately holding on to those time capsule items—fanny packs, parachute pants, beepers, cassette tapes, and a Walkman—trying to retain their relevance in a world of iPhones (super computers that fit in your pocket), skinny jeans, and free downloadable music, then you get an accurate portrait of the challenges that confront the church today. It's time for a remix, and the Holy Spirit is the deejay, going heavy on the air horn—let's get on the floor!

One can survey the field of literature and call this the age of "re"—re-new, re-sign, re-invent, re-imagine, re-model, and the list goes on. But the most important word the church should add into its regular vocabulary is the word *remix*.

In fact, what we know as the church today is a continuous circle of remixes. As we have seen, Christianity itself is a remix of Judaism, Paul's Gentile movement was a remix of the temple-centered church, Antioch was a remix of Jerusalem, Christendom was a remix of the early church, the Protestant reformation was a remix of Catholicism, the Methodist movement was an accidental remix of Anglicanism, and, of course, the US church is in fact a remix of a remix of all these remixes! Each one of these remixes involved the recovery of the two modes of God's presence, stationary and mobile, inherited and emerging. The two live together for a time, until a new creation is birthed.

The church in the twenty-first century is dying for a remix.

For the church to thrive in the West, we need to adapt and respond to our new missional frontier. We need to join in the global collaboration that is transpiring; we need to jump into the new community that is forming around sharing. We need to plant the seeds of the gospel in those micro-communities and establish a transforming presence, green spaces amid those interconnected networks and practice movements.

Our friends in the UK have recognized this need already. In the seminal work of the *Mission-Shaped Church* report, the power of this ecclesial remix was recognized. It reads, "The mixed economy is essential if the Church of England is to fulfill its calling, and most benefices or clusters of parishes have the potential to embody it."[13]

This allows the inherited and emerging forms of church to coexist and give life to each other—the neighborhood theology of a healthy local church, and the network theology, living together.

Let's return to the structure of DNA and the idea that this structure embodies the very relational nature of God. As Lincoln Harvey suggests, if the Trinity serves as the structural model for the church, or "that is to say, the story of the mixed economy is part of the older story of God with his creatures," then we can see something is missing in the "attractional only" form.[14]

It's as if one of the supporting backbones of the double helix is missing. Theologically, if one of the persons of the Trinity is missing,

we have a broken understanding of the relationally dynamic three-in-oneness of God. Ecclesiomissiologically speaking, if a piece of the structure is missing we have a broken structure of church, and the missional potential is crippled.

The *Mission-Shaped Church* author recognized this:

> But the existing parochial system alone is no longer able fully to deliver its underlying mission purpose. We need to recognize that a variety of integrated missionary approaches is required. A mixed economy of parish churches and network churches will be necessary, in an active partnership across a wider area, perhaps a deanery.[15]

So, reimagine the DNA of the church in this threefold way: one backbone of the double helix is the *attractional mode*; the other is the *missional mode*; the rungs are the Spirit working through the *pioneers* connected in the various flows, traveling back and forth between the two with God the living force holding, guiding, and sustaining the emergence together, importing the synergistic energy that perpetuates the cycle of new creation.

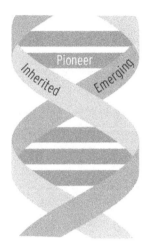

If we only have the inherited church without the emerging forms of church or outlets for the fivefold equippers in the body (apostles, prophets, evangelists, shepherds, and teachers), then we have a broken ladder that no one can climb. Pioneers are left to live on isolated missional islands.

## Leadership (Re)mixed

Contrary to a basic premise of most revitalization literature, the solution to the problem of a declining church is not a better leader. It's not even leadership in the standard understanding. Revitalization begins when the people realize they are all leaders. The focus on leadership—as the influence of a single person on a system identified as a leader—is partly what has gotten us where we are today.

We don't need better leaders; we need better followers. Followership of Jesus, an apostlehood of all believers, is what awakens congregations for resurrection. When we follow Jesus well, we will lead well.

*Leadership is a relational phenomenon that occurs through synergistic interactions between the persons in a community.*

Tod Bolsinger, drawing from Edwin Friedman, says that true adaptive change, true change of heart, true transformation, is the work of the people. The leader only cultivates a process in which the people with the problem internalize the change itself.[16] At different stages of the journey, different members of the community will offer leadership.

To help us process this essential shift in our understanding of leadership, think about the Trinity. Who is the leader in the triune God? Tim Harle says, "A dynamic relational view of leadership is offered by the Christian doctrine of the trinity, which contrasts starkly with the static hierarchies we so often encounter."[17] In the triune God, we see a dynamic, relational, movemental dance of leadership. The Trinity is not a hierarchy, with one person in authority over the other persons, but an interactive, non-linear, relational community.

Thus, in cultivating the blended ecology, we can again learn from the realm of complexity thinking—we can rethink the phenomenon of leadership itself. Leadership is an emergent phenomenon, which occurs in a series of relational interactions among agents; it's not simply a skill that one has, but an exchange of dynamic interactions within a complex system.[18] While this complexity leadership approach moves the focus away from a single individual with concentrated power acting on a system as the leader, it does not in any way minimize the importance of leadership as an organizational phenomenon. More accurately, it recognizes leadership as a phenomenon of a complex adaptive system, where relationships are primarily defined by interactions among heterogeneous agents, rather than hierarchically.[19]

A complexity view suggests a form of distributed leadership that does not lie in a single individual in a managerial role only, but rather in an interactive dynamic in which any particular person will fluctuate between being a leader and a follower. So, leaders enable conditions where a change process can occur, while not being the direct source of that change.[20]

The emerging leadership approach of the twentieth century, called "shared leadership," which has emerged from leadership research in the last twenty-five years, is the fastest growing style of leadership today, particularly in the form of leadership teams.[21] In the midst of the postmodern paradigm shift, scholars like Margaret Wheatley in *Leadership and the New Science* began to wrestle with the implications of the emerging knowledge from physics and how it applied to the structuring, management, and leadership of organizations. She demonstrates how organizational power is purely relational.[22]

In a chapter titled "Newtonian Organization in a Quantum Age," Wheatley challenges long-held assumptions of leadership, which seem to have been built at least partly on faulty assumptions. She writes,

> We need fewer descriptions of tasks and instead learn how to facilitate *process*. We need to become savvy about how to foster relationships, how to nurture growth and development. All of us need to become better at listening, conversing, respecting one another's uniqueness, because these are essential for strong relationships. The era of the rugged individual has been replaced by the era of the team player.[23]

The modern church borrowed heavily from the leadership assumptions of the corporate world—we have bought fully into the "rugged individual" model. The pastor as CEO, a mid-level corporate manager, who develops vision statements, leads board meetings, determines strategic goals, communicates the big ideas from the pulpit, raises funds, all while providing personalized professional chaplaincy care for the aging flock.

The new protest-ant "spiritual, but not religious" dichotomy is in part a response to the overly bureaucratic procedures and overly rationalized institutional forms of the McDonaldized church, in which people serve as cogs in some machine. Robot-like Christians show up weekly to consume their religious goods and services like Bic Macs, but find no real avenue for self-expression, or true community in which to wrestle with the irrationalities of faith, or even opportunities to bring their God-given gifts and abilities.

Thus, this shared leadership flattens the dominating hierarchal mode of denominations. Again, we draw upon the communal life of the Trinity as the model for the kind of leadership we need in the blended ecology. Perichoresis, the relational dance of mutual indwelling, is not about one person of the Trinity ruling over the others. It is a shared mode, each making room for the other, each taking the lead of the divine dance at different times.

Michael Davis demonstrates that for followers of Jesus, shared leadership is much more than an approach to leading others; it is a reflection of the Christian's spiritual growth process that is rooted in the very triune being of God. He writes, "Although shared leadership serves as a contemporary model for the marketplace we may understand it more deeply as an expression of mature Spiritual formation rooted in the biblical doctrine of perichoresis.[24]

Drawing upon Miroslav Volf, who describes the leadership style of the Godhead as "polycentric reciprocity" or a "relationship characterized neither by a pyramidal dominance of the one nor by a hierarchical bipolarity between the one and the many," Davis shows how the life of the Trinity foreshadows the modern model of shared leadership.[25]

Coming back to our parable of the dispersed, polycentric, living vineyard, Jesus says, "Abide in me as I abide in you. Just as the branch cannot bear fruit by itself unless it abides in the vine, neither can you unless you abide in me. I am the vine, you are the branches.

Those who abide in me and I in them bear much fruit, because apart from me you can do nothing" (John 15:4–5). This language demonstrates that one dimension of perichoresis is Jesus' own indwelling of the believer, making life in the Trinity possible.

All Christians share in this mutual indwelling and are to share this life with others. Shared leadership theory helps us understand how each person in a complex system can offer leadership. It is the true design for Jesus' church as the "priesthood of all believers." The blended ecology is a hybrid organizational form in which every follower of Jesus is given opportunity to lead from their giftings, apostles, prophets, evangelists, shepherds, and teachers.

Thus, we all have a part, but Jesus is the true leader. As Bach says, we play the notes as they are written, "but it is God who makes the music." The music we make is less orchestra, with a conductor standing on a podium with pre-decided sheet music and more like a jazz band. We sit down together, choose a tempo and tone, and then just start to play. Doing the creative work together improvisationally.

The community of leaders needs to create habitats where conversations can take place. Organizationally speaking, emergence occurs through a series of conversations. Revitalization is not about implementing strategic goals toward some preconceived outcome. It is not about an appointed leader, operating from a place of positional power, creating a new vision statement, and delegating responsibilities toward its fulfillment. That is the causation thinking of the corporate business world. If we do this action (cause), it will lead to this result (effect).

The concept of cultivation captures this effectuation activity more accurately. It is the journey of cultivating an ecosystem of resurrection in which God is the primary actor. Think of a community of people working together in the triality of caring for the existing tree, seeding new plants, and grafting the organisms together. Or a community planting a garden, tilling the land, planting the seeds, weeding, harvesting, and experimenting with new recipes from what emerges.

Of course, we have a role to play, but we merely offer small contributions to a larger phenomenon of emergence. Just as when we plant a garden, we till, plant, fertilize, and weed, but there are other factors at work beyond our control: climate, pollution, insects, and rodents. Only God can make things grow, the creator and sustainer of life, we simply respond and improvise to emergent changes throughout the process.

Thus, revitalization is not a technical problem that can be solved with the appropriate application of technical solutions. A church is a living organism, not a machine in which broken parts can be swapped out. If that was the case, thousands of churches wouldn't close their doors every year. Rather, revitalization is an adaptive challenge in which a community of leaders must internalize the death-dealing realities and respond to the Spirit's life-giving breath.

This is not only about inherited and emerging modes living together. When all the individual pieces are grafted together, it creates a whole irreducible to the parts. It resembles the complex system of the vineyard, with Jesus' risen life flowing throughout and beyond (John 15). Kingdom fruit is produced. When a local church lives into the mixed economy for a period, a form of emergence takes place, and the greater communal ecosystem is transformed.

## Remixing Your Church—Deep Roots, Wild Branches

This requires the local church to understand itself as a habitat in a larger ecosystem. It may be helpful to reenvision the congregation as a mini-district, with the appointed leader as mini-bishop and missional strategist to the community. Here's a vison of the blended ecology ecosystem, in which every space is a potential church place, and every person a potential pioneer.

## THE BLENDED ECOLOGY ECOSYSTEM

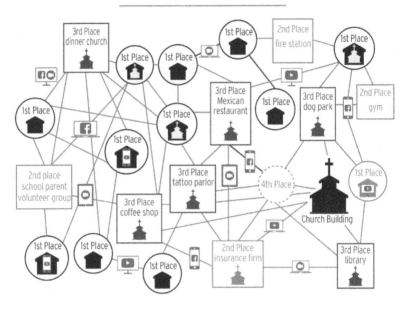

The inherited congregation is the hub of the activity, the home base of operations. The fresh expressions are micro-church plants, tethered to, but distinct from, the inherited congregation. The inherited form is serving within the appropriate leadership framework of the larger system. If it is a denominational congregation, it continues to function within the polity of the denomination, maintaining integrity in that relationship. The fresh expressions are serving in the decentralized, or blockchain, form of dispersed leadership. The local pioneers are released to experiment, self-organize, and replicate. The guiding principle here is low initial training but high ongoing support.[26] This is not about management, controlling, or owning, but seeding, watering, and cultivating.

This allows local churches to harness the potential of both hierarchical and networked modes of being. The church gathered and scattered. While the inherited form appreciates and maintains the hierarchal arrangement, the emerging form operates in a decentralized, blockchain arrangement. Emerging generations no longer experience the world as hierarchically arranged. To unchurched people, submitting to the demands of a mysterious entity whose credibility has eroded and whose authority has been seriously critiqued for decades is a stumbling block.[27]

In post-industrialized Western culture, the pyramids have been replaced by networks.[28] Among the clear majority who have no connection with a church, the hierarchical, patronage view seems to be an older order that stands in tension with the emerging cultural reality that is about being egalitarian, having influence, and intense participation where everyone contributes. Fresh expressions avoid this complexity, offering an alternative form of church that is based on networks and relationships. The fear of the traditional church losing control or becoming unnecessary is unwarranted. Sara Savage says of this fear, "This is a false dichotomy. A mixed economy of church, comprising both traditional and fresh expressions, is indispensable to navigate the cultural shift in which we exist.[29]

This creates a dynamic in which every church can become both congregational and connectional in polity. Through identifying and releasing the people in our pews as God's local mission force, we become a church-planting entity. These little micro-churches may in no way resemble the inherited congregation. Inevitably, some of the people who are engaged in the fresh expressions make their way back to the inherited congregation, and while this is not the goal, it is a welcome outcome.

The chain reaction that occurs is not one of the traditional church now being made unnecessary, but through the power of this structural remix, resurrection energy is released in the form of *emergence*. The inherited church becomes a vibrant green space again. The existing tree is watered, fertilized, and trimmed, as the sowers profusely cast the seeds of the gospel throughout the community.

Fragile little green spaces begin to emerge throughout the larger ecosystem. This is not some new arrangement; this is a remix of the legitimating narrative of our faith.

## Fresh Expressions Team—Disruptive Innovation Department

(Re)missioning is not about scrapping the project and starting over; it's a remix—introducing new elements and blending them together with the old. Where revitalization often involves internal tinkering, tweaking things on the inside, to attract those outside, (re)missioning involves joining what the Spirit is up to in our communities by cultivating fresh expressions. The congregation experiences positive transformation through this missional energy circulating back through feedback loops I will describe in detail in the next chapter.

> **Feedback Loops**: Describes when outputs of a system are routed back as inputs, thus forming a loop. Seemingly small inputs eventually magnify into large-scale transformation.[30]

I spoke earlier of large established institutions creating a disruptive innovation department and the power of fresh expressions to release dual transformation. Living into the blended ecology does not require a large-scale reconfiguration of the local church. This is one of the fatal mistakes of most revitalization approaches, as we all know established congregations with extensive histories cannot be reconfigured easily.

As Tod Bolsinger says, "Well, how do we change *any* DNA? Through sex."[31] Giving birth to new things. It is not easier to give birth than to raise the dead, but giving birth is often a step in the process of raising the dead. Bolsinger reminds us that in changing the DNA of living organisms through birthing something new, the child of that new birthing won't be all one party or the other but a new living culture that combines the past and the future. It's a remix.

Alan Roxburgh says, "The temptation of many leaders remains the need to fix problems with big strategies, more programs, and importing programs from outside. Instead of defaulting to these predictable, manageable solutions that have the appearance of addressing challenges, create experiments around the edge."[32]

A fresh expression forces a congregation to look outside itself. It provides a process to release this experimentation on the edge without giving up on the center. It breaks us open and reconfigures our soul in such a way that it touches our community again. It destabilizes overly fixed systems enough to release innovation. Complexity thinking refers to this concept as the edge of chaos.

> **Edge of Chaos:** In the innovation framework; refers to the sweet spot between enough openness to release change and enough structure to sustain order. Overly stable systems suffocate innovation; conversely, too much rapid change destroys systems. Theologically, this is about the liminal space between creation and new creation, opening ourselves to the Spirit bringing forth a new future, while balancing this with the Spirit's activity in the past.[33]

In *The Innovator's Way: Essential Practices for Successful Innovation*, Peter Denning and Robert Dunham share the story of Louis Pasteur, arguably one of the greatest innovators in history. In the 1870s when cow and sheep populations began to be decimated by a strange disease that threatened to destabilize the economic stability of France, Pasteur was called in to work on the problem. He had already previously shown how to prevent the spoiling of wine (he invented the process that now bears his name, *pasteurization*) and saved the silk industry by identifying the microbe that caused the decimation of French silk worms.[34]

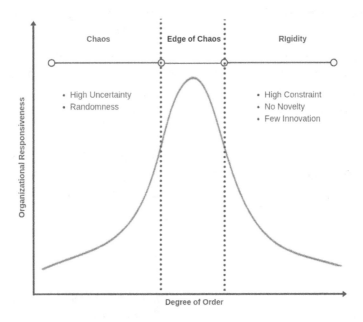

Pasteur had a unique method. He took his laboratory to the site of a major problem out in the field. He produced a series of major innovations in this way in the wine, dairy, silk, and chicken industries. In the case of the cows, he studied how the animals were getting sick on site and through his discovery saved the sheep and cattle industries.[35]

By doing this, he discerned the problem from a position of withness. His perspective was from within the problem, not removed in some ivory tower. His solutions were improvisational. In the case of the dying cows and sheep, through experimentation, he discovered the cause was a microorganism. He devised a way to control the microorganism, then he conducted a dramatic experiment to demonstrate his solution.[36]

Remixing starts with a local church forming a fresh expressions team, an on-site laboratory, and experimenting together through the fresh expressions journey. The small changes produced by this team will feed back into the inherited system through the process of grafting (feedback loops) I will suggest in the final chapter.

## The Fresh Expressions Journey

underpinned by prayer, ongoing listening, and relationships with the wider church

## Stage One: Listening

The first stage of planting fresh expressions within the community is prayerful listening. This cannot be overemphasized. Graham Cray, in a discussion about the "mixed economy" and connecting the center and the edge, reminds us that planting fresh expressions of church starts with an act of "double listening." Double listening includes listening to both God and context.[37]

Fresh expressions begin with the ears, not the eyes. It's the missional practice of surround-sound listening. Not starting with a vision statement but a journey in hearing our community through the ears of faith. We are not walking blindfolded, only using our eyes in a different way. Walking by faith, not by sight, requires using the eyes to hear. We must hear the dubstep the Spirit is mixing up in our communities and join in the rhythms of life there. Rather than assuming we already know, let's take a posture of curiosity and wonder.

Every fresh expression should start with a single question: Who is our *other*? Whose voices do we hear in the community around us that we don't hear in our church? What life-songs are they singing?

What places are they singing them in? What practices are they engaging in those places?

How does your team get started? Start spending time in those places, with those people, and look for the "persons of peace." Jesus sends out the disciples and tells them to find that person (Luke 10:5–6). Give your peace and receive theirs. Notice the reciprocal language here, if they "share in peace, your peace will rest on that person." It's not us bringing to them something they need. They also have what we need. There is a language of exchange, not superiority or dominance.

These are the people who give us an entry way into the community to which we are sent; they translate, contribute, and lead alongside. They open the door to relational potential of that community, and they show us "the way things are done around here." They are the welcomers who offer a safe place. They invite us to the table to be with. They offer us a gift by sharing their lives with us. They teach us the language and the customs of the tribe. As the border-stalkers, we bring good news and presence, but they give us the space to be. It is a reciprocal exchange of blessing and peace.

Connect, a fresh expression with children and youth meeting in the Martin Luther King Jr. building, started with relationships my wife, Jill, was forming in that community and her passion for the inner city. Burritos and Bibles started with a relationship with Adrian, the store manager at Moe's Southwest Grill. Yoga Therapy Church started with Renee's network of Amrit yoga practitioners. Shear Love at Soul Salon started with Krista's skill as a beautician. Tattoo Parlor Church started with Brian, the owner of Fat Kats Artistry, who invited us to come and meet in his tattoo shop. Paws of Praise started with Larry's passion to bring his dog to the dog park and the web of relationships he formed there.

## Stage Two: Loving/Serving

This is simply about finding ways to be with people in our community, loving and serving them with no agenda. As we do so, we may need to stand in the gap to meet physical needs, providing clothing, food, resources, or whatever other lack there may be. However, if the greatest soreness of the sin-fragmented soul is isolation, separation from God and each other, then healing comes through genuinely being with each other. Graham Cray reminds us that if we are planting fresh expressions "as a strategic agenda I think you are doomed from the start—this is God's initiative—it's about his kingdom."[38]

Once we understand this dynamic from a place of genuine withness as needs emerge within the community, we can work together to meet those needs.

My friend Verlon Fosner uses the terminology of "sore neighborhoods" to advocate that local churches need to return to a neighborhood theology: a theology of place. By returning to theology of the neighborhood, churches exist to know and serve the greatest needs of their immediate neighbors.[39] In a network society connected by flows, communities are now a series of interconnected "neighborhoods" or even "micro-communities."

Earlier we expanded the understanding of neighborhood to include *places* and *practices* in a larger network, rather than confining it to geography alone. The blended ecology utilizes both the neighborhood and network theology. The inherited mode primarily serves the larger mission of the neighborhood; the emerging mode serves the larger mission of the network.

Loving and serving is about healing through *withness*, as we join people in the places where they do life, sharing in those practices together. This can occur around tables, sports events, potlucks, service projects, and on park benches. When this is our sincere desire, and it is occurring with increasing regularity with a group, we are moving into the next stage.

## Stage Three: Building Community

Cray calls this approach "long-term incarnational engagement."[40] It is through the repeated patterns of withness that loving and serving becomes authentic community. Time is the fertilizer of relationships. As relationships gain strength, trust begins to build among the group.

A profound sense of connectedness begins to form as we gather around the habitual practices. The community becomes a source of life as we experience the healing of our isolation. Not only do we enjoy being around each other, but it becomes something we look forward to. The relationships have grown beyond whatever hobby, passion, or activity may have initially connected the group. Our sense of purpose and identity among the micro-community finds its fullest expression as we become more and more free to be. We start to find an authentic sense of *belonging*.

Once we sense this kind of belonging and community has formed, we begin to evolve organically into the next stage.

## Stage Four: Exploring Discipleship

In this stage, the group begins to intentionally explore the Christian faith. This occurs through a mixture of both formal learning (intentional conversations) and social learning (simply sharing in the rhythms of life together). More mature believers may begin to form mentorships with younger apprentices, spending time outside the group, discipling them through the messy relational process. There is no formal program, no seven steps to make a disciple. We are operating primarily in the realm of improvisation, sensitive to the nudging of the Holy Spirit, responding and adjusting as we go.

Len Sweet has written an entire book on "nudge evangelism" in which he argues that evangelism in the twenty-first century "will be built on nudges that have more to do with life before death than death and the afterlife, that focus more on the love of Christ than the wrath of God, that worry less about dying than about never having lived."[41]

This kind of evangelism requires us to be sensitive to the fact that God is already at work in every life. We are not simply trying to manipulate someone into a "decision for Christ" as if they were a notch on our belt. It's seeing every encounter with every person, no matter how brief, as an opportunity to be with another child of God in such a way that they will know they are loved. The Spirit does the rest. We are simply being present with people, paying attention, and responding to the movement of the Spirit as we go on the journey together. We are experiencing the unfolding of the good news together, in real time.

Cray reminds us that "evangelism and disciple-making are inseparable. Evangelism calls people to lifelong discipleship, by setting before them a way of life, as a follower of Christ the king."[42] This is utterly a relational approach to discipleship. Jesus models this throughout the Gospels, befriending and coming alongside people of various walks of life. Through their relationship with Jesus, they are experiencing a profound transformation.

When disciples of Christ are beginning to be formed, we are moving fully into *ecclesia*, a community centered around the risen Jesus (a.k.a. the church).

## Stage Five: Church Taking Shape

When people are beginning to enter into relationship with Christ, bend their life to the truth of Scripture, and become passionate about self-giving, other-oriented, and withness, church is taking shape. This may not appear to be our conventional understanding of church. Each fresh expression may be as diverse as the group or practice it is centered around, but the marks of the church begin to become a kind of compass for the journey: *one, holy, apostolic, catholic*—in Fresh Expressions language, we appropriate and remix those words to speak of the essentials as *inward, upward, outward,* and *ofward*. These churches in the flows are incarnational, missional, contextual, and ecclesial.

The missional posture required here is the acceptance of God's saturating presence over every sphere of life. As Len Sweet reminds us, if God can speak through burning bushes, talking donkeys, and crosses, God will speak through "art deco, architecture, abstract expressionism, classic literature like Virgil's *Aeneid*, mass media, disease, Disney, hunger, Twitter, etc."[43] God is also at work through burritos, tattoos, hair salons, running groups, yoga, Star Wars, kayaking, and pickle ball.

The questions become not how do we convert these people and their practices, but how is God working through these people and their practices? Does this practice already point to Jesus? How can church be formed here? Where is the isolation that needs healing through authentic withness? Who is the person of peace for this tribe? Pioneers go out in teams, inhabiting different relational spheres, searching for the already existing life-affirming tendencies, transforming the practices as we go. These churches among the social spaces of connections, structured in the blockchain way, gather and disperse, connecting relationally around the practices in endless contextual variations.[44]

Once we have begun to truly be church, we enter the final stage.

## Stage Six: Do It Again

Fresh expressions are born pregnant. The potential for multiplication is huge. In the McDonaldized church we are often focused on durability—something is healthy if it withstands the test of time. However, a close reading of Scripture and Christian movements in history show that durability is not the main concern. There are periods of the church's life when it flourishes briefly then goes underground or takes a new form, for instance, in Jerusalem or Antioch.

The greater concern is multiplication. While there is certainly a sameness and stability in the church, she has survived the test of time not by staying the same for long periods of time, but through multiplication in an unending array of contextual variations while staying rooted in the first principles revealed in Scripture.

The most fascinating thing is how God is multiplying fresh expressions of church by unleashing the priesthood of all believers. As we saw with early Methodism, the great awakenings of the faith have involved a releasing of the whole people of God. Jürgen Moltmann, reflecting on the missional church in the power of the Spirit, writes, "The whole congregation has 'spiritual' and charismatic gifts, not merely its 'spiritual' pastors. The whole congregation and every individual in it belong with all their powers and potentialities to the mission of God's kingdom."[45]

Fresh expressions shatter the glass ceiling for laity in the institutional church. Typically, when someone within a fresh expression begins to turn their whole life over to Christ, they begin to experience a call to plant another fresh expression with an unreached people group. As we see the ways that God can use ordinary people in their natural passions and practices, we become encouraged that God can use us in a similar way. We begin to hear statements like, "If _____ can do this, then so can I." The more time we spend in the community, the more connections we make, the more the network expands. These missional green spaces multiply themselves and begin to transform the ecosystem at large. The greatest difficulty usually lies in established leaders trusting God enough to release the movement to the people.

FIELD INTERVIEW
# Evelyn Sekajipo

Mama Africana Network

Evelyn Sekajipo is the founder and executive director of the Mama Africana Network. She earned her master of arts at Asbury Theological Seminary and is an experienced movement founder with a demonstrated history of working in the individual and family services industry. Evelyn has used her skills in coaching, social services, and entrepreneurship to plant contextual forms of church with those largely not seen by the church.

## Can you briefly describe the fresh expression(s) of your church?

In a society where black girls and black women are misunderstood, misrepresented, silenced, and devalued, Mama Africana stands as a beacon of hope and light in the city of Tampa. Mama Africana was birthed out of a dire need that my friends and I witnessed while doing work with the neighborhood kids. We wanted to offer a safe space for black girls to express themselves, to grow, and to develop strong sisterhood among themselves all while learning about God's heart for them, their family, and their community. The mission of

Mama Africana is to empower black girls in their ethnic identity and in their relationship with Jesus. We accomplish this through one-on-one and group mentoring, conferences, retreats, academic advocacy, and weekly gatherings. We have existed in the Tampa Bay area since 2005 as a modest yet dynamic grassroots organization/ministry.

### Explain the blended ecology dynamics between the inherited church and your fresh expressions. What kind of tension, if any, goes on between the two?

I believe that a fresh expression like Mama Africana can impact existing congregations if the congregation and its leadership freely allow it to do so. It is problematic when churches take on the responsibility to fix what they believe is wrong about the fresh expression. Unfortunately, we've painfully encountered churches like this, and we've learned to dismiss them, as we nod our heads and smirk #onward. It's not about the fresh expression fitting into the mold of a traditional church but rather the traditional church bending to better serve and learn from the fresh expression, in such a time as this. Many times when I would present Mama Africana to churches, their first inclination is to figure out ways to bring MA into their church—as in serve the girls that already attend their service. MA wasn't designed to operate within a church's blueprint; it was designed as an entity that carries with it the essence of the bride. MA was built to stand beside an existing congregation, reminding its people that its mission is also to those on the outside. Hey! That's where Jesus found his brightest disciples.

### How have you seen the fresh expressions have a positive impact on the existing congregation? In what ways?

When I first started Mama Africana in 2005, the church didn't really know what to do with it. I mean, we promoted Jesus, which was well embraced by congregants, but there was one element that served as some sort of nuisance to them: we were a black ministry, designed for black girls only, operated by black women only. Mama Africana started at a time before the #blacklivesmatter era and sorts came into existence, so many of the white, Latino, Asian, and even black Christians I associated with weren't completely sold on the idea of ethnic specificity. Many secretly believed (they confessed) that Mama Africana was just another way of bringing division to the church, a reawakening of segregation.

In the beginning, it was rough, and it caused me to question the mission of MA and its biblical relevance. There were times I wanted to pull the plug, but dear friends reminded me of the ministry's importance and necessity. The first support we received was from a local black church; the senior pastor, the late Reverend Abe Brown, met with me and my friend in his office to hear about our mission. Reverend Abe Brown was the pioneer of a prison ministry in our city that has existed since 1976. He was our city's gem, and we looked up to him because of his laboring to build up the black community in Tampa. Extremely pleased by what he was hearing, Reverend Abe Brown gave us a donation, saying he believed in our vision. We cherished his words more than his monetary donation.

We were also able to gain support from our friend's church, which was a predominately white family–oriented church. The congregation was overjoyed when they heard stories of how our mentees were progressing; it was as though they were a part of mentoring the girls alongside us. They became familiar with our girls' names and their stories, and they even prayed for them often. There was a time that we brought our girls to service, and they were treated with the utmost respect as if they were a part of the family. It was an affirming experience to feel the support from a church in this way. At the same time, I know that the Mama Africana presence in that congregation sparked up an inspiration that stimulated their understanding of the missional role of the church. I wish I could tell you that people in that church started their own fresh expression; I can only hope.

## Knowing that launching fresh expressions in your congregation involves time, sacrifice, resources, and people power, why do you believe it's worthy to pursue?

Launching a fresh expression is not an easy feat; it comes with several sacrifices, failures, and disappointments. In the end, it is all worth it because:

1. It revitalizes your city. What the church has to offer is unique, eternal, and transformative. Time and history have proven that the value the church brings to a city, to the world, rather, is immense, whether it is through schools, healthcare, or social work. Globally, black girls are hurting and in need of a savior that offers hope when their future seems bleak and uncertain. Mama Africana is an entity that comes alive as it is sent out into the city of Tampa to provide the hope of Jesus to black girls.

2. It revitalizes the church's mission. Often times being internal can be the death of the church. The church is meant to be a vibrant entity that goes out into the world offering the good news of Jesus—you know, like that Isaiah 61 verse Jesus selected to debut his ministry. Yes, of course, it was followed with backlash and discreditation. But if there's one thing I've learned from Jesus, it is that people will get upset when you try to mess up their order of doing church. Mama Africana is one of many beautiful expressions of the church. We eat a meal together, we laugh, we share life, we read Scriptures, we discuss current events, we pray, we share, we cry, we learn, we grow and transform. It is another way of doing church; it is concentrated, and it is invigorating, and it inspires congregations to be the hands and feet of Jesus.

3. It revitalizes your soul. Launching a fresh expression is humbling because we can't do it without the working of the Holy Spirit. When God places a vision on our heart, it can be overwhelming to the point of disarray that leads to a cry for help. It is in this desperation that we confidently approach the throne of grace asking for wisdom. Once we have reached this point, it's time to begin the pioneering work. The best part of Mama Africana for me is when God surprises me with his unfathomable acts. He helps me to remember that Mama Africana is *his*, and I am just a worker, tending to it. One time, a friend of mine in Kenya randomly told me that she and her best friend were going to launch a Mama Africana in Nairobi and in Nakuru. Here I am, strategizing ways that Mama Africana can expand in the city of Tampa, and here Jesus comes, talking about, "No, boo! Hush! The world." This work is God's work. We are privileged to step into it, and we are silly to believe that we have the power to elevate to the place it needs to be. God's plans aren't ours, his ways aren't ours; they are perfectly beyond our imagination. That alone is a reason to pursue launching a fresh expression. It is the opportunity to marvel at our great God and his great heart for the world.

CHAPTER 7

# Symbiosis—
# The Hybrid Organism

> So we cared for you. Because we loved you so much, we were delighted to share with you not only the gospel of God but our lives as well. (1 Thess. 2:8 NIV)

> You have to understand, most of these people are not ready to be unplugged. And many of them are so inured, so hopelessly dependent on the system, that they will fight to protect it.
> —Morpheus in *The Matrix*

Before every local congregation in the US is a choice. The massive shifts will only continue in the coming years. Even churches that are currently thriving in the primarily attractional-only mode of Christendom will soon find themselves plateaued or declining. The choice before us is to die to live. To trust in the power of resurrection. To love those that the church is not reaching so much as "to share with you not only the gospel of God but our lives as well" (1 Thess. 2:8 NIV).

The inherited church can no longer employ only a neighborhood strategy in a network society. We need both.

Furthermore, many churches in decline have ceased serving their neighborhood. The longer a church gathers on the same property, often the more disconnected it becomes from the people who live in that neighborhood just outside its walls. Local churches in the attractional-only mode need to find ways to connect with their neighbors. Also, we need to plant fresh expressions in the practice-centered communities connected by flows.

In the accompanying workbook, I explore the four-stage journey of revitalization: *awakening, futurefitting, planting/grafting,* and *releasing,* with tools, processes, and practices for each stage.

Let's briefly look back over the shifts described earlier and see how the blended ecology allows us to engage a world in the liminality of a paradigm shift.

## 1. Church Identity Crisis
*From Constantine, to US Imperial Corporation, Back to Caves*

The tectonic plates of our history are shifting under our feet. Among the fragmentation, the disruptive work of the Spirit is creating new ecosystems. Fresh expressions of the church are emerging in the cracks. We are going back to the caves, subversively scratching fish on the walls, repurposing our emptying sanctuaries as missional sending hubs. We are finding ways to engage and embody God's love among the spiritual openness in our culture.

The blended-ecology way allows us to protect and preserve the inherited church—the good, beautiful, and true pieces of the Christendom system. The attractional model has worked for most of church history and has significant basis in Scripture. In some places, the attractional model is still working quite well. We don't need to scrap the project and start over; we need a remix that allows us to return to the caves, through releasing our local congregations as missionaries to experiment with emerging forms of church throughout the community.

Those emerging forms of church also transform the existing congregation. We are forced to empty the time capsule of the clutter that doesn't truly reflect the essentials of the church and respond to cultural transformations. Every local church gets to decide what they put in their time capsule. The inherited church shifts to an outward orientation, which allows it to plant the seeds of a new future and create green spaces in the community. The church is futurefitted for mission and finds its identity again.

## 2. Emerging Economy
*From Big Faces to Bitcoin*

Fresh expressions release a transforming energy of traditioned innovation in inherited congregations. Harnessing the winds of change in the current economic milieu is pregnant with missional potential. Practically speaking, fresh expressions don't need buildings. They don't and should not own the spaces where they meet. They share public spaces with others. Typically, they cost nothing, and in many cases, provide a small amount of income for the inherited church to which they are tethered. They don't require professional clergy. In most cases the leaders are not ordained and have no official credentials. They are often led by grassroots indigenous leaders and encourage experimentation and innovation. They greatly resemble the church ecosystem we discover emerging in the New Testament.

As we strengthen the center, stimulate the edge (dual transformation), and go back to the caves, a transformation occurs.

Both the centralized and decentralized forms can exist in the same congregation. The inherited congregation continues to operate as the attractional center, while the emerging fresh expressions harness the dispersed blockchain structure of a network society.

Fresh expressions of church, in most of cases, do not cost anything. There is no fee to rent space. There is no maintenance cost for buildings. No electric bills. However, the benefit is significant to the inherited congregation. The people of God are released to operate into their gifts. The glass ceiling for laity is shattered. No longer is reading liturgy, chairing a committee, or filling in to preach while the pastor is away on vacation the pinnacle of a lay leader's spiritual life. They become pioneering apostles, prophets, evangelists, shepherds, and teachers in their own rite. Also, as disciples are formed in the fresh expressions, some will make their way back to the inherited church. Others will stay in the fresh expression but learn the value of stewardship and the joy of generosity.

Burritos and Bibles met for almost a year before someone finally said, "Hey, isn't this our church? Shouldn't we take an offering or something?" We emptied the chips and salsa basket, passed the plate, and the gathering began to collect offerings that went back to the sending congregation.

Those pioneers who lead the fresh expressions are typically not professional clergy. They are not on the salary of the church. They serve out of their own giftedness in the place of their passions. They extend the presence of the church into the community with masses of people for whom the church is largely inaccessible. They connect people to Christ and create green spaces. This all catalyzes cascading changes in the ecosystem and renews the existing church.

## 3. America (Re)mixed

*From* Leave It to Beaver *to* The Brady Bunch *to* Modern Family

Fresh expressions of church are forming with those dislocated in the current inherited system. The blended-ecology way offers churches the possibility of harnessing these changes in the family life. It offers a new ecclesial ecosystem, which possesses profound potential to bring reconciliation among the generations, races, and social networks. Young and old, dark, light, and blended, cannot only coexist in the same church network, but interact and find unity. Congregations can begin to reflect the diverse singularity of the triune God and the incredible diversity of the (re)mixed America.

Most fresh expressions consist largely of people the inherited church cannot or will not reach. They also reach those who have become disillusioned with the church, the so-called "nones" and "dones." These micro-communities reflect the host networks where they gather, so they reflect the diversity of the people in those networks. Fresh expressions of church, depending on the context, can be heterogeneous or homogeneous. This is part of their power when it comes to a (re)mixed America.

They appeal to people who have interests in certain practices that cross over age, race, and socioeconomic barriers, and so they can be incredibly diverse. Church 3.1 is a fresh expression that gathers to "Pray. Run. Love." They have church and run a 5k together. That group reflects the diversity of the numerous races and ages that have a passion to run. Also, if the heart of the network itself is based in a certain homogeneity, the fresh expression will reflect that contextual reality. For instance, the network of fresh expressions meeting in care facilities throughout the retirement community of The Villages, Florida, reflect the age group of that context. The diversity is determined by the practice movements and flows that connect them.

Fresh expressions allow every church to go multi-site. One shift where they are powerfully able to connect with people beyond the current reach of the attractional model is regarding the emerging realities of families. Fresh expressions take all our eggs out of the Sunday morning basket. There are multiple opportunities throughout the week where people can experience church both in digital and analog ways. This offers a flexible possibility to the busy lives of families and connects with their passions for common practices.

The blended ecology also takes seriously the reality of blended-family dynamics. In shared custody situations, it creates a viable possibility that a family can experience church together weekly. This creates a consistency for children in these arrangements who may alternate weekends with biological parents. The inherited gatherings are still available, but the fresh expressions, which are spread throughout the community meeting at contextually appropriate times for the shared practices, create multiple possibilities for church.

## 4. New *Mayflower*
### From Christendom to Pantheon

Let's come back to Len Sweet's insight that we are always "playing away" now, which means "the church must reconceive itself as a resistance movement and come to terms with the socially disruptive power of the gospel" and "capture the spirit of the times without being captured by or capitulating to it."[1] Fresh expressions give us a team and a strategy to play away games. We are no longer like a team with only defense, holding down our end zone; the inherited church now has a powerful offense as well.

In the incredible religious diversity of the North American landscape, fresh expressions create a counternarrative. The views of the church as a rigid museum-like institution are challenged by the emerging forms of church. Common questions from those exposed to fresh expressions are, "So this is church?" "I didn't know church could meet there!" or "This is what Christians do?" A people for whom the *Mayflower* impulse flows through their veins are exposed to a new revolution.

Fresh expressions of Jesus provide a counternarrative to "new pantheon" thinking. This exposes people to a first encounter, or a fresh encounter. We can enter the post-everything world of emerging generations to provide green spaces where they can have a first taste of the love of God. We can also tap into that impulse toward religious inclusivity while firmly lifting the singularity of Jesus' claim over all spheres. By creating that space where someone who enjoys yoga can hear the Christian gospel, we open opportunities that would have never been possible otherwise.

We can present a fresh offering of spirituality for the "spiritual, but not religious." We can deconstruct the image of Christians as closed-minded, judgmental, and hypocritical by inviting honest dialogue amid the post-pluralism ecosystem. We can offer communal life with Jesus, healing the isolation that suffocates our souls in the deterritorialization of a network society.

## 5. The Digital Ecosystem

*From Morse Code to Virtual Reality*

In an age when a presence in the digital landscape makes a physical building unnecessary, fresh expressions is harnessing social media and networking technologies to create Jesus communities in and among those larger networks. People are connecting and meeting in communal spaces in new relational arrangements that look like the church in Acts. By entering fully into this new digital world and harnessing these technologies, a conversation about reforming the church will be more and more irrelevant. The new conversation will be about reforming "the world as our parish."

The capacity for the church to harness the technological revolution is incredible. The COVID-19 pandemic demonstrated this in profound ways. We can establish a presence on the digital landscape of the network society in much the same way church buildings established a presence in their neighborhoods. Most fresh expressions are organized, promoted, and sustained by harnessing various technologies. We can bypass the traditional ways that churches once relied upon to engage their neighbors. Each local church has an option to embrace this disruptive innovation, harness it, and create a research-and-development department.

By plugging into social media networks, all people can stay connected with those outside the typical church circles. This is completely free and highly underutilized in most congregations. Just as technology is becoming an extension of human beings, so it is becoming an extension of the inherited congregation. Emerging generations who get their news through social media will also have their first encounters with churches through social media.

Most fresh expressions create free pages to describe basic info and location times that can be shared throughout an extensive relational network. Events can be created, and friends invite friends. A relational cascade can stretch out far and wide across the digital landscape. People outside one person's relational network may be reached through another. Some fresh expressions use meetup.com or other similar platforms to create groups and invite new people. The hypoconnectivity that the internet provides can be harnessed to build analog communities in first, second, and third places, or digital communities in the space of flows.

The inherited congregation may have the traditional centralized platform with websites and social media pages. But the fresh expressions serve as kind of decentralized blockchain of relational transactions. Any person who can use social media can start a new fresh expression, organize a movement, or share a message. Wise churches will harness this capacity rather than attack it. While it challenges denominational systems, professional clergy, dedicated facilities, and traditional communication channels, if embraced, it could release the next remixed iteration of the church.

## 6. It's a Beautiful Day in This Network

*From* Mister Rogers' Neighborhood *to Neo's Network Matrix*

Resulting from the previous shift in technology, perhaps the most explosive potential for the blended-ecology way is to sustain the inherited systems while getting out in the flows of a network society. Fresh expressions are already present within the five scapes: ethnoscapes (movement of peoples), mediascapes (media), technoscapes (technology), finanscapes (markets), and ideoscapes (political). Among the fluidity and mobility of culture, fresh expressions are a disruptive innovation to all systems, embedding the church in the communities of shared practices.

Fresh expressions dot the landscape of these dynamic practices that connect people across geographic boundaries within uneven information flows, like green spaces in the communal ecosystems. These incarnational contextual expressions are emerging among the people who journey in and among the many tribes of their daily networks. As we engage this emerging reality, we incarnate the gospel where people live and play, connected by the space of flows. We reach the mass of people for whom the inherited church is largely inaccessible. Unleashing the priesthood of believers as missionaries among these practice movements establishes an incarnational presence within the larger community. The so-called unchurched and dechurched are invited into the reign of God.

Lives are transformed through the other-oriented, patient ferment of walking with. The networked practices themselves are transformed and become signs that point to the diverse singularity of the triune God. An endless kaleidoscope of contextual forms of church are forming all kinds of colorful variations among the native practices, as believers and non-believers do life together. The network of fresh expressions resembles a decentralized blockchain structure, tethered to, but not controlled by, the inherited congregation. The remixed structure provides a life-giving symbiotic exchange as the traditional church functions in ways faithful to the hierarchy.

Traditional congregations are enabled to plant the seeds of the gospel within the fluidity of these cultural flows by futurefitting in the blended-ecology way. The apostles, prophets, evangelists, shepherds, and teachers (Eph. 4) in our pews are released into the larger ecosystem, creating trophic cascades that renew the community. They turn their passions and practices into forms of church. Ordinary heroes of the traditional congregation discover their calling as pioneers and connect with other pioneers on the edge.

People within the fresh expressions of church are taken through the life of grace, become disciples, and catalyze more new churches. The force of multiplication is released and the movemental nature of the church is recovered. Harnessing the latest technologies, connected by digital networks, the movement is organized primarily in the third places around common hobbies, interests, and bundled practices. The local congregation moves from only being a once-per-week gathered model, to a dispersed, daily, scattered model.

Fresh Expressions is harnessing those networks, offering communal life with Jesus in the first, second, and third places of the interconnected ecosystems of neighborhoods and networks. We are finding ways to enter those technology-enabled relational webs, coming empty-handed with open ears. We are locating the "persons of peace" in these networked communities (Luke 10:1–8), those that have the key to unlock the relational potential there. We do so while simultaneously remaining ever neighbor-oriented. In a world that is forgetting the value and beauty of neighboring and placefulness, too lost in the blazing 5G, 24/7 anxiety work cycle, we present a counternarrative of what communities can look like. We approach the people outside the walls of our churches, where the Spirit is already working, and we ask the gentle questions like "Who is my other?" and "Won't you be my neighbor?"

The blended ecology recovers the withness embodied in the Trinity and the faithful pattern of that presence throughout Scripture and history. God sings people to himself through both the stationary and mobile modes.

As we employ the best thinking of the new science, the dual transformation way—we harness the power of institution and movement, fertilize the tree, and plant the new organisms—the larger communal ecosystem is transformed and the inherited church can potentially experience renewal.

## Grafting

Earlier we explored the process of how fresh expressions form. For those futurefitting existing congregations in the blended-ecology way, you may want to consider a seventh stage. The team planting fresh expressions from the local church needs to find creative ways to keep them tethered to the anchor congregation. Like the structure of the Möbius strip, the life of the church should be flowing out into the community and the life of the community flowing back into the church. This becomes a continuous open loop of cocreation.

Steven Croft notes three major focuses of activity if the mixed economy is to work: (1) sustaining and developing traditional churches, (2) developing fresh expressions of church, and

(3) connecting everything together.[2] Very little attention has been paid to item three.

Remember in dual transformation, "Transformation A" repositions the core business, adapting its current business model to the altered marketplace. "Transformation B" creates a separate, disruptive business to develop the innovations that will become the source of future growth. "Transformation C," or the "capabilities link," involves the grafting together of these dual processes.[3]

Insight from the business world shows that in dual transformation, the greatest challenge lies not in finding creative ways to better service existing customers, or finding fresh ways to reach new customers outside core markets, but in the combining and leveraging a company's valuable assets to simultaneously release entrepreneurial creativity ("Transformation C"). It's the merging

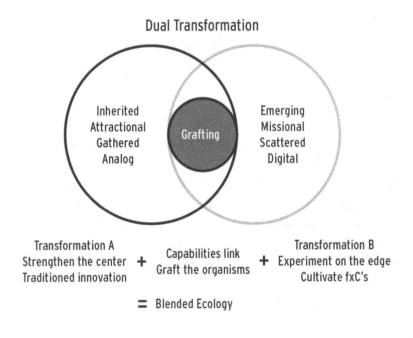

together of these two simultaneous transformations to reinforce each other that is often most difficult.[4]

The focus of this book has been to introduce local churches to navigating the symbiotic relationship between inherited and emerging modes of church. What I offer here is born out of our own experimentation at Wildwood, learnings from other pioneers across the West, integrated with research in the field. It's unanimous: "grafting" or living in the tension of these dual transformations is the greatest challenge.

In a subsection of his essay titled "A Test for the Whole Mixed Economy," Graham Cray says, "The continuing challenge facing all churches is to remain missional, to be communities for the kingdom, and not revert to the maintenance of their own existence."[5] While the focus of fresh expressions is not to revitalize the existing congregation, they provide a viable means for the local church to recover and retain a missional posture.

In a journey of transformation, this grafting is what keeps us on the edge of chaos without tearing the system apart. Room is made for experimentation and change, while the inherited congregation is nurtured in new ways. The fresh expressions will transform the inherited congregation, and the inherited congregation will transform the fresh expressions. It is this symbiosis, and the mysterious importation of energy by the Spirit, that leads to the emergence of the new ecosystem.

Michael Moynagh proposes that these new expressions of Christian community are understood to be church "so long as they are engaged in the four interlocking sets of relationships that constitute the church—with God, the world, the living Christian tradition, and within the gathering."[6] My experience, both as a practitioner and as a coach of practitioners, is that fresh expressions have the greatest potential when connected with inherited congregations.

I have taken great pains to demonstrate how both the inherited and emerging modes have functioned throughout history, sometimes in collaboration—temple and synagogue, Jerusalem and Antioch, Anglican and Methodist revival, attractional and emerging, gathered and scattered, old and new wineskins. This diverse singularity reflects the personhood of the triune God.

Most of the fresh expressions that demonstrate longevity and the cultivation of disciples operate in the blended-ecology way. Creating a disruptive innovation department, an on-site laboratory, in our church and sending "go" teams into the community allows a church to embody both gathered and scattered modes of being. What Moynagh refers to as "pockets in the same trousers," I refer to as living organisms, grafted in the one true vine.

Back to the words of Stuart Murray, in *Church after Christendom*, "The brightest hope for the church after Christendom is a symbiotic relationship between inherited and emerging churches."[7]

The focus of grafting is captured by the phrase "symbiotic relationship." When local churches plant fresh expressions and live in the mixed economy for a period of time, tending the symbiotic relationship between the inherited and emerging modes of church, a new creation is birthed . . . the blended ecology. This symbiosis is a form of revitalization. Grafting is all about the tending of that relationship. New learnings from our friends in the Leicester Diocese of the Church of England can help us here.

I had the opportunity to share and learn at the 2018 National Pioneer Gathering in Leicester, United Kingdom. The Leicester Diocese has been living into the blended ecology for more than a decade. In the fresh expressions process, they are noticing the emergence of two distinct phenomena they refer to as *edgelands* (missional enterprises that may or may not become "church") and

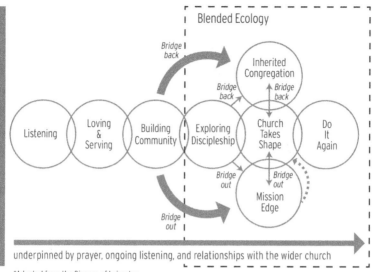

*Adapted from the Diocese of Leicester

*bridge backs* (fresh expressions in process that connect people back to an inherited church).

While the focus of a fresh expression is to become the fullness of the church in the larger communal ecosystem of first, second, and third places, some fresh expressions effectively connect people back to the local congregation for discipleship and connect people from the inherited church to people and culture outside of it. The bridge back is thus a two-way, not a one-way street. Furthermore, people that come to faith in the fresh expressions of church often find their way back into inherited congregations as well. While some fresh expressions purists believe this muddies the missional waters, so to speak, I find no rational explanation for why we should not encourage and actively facilitate this kind of exchange.

Returning to Jesus' parable of the vineyard, a fitting analogy for this process is grafting in the vineyard (John 15). As we plant the scions (fresh expressions) we need to continually connect them back to the rootstock (inherited congregation). Michael Moynagh reminds us that organizations are sequences of conversations, in which any individual's contribution can catalyze change in the whole system. In organizational transformation language, grafting creates *feedback loops*, in which outputs of a system are routed back as inputs, thus forming a loop. Again, seemingly small inputs eventually magnify into large-scale transformation.[8]

The existing congregation as the *rootstock* is being grafted with the *scions* to create an abundant harvest. The key here is not trying to manage, own, or fix, but to rest in the abiding together. How can we create ways that inherited and emerging modes of church can abide together? How can we create a significant witness between the tree and the green spaces to cultivate new generative communal ecosystems?

Following are some suggested practices for grafting the inherited and emerging mode.

## 1. Tell Stories

What made Pasteur so successful as an innovator where others failed? The genius of establishing laboratories at the problem site, living in the phenomena, and improvising solutions was certainly part of his effectiveness. Yet those things in and of themselves don't guarantee the adoption of a new way by a community or the resulting deep culture change. It was how he shared his learnings, by storifying the data and attracting support, that became the feedback loops that transformed industries. Pasteur was called the master of the "theater of experiment." His ability to draw others into the experiment, and show how his discoveries could add value, set him apart as an innovator. He not only invented, he attracted powerful allies who supported his science.[9]

Not only do we need to cultivate fresh expressions that offer communal life with Jesus, we must show the inherited congregation the value of this activity and involve them. If the inherited congregation is not brought along in the journey and willing to adopt and support these innovations, there is a strong likelihood of death on the vine.

Stories from the fresh expressions give life to the sending hub of the congregation. The congregation begins to understand the impact they are having on the community. They hear the stories of the young lady receiving Christ by the ice machine in Moe's, or the tattoo artist taking Communion for the first time, and it has an awakening affect. It reminds us of why we exist and excites us to know we are having an impact in the community beyond our walls. We have built into our inherited worship gatherings at Wildwood a weekly "missions' moment." We tell a quick story from something that happened in our fresh expression, show a picture, or a clip from a gathering. In this way, we bring the congregation along in the "theater of experiment."

## 2. Invite

We invite members of the congregation to visit the fresh expressions and vice versa. This must be handled carefully. There have been times when we had to tell inherited church people to stop coming because they were overwhelming a gathering. One of the admission fees is to bring a not-yet-Christian or nominally religious friend with you to a gathering. We find people are much more open to checking out some crazy Christians gathering in a Mexican restaurant, dog park, or yoga studio than a steeple on Sunday morning. We also encourage those participating in the fresh expressions to come check out the rest of their big, blended family some time. Not to extract them from the incarnational community, but to meet their relatives occasionally.

## 3. Measure in Story

It is very easy to try to institutionalize a movement of the Holy Spirit; it has happened to every great awakening of the faith in history. One surefire way to do that is with measurement. When we start trying to quantify, measure, and create data categories for the movement of the Holy Spirit, we quench the fire. Measurement is fine for science experiments, just not human lives. Measurement is not neutral; we measure what matters to us, and the experiment in quantum physics I mentioned earlier shows that we affect what we attempt to measure (see the *intelligent observer paradox*, for instance).[10]

JR Woodward reminds us that story is the measurement of community.[11] When someone asks, "How many?" then respond by saying, "Let me tell you what happened to _____ the other day!" When people begin to question whether spiritual growth is taking place, we can only respond with stories of transformed lives; there are no metrics. I understand that we all need to record data and numbers can indicate health. What I'm suggesting here in grafting for the blended-ecology way is that we measure in story. Just one is enough (Luke 15:7).

## 4. Know That They May Never Come Here

The death-dealing question that will ultimately come for every blended ecology scenario is, "So when are those people going to start coming to *real church*?" It seems that the fresh expressions approach is so outside lifelong church members' experience, they will never see the gatherings in the green spaces as church. In my experience, it is a waste of time and energy trying to convince people the world is flat when it's round.

We do, however, need to set a healthy boundary right up front: the truth is, most people in our fresh expressions will never come back to the "real church." Just firmly establish that with the inherited congregation. This is not some bait-and-switch tactic to get people back to the church compound. The clearer you can make that to a congregation, the better. We are being the church with them, whether they ever come back or not. *And* yet, some do come back!

## 5. Celebrate the Inherited Congregation

I often remind folks that "bad Christians happen to good people." In pioneering fresh expressions, I have heard the horror stories of "dones" and how they were treated by so-called Christians and existing churches. In the moments of deep sharing, we need to honor their feelings, empathize with their pain, and offer authentic withness. It is sad and heartbreaking.

There have been times when the energy of the fresh expression turned to an inherited church-bashing session. We always redirect that energy by saying things like "Glad that doesn't happen at our church" or "Good thing God has a no only-perfect-people-allowed policy" or "I'm sorry you had that experience. It reminds me that the church is a wellness center for sinners, not a nursing home for saints." We try to find ways to tell stories about the God-loving, faithful people back at the inherited hub as well. Storytelling is not a one-way street.

## 6. Encourage Exploration of the Inherited Congregation

Some people who pioneer fresh expressions act as if it's a curse word to invite people back to the inherited congregation. This has not been my experience. If people have an issue with that invitation, they will let you know. We find a real inquisitiveness about the traditional church in most of our groups. In fact, when someone is ready to get baptized, marry, or loses a loved one, I encourage them to share those significant moments back at the inherited congregation. I have no problem serving Communion, and even baptizing folks in tattoo parlors, community centers, jail, and restaurants—if it is happening in the community that they call church. However, I often encourage folks with things like, "You know, baptism is a pretty big step. I would love for you to share that with the big, messy blended family you haven't met yet!"

Further, emerging generations love to get involved with projects that meet human need. While they may be opposed to attending a Sunday morning worship event, they are often quite excited to come volunteer at the food pantry, help with a scout troop, join a recovery fellowship, or show up for a church workday. Frequently, when they form relationships with church members in those hands-on times, their disposition about traditional church can be changed.

## 7. Transform Inherited Space

It is a misconception that fresh expressions can only occur in first, second, and third places and not a church building. I try to help the churches I work with understand that your facility may be the only "third place" in the community (as noted earlier, particularly in a rural context). The new protest-ant "spiritual, but not religious" movement is not pushing against Jesus or buildings, but hypocritical Christians and rigid institutionalism.

Angela Shier-Jones makes a compelling case for utilizing church property as one of our greatest assets. She proposes asking a series of questions about what each space communicates about God to visitors. Those spaces can be repurposed for mission. She documents trends among emerging generations that they are in fact drawn to sacred spaces. She writes, "The familiarity and yet distinct 'otherness' of church buildings and their interiors can and does speak of a timeless truth which cannot be silenced or hidden away, regardless of how the world may change."[12]

Our buildings are some of our greatest assets; we just need to stop seeing them as colonies from which we extract people from the community and understand them as habitats of a larger communal ecosystem. While I do see the value in maintaining inspiring structures that point to the majesty and power of God, I see a greater value in some cases in minimizing the intimidation factor of church buildings. Church compounds can be repurposed in a way that people feel comfortable about doing life there, not just for a worship service.

We have multiple fresh expressions that meet at our church facility, where people in our community who are not connected to the inherited congregation feel free to join us. Our buildings are the places where they come pick up their weekly groceries, shop for free clothing, stop at Shear Love at Soul Salon for a free haircut, gather for a weekly community dinner, and host Wednesday yoga sessions. The true challenge of transforming inherited space is intentionally recreating each room as a graceful place where people can feel accepted, spill coffee, and children can break stuff. Sacred places where people throw cigarette butts in the parking lot, drop f-bombs, and encounter the living God.

## 8. Digital Space Can Be a "Third Place"

I referenced earlier the massive social shifts that have literally transformed the human experience of space and time. We explored the difference between two kinds of space—the *space of place* and the *space of flows*, with the latter referring to the amalgamation of technologies that create simultaneity of social relationships at a distance, or "distanced contact."

I described at length the importance of the first, second, and third places in cultivating fresh expressions. First place: The home or primary place of residence. Second place: The workplace or school. Third place: The public places separate from the two usual social environments of home and workplace, which "host regular, voluntary, informal, and happily anticipated gatherings of individuals" (cafes, pubs, theaters, parks, and so on).[13]

I also referenced how when COVID-19 struck, for those of us who are fresh expressions practitioners, our two primary mission spaces were closed off—the second and third places were shut down. We could not have Tattoo Parlor Church; the tattoo parlor was closed. We couldn't gather in Moe's Southwest Grill for Burritos and Bibles; they were doing take-out only. The dog park was empty as people were quarantined at home, therefore no Paws of Praise.

This limited us to the only spaces we had left:

1. The first place, or the home place.
2. The digital place, or the "space of flows."

In the pandemic, we discovered that digital space is its own kind of "third place"—a neutral, communal gathering location.

These technologies enable us to be present to some degree across the world at any given moment. A part of us, our technologically extended mind, is inhabiting both digital and analog space simultaneously. The technology enables a kind of extension of ourselves to be present on the digital frontier. This leads to the compression and transformation of time and what Castells references as "timeless time" in the "real virtuality."[14]

We need to seriously consider how we can be an incarnational presence in this digital space. We are finding that many people we engage in our digital fresh expressions are bridging back to our inherited congregation, and people in our inherited congregation are pioneering new forms of church on the digital frontier.

A blended ecology of attractional (inherited) and incarnational (missional) modes of church is necessary. Yet COVID-19 showed us we need to add another dimension to the blended ecology: physical (or analog) and digital (or virtual). Growing the inherited church, while planting fresh expressions in the community, must certainly include this digital dimension.

We had to redefine the center and create new ways to care for our people in a pandemic world. Additionally, we learned to cultivate new digital and hybrid forms of church. For instance, *Supper Table Church*, was created out of the need of parents who became homeschool teachers overnight to connect with other parents. Every Wednesday during quarantine, they prepared meals and sat at the dinner table with a screen. Through Zoom, they connected with others across the country to converse, pray, and share in a Jesus story. This community that formed in digital space during the initial raging of the Coronavirus still meets weekly today.

Perhaps you will find this axis helpful as you think about this work, every church will need to be engaged in mission in each quadrant on this new missional frontier.

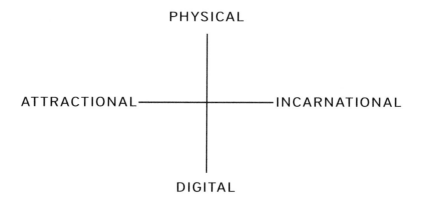

## 9. Create a Fourth Place

We discovered many people in our fresh expressions were starting to matriculate back to the inherited worship experience. However, they would come and never come back. The very traditional experience at Wildwood was not connecting with many of these visitors. We started hearing things like, "All the candles and ritual stuff seems sketchy" or, "That old lady yelled at my kids" or, "That gentleman passed me a note telling me how rude it was to be on my technological device when I was following along in the Bible."

For us, we needed to create what I now call a "fourth place." The fourth place is a neutral space that blends together a fresh expression and an inherited gathering. For us, we call that place New Life, a blended worship experience, which is as intentionally non-institutional as we can get. This seems to be a soft place to land for the so-called "nones" and "dones" of our community. New Life meets in a renovated fellowship hall and is a kind of middle-space for the people who encounter Jesus in our fresh expressions and is now our most attended worship experience.

We have baptized most of the people in that room or walked them home from a once fragmented relationship with the church. New Life is a mess; children and youth are running around everywhere as families sit around tables for breakfast. The WildOnes Band consists of pastors singing and playing guitar beside folks who were shooting heroine a couple weeks before. Teenagers play in the band and draw on easels as a worship offering. We have a "sacred in the secular" song time, a "coffee toast," "social media moments"; we encourage children to play, and feature dubstep club music for "connect time."

People spill coffee next to others spilling their guts, weeping at the altar in the same makeshift worship space. There was some debate about where it should take place. My team overruled me that it could happen on church property. They were right! We took our old "bingo hall" as it became commonly known, renovated it into a makeshift worship space, and then asked our so called "nones" and "dones" what worship would look like for them. I think many churches who embrace the blended-ecology way would benefit from having a fourth place.

These nine suggestions may be helpful as we engage in the work of fertilizing the existing tree, planting the seeds of green spaces, and grafting the rootstock and scions together. In this way, every church can become a multi-site, and every community can become a thriving vineyard.

Here's a diagram to help us visualize how pioneer teams move through the five spheres of our communities.

### THE BLENDED ECOLOGY ECOSYSTEM

How Pioneers Move Through the Five Spheres

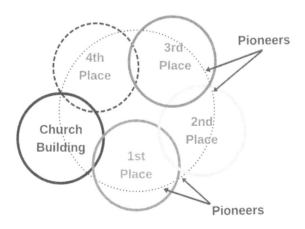

FIELD INTERVIEW
# Jonathan Dowman

Pioneer Development Worker
Diocese of Leicester (Church of England)

Jonathan Dowman works full time in training, supporting, and encouraging both lay and ordained pioneer leaders of fresh expressions of church in Leicester Diocese (Church of England) in the UK. They have more than fifty-six licensed lay pioneers, who are mostly voluntary, and a further five pioneers who are training for the priesthood (as pioneers). There are probably an additional hundred-plus lay pioneers who are unlicensed, and many are quite happy being so!*

As part of Jonathan's work, he spends 20 percent of his time as a practitioner so that he practices what he preaches, modeling what he encourages others to do and puts his own shoulder to the wheel. He is a permanent member of diocesan staff and a training incumbent (the ministerial oversight lead for new deacons and priests) for four newly ordained pioneers.

(*The Leicester Diocese licenses pioneers as they do lay leaders and other such ministries. This gives them access to diocesan support and training, working agreements, and the bishop's authority to minister. Many pioneers don't want or seek this recognition though, but the Leicester Diocese still supports them.)

## Can you briefly describe the fresh expression(s) of your church?

My wife, Emma, and I are the leaders of Watershed.

*A watershed is a ridge of land that separates waters flowing in different directions. It is also an important event that represents a change in how people do or think about something.*

A few miles west of Market Harborough (our home) sit the Hothorpe Hills. These hills mark Great Britain's east/west watershed, with rain water eventually flowing out to the Wash and the North Sea to the east, or the Avon and the Bristol Channel to the west. Our connection with this local landscape caused a small group of us to question our spiritual way of living as families and individuals: Which way was our life flowing? Was there anything we could do together to live happily and holistically?

Watershed emerged as a community of all ages, gathering throughout the year to retreat from the hectic pace and pressures of the everyday. We plant, discover, create, harvest, and celebrate life through the seasons, spending time in the beauty and flow of God's creation instead of merely passing through it.

Meeting monthly in the beautiful grounds of Launde Abbey, space and time are created for refreshed perspectives and direction to be kindled.

We gather on Sunday afternoons and are joined by between 30 to 60 regularly, many of these coming from smaller local villages and generally consisting of people who want to engage in something soulful. For two-thirds of our regulars Watershed is their only connection to Christian community or church. We are growing, largely through invitation and word of mouth.

Each time we gather we have a central meeting purpose—for example, building bird boxes. This is usually linked to the season. We'll do this together, while also allowing people to explore the grounds, for children to play and friends to catch up. Toward the end of the afternoon we'll gather people in a small chapel or around a campfire and share a Christian reflection based around the activity we have been doing together. This will be all-aged and will offer a time of reflection, prayer, and Scripture, and will usually have a practical application (something simple to take away and put into action in the week). This time is always optional, but most people at Watershed join us and contribute to it. We always end with tea and cake.

We don't yet consider ourselves to be a Fresh Expression of Church (FxC). Although we are working toward being a FxC, we feel (even three years in) that this would be to make Watershed something we have no right to make it yet. Watershed is based around relationships, our shared environment, the land, the seasons, and those natural activities or points of the year where earth and heaven seem close. Our prayer is that we grow and deepen, and that one day we will start to meet with a smaller group from Watershed who are saying "and this is how we want to live." This smaller group, meeting in a Watershed way might become church

## Explain the blended ecology dynamics between the inherited church and your fresh expressions. What kind of tension, if any, goes on between the two?

In Leicester Diocese we have more than sixty recognized fresh expressions of church. These meet at least monthly, are missional, see themselves as church, have clear discipleship taking place and show loving service to the world. Watershed covers most of these, but those who come do not *yet* see it as church. Out of these sixty, about 75 percent remain within the local parish boundaries. They remain linked with the sending and resourcing church (though the church may be smaller than the fresh expression at times!).

This link can work very well in smaller rural communities, where numbers are smaller and the wider community may also be small. Many of our churches have multiple small congregations, so a fresh expression meeting in a pub, school, or library (for example) can simply be an extension of that church, though it meets in a different way.

In addition to our recognized FxCs, we have approaching two hundred pioneering missional activities (PMA). These PMA activities are neither the existing church community nor yet a FxC. Some of these PMAs end up becoming fully fledged FxCs, but some end up changing the existing church instead. Either is good, but what unites both the PMAs and FxC is:

- The activity is missional.
- It is new; we've never tried it before.
- It is probably lay-led.
- We're dependent on finding people of peace and working with them (rather than doing to or for them).
- We'll go where the Holy Spirit leads us.
- It will be costly—either as we are called to become a FxC or people start joining the existing church . . . we will change and sometimes it will be hard!

We find that this approach opens new possibilities with churches. It releases them from trying to imagine a FxC from the outset or trying to force one into being and instead frees them to think about who God might be leading them to serve and what the first steps of pioneering might look like.

As most of our fresh expressions are rooted in their parishes, most relationships are good. They become strained when both the

FxC and the existing church make assumptions about worship, people, and expectations.

## Worship

Many assumptions are made, and FxCs can land themselves with serious problems because questions like, "Can we baptize people in the woods?" have never been worked out with the sending church until it becomes a pressing issue. There is often no right answer, but there is an issue about not working it out until the week before an answer or policy is needed! The same can be said for Communion, sermons, sung worship, etc.

## People

Tensions can arise when practicing Christians end up joining the FxC, which changes the charism significantly unless they are called to the particular mission of the FxC. These Christians can often be seeking alternative church, rather than a FxC to serve.

Tensions can also arise when members of the FxC end up seeking to join the existing church. Many FxC leaders have read all the right books and can be distressed when people show up to the things they are not supposed to be interested in!

## Expectations

Tensions can arise when there is little understanding regarding where the FxC could lead in the future. Should it become a new Church of England church within the parish (through a process called a Bishop's Mission Order), should the FxC be temporary, for a time and a season, or should it actually remain a PMA and not develop into a FxC are all things that need to be considered and reviewed in partnership.

We tend to use the phrase "mixed ecology" rather than "mixed economy." For us, the metaphor of the garden with many complementary plants is more helpful than a monetary image.

For Watershed, we experience tension as being part of the other 25 percent of our pioneering communities who don't sit within parish boundaries!

Our community comes from fourteen different settlements over a large (for the UK) geographical area. This together with how we meet means that we don't fit easily within our existing ecclesial governance structures.

## How have you seen the fresh expressions have a positive impact on the existing congregation? In what ways?

We see many of our existing congregations begin further PMAs and FxCs—about 25 percent at present. Often it seems that the initial pioneers then encourage others to follow.

About two-thirds of our PMAs seem to gravitate toward growing the existing church congregation in some way, though this will (in most instances) lead that congregation into change.

More than 80 percent of all of our pioneering in the diocese comes out of churches with congregations of less than one hundred people. Increasingly we are seeing much smaller churches begin to explore pioneering and fresh expressions, some because they need to do so in order to survive, but many others because they see other churches like theirs giving it a go and if they can do it, why can't we?

For the third of the members who are already Christian, Watershed gives them something to invite friends and family to (rather than church), and it helps them to remain rooted in their small rural church where they may be the only family. Being dispersed, Watershed is able to serve the wider deanery (a larger group of parishes—thirty-seven in ours) and in the future hopefully work to complement their work.

## Knowing that launching fresh expressions in your congregation involves time, sacrifice, resources, and people power, why do you believe it's worthy to pursue?

I grew up in the Church of England (my father is a priest), and I loved it. Being part of the church gave me a narrative for life, a community to belong to, and introduced me to the Creator, Redeemer, and Sustainer of the world. I think I came to faith several times in my teenage years, as I understood better who I was and who God is . . . and I guess I still am.

Today, however, the families I work with are often now four generations removed from church. That doesn't bother me too much, but what does is that they are possibly four generations removed from knowing and walking with Jesus Christ.

For myself (and Emma too), our calling has been to honor, celebrate, and yet leave the church that loved and formed us and set out to create new Christian community with those (not to them), who are yet to share in knowing Jesus. This isn't to say we won't ever end up back in traditional ministry as this is calling away from, so we may well be called back in the future.

Jonny, a member of Watershed (whom I married last year—a great privilege) said to me recently, "Jonathan, Isabella and I just want to know what it means to live a wholesome life." Knowing something of their context I knew this wholesome life encompassed the spiritual, material, and emotional aspects of personal family and community life. My response was "So do we (Emma and our children), but we find that hard to do on our own." I then shared why we started Watershed—in part to help people do just that together, and that in our experience seeking to follow

Jesus helped us to live that wholesome life—so why not explore this together?

Jonny and his family are not part of any church, and they have never been. Yet his statement is essentially one of discipleship. It reminded me of John 10:10 (life to the full). At this stage, they are not looking for church, they are looking for life.

For us, this is reason alone to journey *to* them and not them to us.

CLOSING VISION
# Tree of Life (Re)mixed

We began our journey with an opening vision of the tree of life and mixing our metaphors with Paul's image of the church as a living tree in which Jew and Gentile are grafted together in a remixed new creation (Rom. 11:17–21). We saw ancient olive trees, who thrive across millennia, not by staying the same, but through continuously birthing new shoots from the root ball. We considered how Paul employs this image to describe the church, a living organism that is both deep and wild.

Further, we reflected on John 15:1–6. I asked: What if local congregations could find their deepest story again and base themselves, structurally speaking, on Paul's olive tree, or Jesus' parable of the vine, rather than some corporate entity? What does the local church look like as a living composite organism that is an interweaving, organic, polycentric, dispersed, networked system?

I want to conclude by synthesizing all our learnings in a closing vision of the (re)mixed tree of life.

Again, Paul takes up the language of grafting to describe the new composite reality of God's people as both Gentile and Jew (Rom. 11:17–21). Deep roots and wild branches.

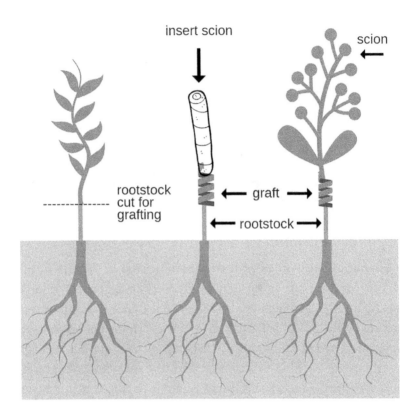

This grafting technique leads to the formation of the graft union of the scion and rootstock. A research study concluded that genomic-scale mRNA was exchanged across graft junctions, occurring in grapevines in a passive or genotype and environment-dependent manner.[1] Meaning, grafting leads to an exchange of genetic material between the scion and rootstock, resulting in the formation of a unique organism.

**mRNA:** The template for protein synthesis; the form of RNA that carries information from DNA in the nucleus to the ribosome sites of protein synthesis in the cell. Abbreviated form for messenger ribonucleic acid, the type of RNA that codes for the chemical blueprint for a protein (during protein synthesis).

Thus, through this grafting process, there is an exchange at the fundamental level between the scion and the rootstock. The two species not only enter a symbiotic union, but they actually transform each other through an exchange of the foundational building blocks of their being.

What does this remixed tree of life look like?

Well, coming back to the single organism that can provide both ketchup and fries, Lynda Ly shares about a new species of plant created through grafting. This plant grows cherry tomatoes above ground and white potatoes below ground.[2] Now you may find this amalgamation of two of your favorite things growing on the same plant an abomination. But this describes the emergent structural reality of the blended ecology: the inherited church is growing healthy vegetables just below the surface where the roots run deep, while the wild, colorful, emerging vegetables are growing above!

Every church can embody the (re)mixed tree of life.

When existing congregations plant fresh expressions of church in the community and graft those new lifeforms together, a new

creation can emerge. On the new missional frontier, we need inherited and emerging modes of church living in symbiosis. Every church can offer both attractional and missional modes of God's withness in the world. Over time, this new organism takes on a life of its own. Who knows what splendid new creations may be born out of this symbiosis; perhaps the future church is emerging right before our eyes.

We followers of Jesus call the power that brings forth that new life resurrection. It also goes by another name . . . revitalization. When we join what the Spirit is up to in our communities, this occurs through the process of (re)missioning from the outside in. That is my deepest prayer for your church.

God has called us to be stewards of a very precious, life-transfiguring gospel. He has entrusted us with the seeds. A seed is just a seed without a context. Its potential can only be released by being planted. A tree is the result of a symbiotic relationship. A tree is only a dream without soil, atmospheric conditions, rain, oxygen, sunlight, and so on. Fresh expressions allow us to plant the seeds of the gospel in real contexts, with real people, and let it grow wild. When we do that, we somehow contribute to that final vision at the tree of life, where all the nations gather to worship the living God (Rev. 22).

I look forward to seeing you there!

FIELD INTERVIEW
# Mike Snedeker

Lead Pastor, Community Evangelical Church

Mike Snedeker has been the lead pastor of Community Evangelical Church in Reading, Pennsylvania, for the past six years. He has served there for twenty-five years as the youth pastor and discipleship pastor before moving into his current role. The church is a part of a small denomination of about 120 churches with the majority of the churches in decline and on the verge of shutting their doors. Mike's congregation has a wide range of ages and runs approximately four hundred people on a Sunday morning. They have one liturgical worship service and two contemporary services. Community Evangelical Church has engaged in the Fresh Expressions adventure for about four years now.

### Can you briefly describe the fresh expression(s) of your church?

We currently have five fresh expressions of church with two or three in the oven. Each of the current fresh expressions is in a various stage of its life cycle.

*Triple Tree:* This is our biker ministry, which is a concentrated outreach to the 1 percent motorcycle culture. Triple Tree engages in multiple events and rides each year, which brings them in close contact with the motorcycle clubs from around the area. These events are primarily relationship-building events. Thursday night is Biker Church, which is a gathering of bikers to seek Jesus together.

*First Responders Connect*: This is our ministry to first responders. This fresh expression started as a gathering of various member of the first responder community. The purpose was to create a safe place for first responders to connect and share the struggles unique to their line of work. They share each other's burdens and help to encourage each other through prayer and sharing Scripture together.

*Open Hands House Church:* This began as a typical house church but has morphed into a house dinner church. The host family opens their home every Tuesday night to their neighborhood for dinner and conversation. They share stories of Jesus' life and talk about the impact of those stories on their lives.

*Early Inspiration:* This is a new fresh expression for our church. It happens at the local YMCA twenty minutes before opening time (5:30 a.m.) and is a time of challenge and inspiration from God's Word, as well as sharing prayer concerns and questions.

*Sportsman's Launch:* This group is in the process of loving/serving and building community at a local sportsman's club. They are involved in helping with archery shoots and youth education programs, as well as just serving everywhere possible at the club. They have begun to meet with groups there to discuss life and sharing from their own lives what faith in Jesus has meant to them. They have recently begun to be asked to pray at various club events and are developing a regular club meeting for the sake of specific Jesus-centered conversation.

## Explain the blended ecology dynamics between the inherited church and your fresh expressions. What kind of tension, if any, goes on between the two?

When we decided to pursue healthy multiplication as a church, fresh expressions of church seemed to be not only the best fit for our congregation, but it also seemed to resonate with our leadership as the future of the church in America. Being a mixed-economy church is not always easy. We strive to do our established church ministries with excellence. We want to be sure that anyone who comes to the church finds Jesus through the ministries we offer. We strive to have excellent worship and preaching on a weekly basis, as well as active and engaging children and youth ministries, and effective small-group ministries. At the same time, as we recognize these ministries are not effective at engaging a large population of our culture, thus the need for fresh expressions of church. In order to do our best to make sure both of these facets of ministry are thriving, we offer try to engage people and leadership in shared ministry and stories. While we never expect anyone from a fresh expression to become active and involved in our established church, we do want to make sure the two groups know about and love each other as the body of Christ. We have leaders and participants in our fresh expression churches on a monthly basis involved in the worship service of the established church in order to keep up the excitement for the fresh expressions of church. We have them shares stories, prayer concerns, and updates. This has helped create a culture of cooperation and partnership between the groups.

One of the tensions that we are regularly dealing with is jealousy. We will hear from congregation members of the established church comments like, "Those fresh expressions are great but don't forget about taking care of us!" While this spirit of discontent is rare, it is still present and a normal tension in ministry. On the flip side, we have had a dedicated staff working with our fresh expressions until recently. The lessened attention from staff has caused some tension there as well with expectations of support and effort from the paid professionals.

## How have you seen the fresh expressions have a positive impact on the existing congregation? In what ways?

A couple of real benefits of the fresh expression work on our existing congregation have been:

1. A heart for the world around them is developing. Our county in Pennsylvania has not been known for its kindness and hospitality. Fresh expressions has given people who are typically shy and removed the motivation to see others through Jesus' eyes. Even those who readily admit to not being called into fresh expressions of church are feeling moved to engage their neighborhood in conversation and, at times, invite them into the established church.

2. A new openness to what church looks like. While we still fight the "we've never done it that way before" battles, people are much more willing to explore ministry creativity and innovation in the established church.

## Knowing that launching fresh expressions in your congregation involves time, sacrifice, resources, and people power, why do you believe it's worthy to pursue?

First and foremost, Jesus specifically called his church to reach the world with the gospel. He never called his church to a life of ease or wealth or comfort. To be obedient to one of Jesus' greatest commands requires time, sacrifice, resources, and people power. Secondly, one of the main themes you will hear in my preaching is walking in Jesus' footsteps as his followers. Fresh expressions of church is how Jesus lived his life. Not inside the walls of the temple or synagogues. He lived out among people, meeting them where they are. Finally, Jesus always calls his followers to selflessness. Any excuse that prevents us from pursuing fresh expressions of church probably has, at its core, selfishness.

# Bibliography

Alexander, T. Desmond, and David W. Baker, eds. *Dictionary of the Old Testament: Pentateuch*. Downers Grove, IL: InterVarsity Press, 2003.

Allen, Roland. *Missionary Methods: St. Paul's or Ours?* Grand Rapids, MI: W. B. Eerdmans Publishing, 1962.

Appadurai, Arjun. *Modernity at Large: Cultural Dimensions of Globalization*. Minneapolis: University of Minnesota Press. 1996.

Avis, Paul D. *The Oxford Handbook of Ecclesiology*. Oxford: Oxford University Press, 2018.

Backert, Chris. "Emerging Church and Missional Church: Same Difference?" *Fresh Expressions US*. April 18, 2016. http://freshexpressionsus.org/2016/04/18/emerging-church-missional-church-difference/. Accessed July 2017.

———. https://freshexpressionsus.org/2018/12/10/fresh-expressions-us-year-end-review-2018/.

Baker, Jonny, and Cathy Ross. *The Pioneer Gift: Explorations in Mission*. Norwich, UK: Canterbury Press, 2014.

Barraclough, Geoffrey, ed. *The Times Atlas of World History*. Edinburgh: Collins Bartholomew, 1978.

Bayes, Paul, et al. *Mission-Shaped Parish: Traditional Church in a Changing World*. New York: Seabury Books, 2010.

Bevans, Stephen B., and Roger P. Schroeder. *Constants in Context: Theology of Mission for Today*. Maryknoll, NY: Orbis, 2004.

Bevans, Stephen. "Ecclesiology and Missiology: Reflections on Two Recent Documents from the World Council of Churches." *Dialog:*

*A Journal of Theology* 54, no. 2 (June 2015): 126–34. doi:10.1111/dial.12168.

Billings, Todd. *Union with Christ: Reframing Theology and Ministry for the Church*. Grand Rapids, MI: Baker Academic, 2011.

Bolger, Ryan K. "Practice Movements in Global Information Culture: Looking Back to McGavran and Finding a Way Forward." *Missiology* 35, no. 2 (2007): 181–93. Accessed December 11, 2017. http://journals.sagepub.com.georgefox.idm.oclc.org/doi/pdf/10.1177/009182960703500208.

Bolsinger, Tod E. *Canoeing the Mountains: Christian Leadership in Uncharted Territory*. Downers Grove, IL: IVP Books, 2016.

Bolton, Bill, and John Thompson. *Entrepreneurs: Talent, Temperament and Opportunity*. London: Routledge, 2013.

Bosch, David J. *Transforming Mission: Paradigm Shifts in Theology of Mission*. Maryknoll, NY: Orbis Books, 1991.

Boyd, Gregory A. *The Myth of a Christian Nation: How the Quest for Political Power Is Destroying the Church*. Grand Rapids, MI: Zondervan, 2005.

Brandt, Anthony K., and David Eagleman. *The Runaway Species: How Human Creativity Remakes the World*. New York: Catapult, 2017.

Brubaker, Pamela. *Globalization at What Price?: Economic Change and Daily Life*. Cleveland: Pilgrim Press, 2007.

Brueggemann, Walter. *God, Neighbor, Empire: The Excess of Divine Fidelity and the Command of Common Good*. Waco, TX: Baylor University Press, 2016.

Carter, Ken. "Church Vitality." https://www.flumc.org/church-vitality. Last accessed June 12, 2020.

Castells, Manuel. *The Rise of the Network Society*. Oxford Malden, MA: Blackwell Publishers, 2000.

Collins, Travis. *From the Steeple to the Street: Innovating Mission and Ministry through Fresh Expressions of Church*. Franklin, TN: Seedbed Publishing, 2016.

Cray, Graham. "Connecting the Centre to the Edge." *Anglican Church Planting Initiatives*. July 26, 2017. https://acpi2017.wordpress.com/2017/07/26/connecting-the-centre-to-the-edge-graham-cray/. Last accessed September 2017.

———. *Mission-Shaped Church: Church Planting and Fresh Expressions in a Changing Context*. New York: Seabury Books, 2010.

Cray, Graham, Ian Mobsby, and Aaron Kennedy. *Fresh Expressions of Church and the Kingdom of God*. Norwich, UK: Canterbury Press, 2012.

Croft, Steven J. *The Future of the Parish System: Shaping the Church of England for the Twenty-First Century*. London: Church House, 2006.

———. *Mission-Shaped Questions: Defining Issues for Today's Church*. New York: Seabury Books, 2010.

Davis, Michael L. "Spiritual Formation: Retrieving Perichoresis as a Model for Shared Leadership in the Marketplace." *Journal of Religious Leadership* 14, no. 1 (2015): 105–26 (106). https://georgefox.idm.oclc.org/login?url=http://search.ebscohost.com/login.aspx?direct=true&db=lsdar&AN=ATLAn3793997&scope=site.

Davison, Andrew, and Alison Milbank. *For the Parish: A Critique of Fresh Expressions*. London: SCM Press, 2010.

Dean, Kenda C. *Almost Christian: What the Faith of Our Teenagers Is Telling the American Church*. Oxford: Oxford University Press, 2010.

Denning, Peter J., and Robert Dunham. *The Innovator's Way: Essential Practices for Successful Innovation*. Cambridge, MA: MIT Press, 2010.

Downing, Crystal. *Changing Signs of Truth: A Christian Introduction to the Semiotics of Communication*. Downers Grove, IL: IVP Academic, 2012.

Ferguson, Niall. *Civilization: The West and the Rest*. New York: Penguin Press, 2011.

Flynn, James T. "MOOCs: Disruptive Innovation and the Future of Higher Education." *Christian Education Journal* 10, no. 1 (2013): 149–62.

Fosner, Verlon. *Dinner Church: Building Bridges by Breaking Bread*. Franklin, TN: Seedbed Publishing, 2017.

———. *The Dinner Church Handbook: A Step-By-Step Recipe for Reaching Neighborhoods*. Franklin, TN: Seedbed Publishing, 2017.

Frank, Robert. "Richest 1% Now Owns Half the World's Wealth." November 14, 2017. https://www.cnbc.com/2017/11/14/richest-1-percent-now-own-half-the-worlds-wealth.html.

Friedman, Edwin H., Margaret M. Treadwell, and Edward W. Beal. *A Failure of Nerve: Leadership in the Age of the Quick Fix*. New York: Seabury Books, 2007.

Fujimura, Makoto. *Culture Care: Reconnecting with Beauty for our Common Life*. New York: Fujimura Institute, 2014.

Gaze, Sally. *Mission-Shaped and Rural: Growing Churches in the Countryside*. London: Church House Publishing, 2006.

Gibbs, Eddie, and Ryan K. Bolger. *Emerging Churches: Creating Christian Community in Postmodern Cultures*. Grand Rapids, MI: Baker Academic, 2005.

Goodhew, David, Andrew Roberts, and Michael Volland. *Fresh!: An Introduction to Fresh Expressions of Church and Pioneer Ministry*. London: SCM Press, 2012.

Green, Joel B., Scot McKnight, and I. H. Marshall. *Dictionary of Jesus and the Gospels*. Downers Grove, IL: InterVarsity Press, 1992.

Greenfield, Susan. *Mind Change: How Digital Technologies Are Leaving Their Mark on Our Brains*. New York: Random House, 2015.

Guder, Darrell L., and Lois Barrett. *Missional Church: A Vision for the Sending of the Church in North America*. Grand Rapids, MI: Eerdmans Publishing, 1998.

Gunkel, David J. "Rethinking the Digital Remix: Mashups and the Metaphysics of Sound Recording." *Popular Music & Society* 31, no. 4 (2008): 489–510. http://dx.doi.org/10.1080/03007760802053211.

Hadaway, C. Kirk, and Penny Long Marler. "How Many Americans Attend Worship Each Week? An Alternative Approach to Measurement." *Journal for the Scientific Study of Religion* 44, no. 3 (September 2005): 307–22. http://doi.wiley.com/10.1111/j.1468-5906.2005.00288.x.

Harari, Yuval Noah. *Homo Deus: A Brief History of Tomorrow*. New York: HarperCollins, 2017.

Harle, Tim. "The Formless Void as Organizational Template." *Journal of Management, Spirituality & Religion* 9, no. 1 (2012): 103–21. DOI: 10.1080/14766086.2012.641100.

Harnish, James A. *You Only Have to Die: Leading Your Congregation to New Life*. Nashville, TN: Abingdon Press, 2004.

Heath, Elaine A., and Scott T. Kisker. *Longing for Spring: A New Vision for Wesleyan Community*. Eugene, OR: Cascade Books, 2010.

Heitzenrater, Richard P. *Wesley and the People Called Methodists*. Nashville, TN: Abingdon Press, 1995.

Hiebert, Paul G. *The Gospel in Human Contexts: Anthropological Explorations for Contemporary Missions*. Grand Rapids, MI: Baker Academic, 2009.

Hirsch, Alan. *5Q: Reactivating the Original Intelligence and Capacity of the Body of Christ*. 100 Movements Publishing, 2017.

———. *The Forgotten Ways: Reactivating the Missional Church*. Grand Rapids, MI: Brazos Press, 2006.

Hirsch, Alan, and Dave Ferguson. *On the Verge: A Journey into the Apostolic Future of the Church*. Grand Rapids, MI: Zondervan, 2011.

Hirsch, Alan, Tim Catchim, and Mike Breen. *The Permanent Revolution: Apostolic Imagination and Practice for the 21st Century Church*. San Francisco: Jossey-Bass, 2012.

Holmes, Michael W., ed. "Epistle to Diognetus 11:4." In *The Apostolic Fathers, Greek Texts and English Translations of Their Writings*. 2nd edition. Translated by J. B. Lightfoot and J. R. Harmer. Grand Rapids, MI: Baker, 1992.

Hughes, Richard A. "'Make Us One with Christ': Essay on the Anglican-Methodist Dialogue." *Journal of Ecumenical Studies* 49, no. 3 (2014): 443–57. https://georgefox.idm.oclc.org/login?url=http://search.ebscohost.com/login.aspx?direct=true&db=aph&AN=99140861&scope=site.

Hunter, George G. *The Apostolic Congregation: Church Growth Reconceived for a New Generation*. Nashville, TN: Abingdon Press, 2009.

———. "The End of the Home Field Advantage." *Epworth Review* 19 (May 1992): 69–76.

Johnson, Luke T. *The Creed: What Christians Believe and Why It Matters*. New York: Doubleday, 2003.

Jones, Angela. *Pioneer Ministry and Fresh Expressions of Church*. London: SPCK, 2009.

Jones, L. Gregory. *Christian Social Innovation: Renewing Wesleyan Witness*. Nashville, TN: Abingdon Press, 2016.

Kelly, Kevin. *The Inevitable: Understanding the 12 Technological Forces That Will Shape Our Future*. New York: Penguin Books, 2017.

Kreider, Alan. *The Patient Ferment of the Early Church: The Improbable Rise of Christianity in the Roman Empire*. Grand Rapids, MI: Baker Academic, 2016.

Küng, Hans. *Christianity: Essence, History and Future*. New York: Continuum, 1995.

———. *The Church*. Garden City, NY: Image Books, 1976.

Kutz, Matthew R. *Contextual Intelligence: Smart Leadership for a Constantly Changing World*. Perrysburg, OH: RTG Publishing, 2013.

Lichtenstein, Benyamin B., Mary Uhl-Bien, Russ Marion, Anson Seers, James Douglas Orton, and Craig Schreiber. "Complexity Leadership Theory: An Interactive Perspective on Leading in Complex Adaptive Systems." *Emergence: Complexity & Organization* 8, no. 4 (2006): 2–12. https://georgefox.idm.oclc.org/login?url=http://search.ebscohost.com/login.aspx?direct=true&db=bth&AN=24083897&scope=site.

Ly, Linda. "Grafting Gone Wild: Grow Your Ketchup and Fries on the Same Plant." KCET. February 26, 2015. https://www.kcet.org/home-garden/grafting-gone-wild-grow-your-ketchup-and-fries-on-the-same-plant.

Male, David. *Pioneers 4 Life: Explorations in Theology and Wisdom for Pioneering Leaders*. Abingdon, UK: Bible Reading Fellowship, 2011.

———. "Do We Need Pioneers?" 2017. https://freshexpressions.org.uk/get-started/pioneer-ministry/.

McGavran, Donald A. *The Bridges of God: A Study in the Strategy of Missions*. Eugene, OR: Wipf & Stock, 2005.

McGavran, Donald A., and C. Peter Wagner. *Understanding Church Growth*. Grand Rapids, MI: W. B. Eerdmans, 1990.

McGrath, Alister E. *Christian Theology: An Introduction*. Chichester, UK: Wiley-Blackwell, 2011.

McIntyre, Dean. "Did the Wesleys Really Use Drinking Song Tunes for Their Hymns?" n.d. https://www.umcdiscipleship.org/resources/debunking-the-wesley-tavern-song-myth

Meeks, Wayne A. *The First Urban Christians: The Social World of the Apostle Paul*. New Haven: Yale University Press, 1983.

Meyers, Robin R. *Spiritual Defiance: Building a Beloved Community of Resistance*. New Haven: Yale University Press, 2016.

Migliore, Daniel L. *Faith Seeking Understanding: An Introduction to Christian Theology*. Grand Rapids, MI: W. B. Eerdmans Publishing, 2014.

Minear, Paul S. *Images of the Church in the New Testament*. Philadelphia: Westminster Press, 1970.

*Mixmag.* "What Is the Greatest Dance Track of All Time?" February 2013. http://mixmag.net/read/what-is-the-greatest-dance-track-of-all-time-features. Accessed September 2017.

Moltmann, Jürgen. *The Church in the Power of the Spirit: A Contribution to Messianic Ecclesiology.* Minneapolis, MN: Fortress Press, 1993.

Moot: A New-Monastic Community. http://www.moot.uk.net/.

Mortensen, Viggo, and Andreas Nielsen. *Walk Humbly with the Lord: Church and Mission Engaging Plurality.* Grand Rapids, MI: W. B. Eerdmans Publishing, 2011.

Moynagh, Michael. *Being Church, Doing Life: Creating Gospel Communities Where Life Happens.* Oxford, UK: Monarch Books, 2014.

———. *Church in Life: Emergence, Ecclesiology and Entrepreneurship.* London: SCM Press, 2017.

Moynagh, Michael, and Philip Harrold. *Church for Every Context: An Introduction to Theology and Practice.* London: SCM Press, 2012.

Moynagh, Michael, and Richard Worsley. *Going Global: Key Questions for the Twenty-First Century.* London: A & C Black, 2008.

Murray, Stuart. *Church after Christendom.* Milton Keynes, UK: Paternoster Press, 2004.

Nelstrop, Louise, and Martyn Percy. *Evaluating Fresh Expressions: Explorations in Emerging Church: Responses to the Changing Face of Ecclesiology in the Church of England.* Norwich, UK: Canterbury Press, 2008.

Newbigin, Lesslie. *Foolishness to the Greeks: The Gospel and Western Culture.* Grand Rapids, MI: W. B. Eerdmans Publishing, 1986.

Norberg, Johan. *Progress: Ten Reasons to Look Forward to the Future.* London: Oneworld Publications, 2017.

Oldenburg, Ray. *The Great Good Place: Cafés, Coffee Shops, Bookstores, Bars, Hair Salons, and Other Hangouts at the Heart of a Community.* Berkeley, CA: Marlowe, 1999.

Pearce, Craig, and Jay A. Conger. *Shared Leadership: Reframing the Hows and Whys of Leadership.* Thousand Oaks, CA: Sage Publications, 2003.

Peterson, Eugene. "*Eat This Book: A Conversation in the Art of Spiritual Reading.* Grand Rapids, MI: W. B. Eerdmans Publishing, 2006.

Plowman, Donde, LaKami Baker, Tammy E. Beck, Mukta Kulkarni, Stephanie Thomas Solansky, and Deandra Villarreal Travis. "Radical Change Accidentally: The Emergence and Amplification of Small Change." *The Academy of Management Journal* 50, no. 3, (2007). https://doi.org/10.5465/amj.2007.25525647.

Potter, Phil. *Pioneering a New Future: A Guide to Shaping Change and Changing the Shape of Church*. Abingdon, UK: Bible Reading Fellowship, 2015.

Putnam, Robert D. *Bowling Alone: The Collapse and Revival of American Community*. New York: Simon & Schuster, 2000.

Rainer, Thom S. *Autopsy of a Deceased Church: 12 Ways to Keep Yours Alive*. Nashville, TN: B & H Publishing Group, 2014.

*Religion*. https://news.gallup.com/poll/1690/religion.aspx.

Rendle, Gilbert R. *Back to Zero: The Search to Rediscover the Methodist Movement*. Nashville, TN: Abingdon Press, 2011.

———. *Quietly Courageous: Leading the Church in a Changing World*. Lanham, MD: Rowman & Littlefield, 2019.

Roxburgh, Alan J. *Missional: Joining God in the Neighborhood*. Grand Rapids, MI: Baker Books, 2011.

———. *Missional Map-Making: Skills for Leading in Times of Transition*. San Francisco, CA: Jossey-Bass, 2010.

———. *Structured for Mission: Renewing the Culture of the Church*. Downers Grove, IL: InterVarsity Press, 2015.

Savage, Sara B., and Eolene M. MacMillan. *The Human Face of Church: A Social Psychology and Pastoral Theology Resource for Pioneer and Traditional Ministry*. Norwich, UK: Canterbury Press, 2007.

Selbie, Joseph. *The Physics of God: Unifying Quantum Physics, Consciousness, M-Theory, Heaven, Neuroscience, and Transcendence*. Wayne, NJ: Career Press, 2017.

Sinek, Simon. *Start with Why: How Great Leaders Inspire Everyone to Take Action*. New York: Portfolio, 2009.

Smith, Gregory. "America's Changing Religious Landscape: Christians Decline Sharply as Share of Population; Unaffiliated and Other Faiths Continue to Grow." Pew Research Center. May 12, 2015. http://www.pewforum.org/2015/05/12/americas-changing-religious-landscape/.

Soto, D. J. "Virtual Reality Church: Taking Church to the People." Medium. June 16, 2016. https://medium.com/virtual-reality-church/virtual-reality-church-7569baed4c2a.

Sumner, George. "Wesley and Anglican Mission." 2014. https://livingchurch.org/2014/10/14/wesley-and-anglican-mission/.

Sweet, Leonard I. *11 Indispensable Relationships You Can't Be Without*. Colorado Springs, CO: David C. Cook, 2008.

———. *From Tablet to Table: Where Community Is Found and Identity Is Formed*. Colorado Springs, CO: NavPress, 2014.

———. *Nudge: Awakening Each Other to the God Who's Already There*. Colorado Springs, CO: David C. Cook, 2010.

———. *Quantum Spirituality: A Postmodern Apologetic*. Dayton, OH: Whaleprints, 1991.

Sweet, Leonard I., and Frank Viola. *Jesus: A Theography*. Nashville, TN: Thomas Nelson, 2012.

Taleb, Nassim N. *Antifragile: Things That Gain from Disorder*. New York: Random House Trade Paperbacks, 2014.

Taylor, Paul. *The Next America: Boomers, Millennials, and the Looming Generational Showdown*. New York: Public Affairs, 2015.

*The United Methodist Hymnal*. Nashville, TN: The United Methodist Publishing House, 1989.

Turner, Edith. "Exploring the Work of Victor Turner: Liminality and Its Later Implications." *The Journal of the Finnish Anthropological Society* 33, no. 4 (2008): 26–44. https://georgefox.idm.oclc.org/login?url=http://search.ebscohost.com/login.aspx?direct=true&db=mlf&AN=EIS36604470&scope=site.

Unchurching: Christianity without Churchianity. http://www.unchurching.com/.

Valentinov, Vladislav, Stefan Hielscher, and Ingo Pies. "Emergence: A Systems Theory's Challenge to Ethics." *Systemic Practice & Action Research* 29, no. 6 (2016): 597-610.

Weems, Lovett H. *Focus: The Real Challenges That Face the United Methodist Church*. Nashville, TN: Abingdon Press, 2011.

Wells, Samuel. *Incarnational Mission: Being with the World*. Grand Rapids, MI: W. B. Eerdmans Publishing, 2018.

———. *Power and Passion: Six Characters in Search of Resurrection*. Grand Rapids, MI: Zondervan, 2007.

———. "Rethinking Service." Special issue, *The Cresset* LXXVI, no. 4 (2013): 6–14. http://thecresset.org/2013/Easter/Wells_E2013.html.

Wesley, John. "Reasons against a Separation from the Church of England." 1758. http://anglicanhistory.org/wesley/reasons1760.html.

Wheatley, Margaret J. *Leadership and the New Science: Discovering Order in a Chaotic World*. San Francisco: Berrett-Koehler Publishers, 1999.

Willard, Dallas. *The Divine Conspiracy: Rediscovering Our Hidden Life in God*. London: Fount, 1998.

Williams, Rowan. "Making the Mixed Economy Work." May 6, 2011. http://aoc2013.brix.fatbeehive.com/articles.php/2044/making-the-mixed-economy-work.

Wilson, Len. "Top 25 Fastest Growing Large United Methodist Churches, 2017 Edition". lenwilson.us. January 10, 2017. http://lenwilson.us/top-25-fastest-growing-large-umc-2017/.

Womack, James. "A Comparison of Perichoresis in the Writings of Gregory of Nazianzus and John of Damascus," quoted in Davis, Michael L. "Spiritual Formation: Retrieving Perichoresis as a Model for Shared Leadership in the Marketplace." *Journal of Religious Leadership* 14, no. 1 (2015): 105–26.

Woodward, J. R. *Creating a Missional Culture: Equipping the Church for the Sake of the World*. Downers Grove, IL: IVP Books, 2012.

Wright, N. T. *Surprised by Hope: Rethinking Heaven, the Resurrection, and the Mission of the Church*. New York: HarperOne, 2008.

Yezdani, Omer, Louis Sanzogni, and Arthur Poropat. "Theory of Emergence: Introducing a Model-Centered Approach to Applied Social Science Research." *Prometheus* 33, no. 3 (2015): 305–22.

Yingzhen, Yang, Mao Linyong, Yingyos Jittayasothorn, Kang Youngmin, Jiao Chen, Fei Zhangjun, and Zhong Gan-Yuan. "Messenger RNA exchange between scions and rootstocks in grafted grapevines." *BMC Plant Biology* 15 (2015): 1–14.

Zscheile, Dwight J. "Disruptive Innovations and the Deinstitutionalization of Religion." *Journal of Religious Leadership* 14, no. 2 (Fall 2015): 5–30. https://georgefox.idm.oclc.org/login?url=http://search.ebscohost.com/login.aspx?direct=true&db=rfh&AN=ATLAn3830239&scope=site#.Wi7.

# Notes

*Foreword*

1. Epistle to Diognetus 11:4, *The Apostolic Fathers, Greek Texts and English Translations of Their Writings*, ed. and trans. J. B. Lightfoot and J. R. Harmer, 2nd ed. (Grand Rapids, MI: Baker Book House, 1992), 551.
2. Anthony K. Brandt and David Eagleman, *The Runaway Species: How Human Creativity Remakes the World* (New York: Catapult, 2017), 47–48.

*The Opening Vision: The Tree of Life*

1. Linda Ly, "Grafting Gone Wild: Grow Your Ketchup and Fries on the Same Plate," *KCET* (February 26, 2015), https://www.kcet.org/home-garden/grafting-gone-wild-grow-your-ketchup-and-fries-on-the-same-plant, last accessed January 27, 2020.

*Trailer*

1. George G. Hunter, *The Apostolic Congregation: Church Growth Reconceived for a New Generation* (Nashville, TN: Abingdon Press, 2009), 1.
2. See *The Great Opportunity: The American Church in 2050* report, https://cdn2.hubspot.net/hubfs/4245467/The%20Great%20Opportunity.pdf.

3. Alan J. Roxburgh, *Structured for Mission: Renewing the Culture of the Church* (Downers Grove, IL: InterVarsity Press, 2015), 32.
4. Ibid.
5. Alan Hirsch and Dave Ferguson, *On the Verge: A Journey into the Apostolic Future of the Church* (Grand Rapids, MI: Zondervan, 2011), 27–29.
6. Ibid., 250–51.
7. Michael Moynagh, *Being Church, Doing Life: Creating Gospel Communities Where Life Happens* (Oxford, UK; Grand Rapids, MI: Monarch Books, 2014), 29.
8. Alan J. Roxburgh, *Missional: Joining God in the Neighborhood* (Grand Rapids, MI: Baker Books, 2011), 16.
9. Alan Hirsch, *The Forgotten Ways: Reactivating the Missional Church* (Grand Rapids, MI: Zondervan, 2006), 66.
10. Chris Backert, "Emerging Church and Missional Church: Same Difference?" *Fresh Expressions US*, April 18, 2016, http://freshexpressionsus.org/2016/04/18/emerging-church-missional-church-difference/, last accessed January 2020.
11. Stephen Bevans, "Ecclesiology and Missiology: Reflections on Two Recent Documents from the World Council of Churches," *Dialog: A Journal of Theology* 54, no. 2 (June 2015): 126–34, doi:10.1111/dial.12168.
12. Paul D. Avis, *The Oxford Handbook of Ecclesiology* (Oxford: Oxford University Press, 2018), 13.
13. C. Kirk Hadaway and Penny Long Marler, "How Many Americans Attend Worship Each Week? An Alternative Approach to Measurement," *Journal for the Scientific Study of Religion* 44, no. 3 (September 2005): 307–22.
14. Borrowing from concepts first developed by Thomas Kuhn, *The Structures of Scientific Revolutions* (Chicago: University of Chicago Press, 1962), see David J. Bosch, *Transforming Mission: Paradigm Shifts in Theology of Mission* (Maryknoll, NY: Orbis Books, 1991), 185.
15. Ibid.
16. Leonard I. Sweet, *Quantum Spirituality: A Postmodern Apologetic* (Dayton, OH: Whaleprints, 1991), 8.

17. Ibid., 6–7.
18. Margaret J. Wheatley, *Leadership and the New Science: Discovering Order in a Chaotic World* (San Francisco: Berrett-Koehler Publishers, 1999), xiii.
19. Sara B. Savage and Eolene M. MacMillan, *The Human Face of Church: A Social Psychology and Pastoral Theology Resource for Pioneer and Traditional Ministry* (Norwich, UK: Canterbury Press, 2007), 37.
20. Michael Moynagh, *Church in Life: Emergence, Ecclesiology and Entrepreneurship* (London: SCM Press, 2017), 11, 21.
21. John Drane, "Resisting McDonaldization: Will 'Fresh Expressions' of Church Inevitably Go Stale,'" in *Walk Humbly with the Lord: Church and Mission Engaging Plurality*, eds. Viggo Mortensen and Andreas Nielsen (Grand Rapids, MI: W. B. Eerdmans Publishing, 2011), 157.
22. Moynagh, *Being Church, Doing Life*, 432.
23. Lynda Barley, "Can Fresh Expressions of Church Make a Difference?" in *Mission-Shaped Questions: Defining Issues for Today's Church*, ed. Steven J. Croft (New York: Seabury Books, 2010), 170.
24. Omer Yezdani, Louis Sanzogni, and Arthur Poropat, "Theory of Emergence: Introducing a Model-Centered Approach to Applied Social Science Research," *Prometheus 33*, no. 3 (2015): 305–22 (306).
25. Vladislav Valentinov, Stefan Hielscher, and Ingo Pies, "Emergence: A Systems Theory's Challenge to Ethics," *Systemic Practice & Action Research* 29, no. 6 (2016): 597–610 (597).
26. Donde Plowman, LaKami Baker, Tammy E. Beck, Mukta Kulkarni, Stephanie Thomas Solansky, Deandra Villarreal Travis, "Radical Change Accidentally: The Emergence and Amplification of Small Change," *The Academy of Management Journal*, 50. no. 3 (2007): 515–43.
27. Louise Nelstrop and Martyn Percy, eds., *Evaluating Fresh Expressions: Explorations in Emerging Church: Responses to the Changing Face of Ecclesiology in the Church of England* (Norwich, UK: Canterbury Press, 2008), 3–5.
28. Stuart Murray, *Church after Christendom* (Milton Keynes, UK: Paternoster Press, 2004), 122.
29. Quoted in Paul Bayes, et al., *Mission-Shaped Parish: Traditional Church in a Changing World* (New York: Seabury Books, 2010), ix.

30. Rowan Williams, "Making the Mixed Economy Work," May 2011, http://aoc2013.brix.fatbeehive.com/articles.php/2044/making-the-mixed-economy-work, last accessed January 2020.
31. Jonny Baker and Cathy Ross, eds., *The Pioneer Gift: Explorations in Mission* (Norwich, UK: Canterbury Press, 2014), 2–3.
32. Anthony Brandt and David Eagleman, *The Runaway Species: How Human Creativity Remakes the World* (New York: Catapult, 2017), 47–48.
33. Doug Gay notes the mixed economy will require some "mixed polity" and a re-mixed understanding of vocation. We will do some of this remixing later. See Doug Gay, "Prospective Practitioners," in *The Pioneer Gift: Explorations in Mission*, eds. Jonny Baker and Cathy Ross (Norwich, UK: Canterbury Press, 2014), 45.
34. Sally Gaze, *Mission-Shaped and Rural: Growing Churches in the Countryside* (London: Church House Publishing, 2006), xviii.
35. Nassim Nicholas Taleb, *Antifragile: Things That Gain from Disorder* (New York: Random House Trade Paperbacks, 2014), 6.
36. David J. Bosch, *Transforming Mission: Paradigm Shifts in Theology of Mission* (Maryknoll, NY: Orbis Books, 1991), 380.
37. Gilbert R. Rendle, *Back to Zero: The Search to Rediscover the Methodist Movement* (Nashville, TN: Abingdon Press, 2011), 83.
38. Len Wilson, "Top 25 Fastest Growing Large United Methodist Churches, 2017 Edition," lenwilson.us (January 2017), http://lenwilson.us/top-25-fastest-growing-large-umc-2017/, last accessed January 2020.
39. Taleb, *Antifragile*, 12–14.
40. Ibid., 14.
41. Tod E. Bolsinger, *Canoeing the Mountains: Christian Leadership in Uncharted Territory* (Downers Grove, IL: IVP Books, 2016), 191.

*Chapter 1: The New Missional Frontier*

1. Vincent J. Donovan, *Christianity Rediscovered* (Maryknoll, NY: Orbis Books, 2003), 59.

2. Richard P. Heitzenrater, *Wesley and the People Called Methodists* (Nashville, TN: Abingdon Press, 1995), 93.
3. Manuel Castells, *The Rise of the Network Society* (Oxford Malden, MA: Blackwell Publishers, 2000), xvii–xviii.
4. Ibid., 442.
5. Lesslie Newbigin, *Foolishness to the Greeks: The Gospel and Western Culture* (Grand Rapids, MI: W. B. Eerdmans Publishing, 1986), 4.
6. David J. Bosch, *Transforming Mission: Paradigm Shifts in Theology of Mission* (Maryknoll, NY: Orbis Books, 1991), 182–83.
7. Stephen Sykes, John Booty, and Jonathan Knight, eds., *The Study of Anglicanism*, rev. ed. (Minneapolis, MN: Fortress Press, 1998), 32–33.
8. Vincent J. Donovan, *Christianity Rediscovered* (Maryknoll, NY: Orbis Books, 2003), 112.
9. Leonard I. Sweet, *Quantum Spirituality: A Postmodern Apologetic* (Dayton, OH: Whaleprints, 1991), 1–4.
10. David Bosch examines the critiques of Hoekendijk, Hutchison, and others in Bosch, *Transforming Mission*, 384.
11. Ibid., 349.
12. Edith Turner, "Exploring the Work of Victor Turner: Liminality and Its Later Implications," *The Journal of the Finnish Anthropological Society* 33 (2008): (26–44), 36.
13. Ibid., 35.
14. Joseph Selbie, *The Physics of God: Unifying Quantum Physics, Consciousness, M-theory, Heaven, Neuroscience, and Transcendence* (Wayne, NJ: Career Press, 2017), 24.
15. Ibid., 24–29, 136–37.
16. Alan Hirsch and Dave Ferguson, *On the Verge: A Journey into the Apostolic Future of the Church* (Grand Rapids, MI: Zondervan, 2011), 26–30.
17. James Thomas Flynn, "MOOCs: Disruptive Innovation and the Future of Higher Education," *Christian Education Journal* 10, no. 1 (2013): 149–62.

18. Scott Anthony, Clark Gilbert, and Mark Johnson, "Dual Transformation," https://www.innosight.com/wp-content/uploads/2017/04/Final_Dual-Transformation_Mini-Book.pdf.
19. Alan J. Roxburgh, *Structured for Mission: Renewing the Culture of the Church* (Downers Grove, IL: InterVarsity Press, 2015), 32.
20. L. Gregory Jones, *Christian Social Innovation: Renewing Wesleyan Witness* (Nashville, TN: Abingdon Press, 2016), 3–5.
21. Ibid., 73.
22. Ibid., 51.
23. Dwight J. Zscheile, "Disruptive Innovations and the Deinstitutionalization of Religion," *Journal of Religious Leadership*, 14, no. 2 (Fall 2015): 5–30.
24. Ibid.
25. Quoted in Crystal Downing, *Changing Signs of Truth: A Christian Introduction to the Semiotics of Communication* (Downers Grove, IL: IVP Academic, 2012), 45.
26. Quoted in Tod E. Bolsinger, *Canoeing the Mountains: Christian Leadership in Uncharted Territory* (Downers Grove, IL: IVP Books, 2016), 38.
27. Leonard Sweet and Michael Beck, *Issachar's Secret: Contextual Intelligence for Jesus Followers* (Oviedo, FL: Higher Life Publishing, 2020).
28. Matthew R. Kutz, *Contextual Intelligence: Smart Leadership for a Constantly Changing World* (Perrysburg, OH: RTG Publishing, 2013), 8–9.
29. Leonard I. Sweet, *Nudge: Awakening Each Other to the God Who's Already There* (Colorado Springs, CO: David C. Cook, 2010), 41.
30. Hans Küng, *Christianity: Essence, History and Future* (New York: Continuum, 1995), 7.
31. Beth Keith, "The Gift of Troublesome Questioning: Pioneers and Learning," in David Male, *Pioneers 4 Life: Explorations in Theology and Wisdom for Pioneering Leaders* (Abingdon, UK: Bible Reading Fellowship, 2011), 57.

32. Hans Küng, *The Church* (Garden City, NY: Image Books, 1976), 34.
33. Darrell L. Guder, ed., *Missional Church: A Vision for the Sending of the Church in North America* (Grand Rapids, MI: W. B. Eerdmans Publishing, 1998), 114.
34. Paul Taylor, *The Next America: Boomers, Millennials, and the Looming Generational Showdown* (New York: PublicAffairs, 2015), 164.
35. Robert D. Putnam, *Bowling Alone: The Collapse and Revival of American Community* (New York: Simon & Schuster, 2000), 71.
36. Taylor, *The Next America*, 164.
37. The research from David T. Olson and the American Church Project shows that less than 20 percent of the US population attends a Christian church on any given Sunday, far below what pollsters report. The national average of regular churchgoing is 17 percent. The American Church Research Project, 2010. See www.TheAmericanChurch.org.
38. This graph was reconstructed from the research of Thom Rainer in 2000. Researchers interviewed 1,300 people from four generations: of the Builder generation, 65 percent were Christians; Boomer generation, 35 percent; Buster generation, 15 percent; and Bridger generation, only 4 percent. See http://www.bpnews.net/6704/survey-notes-heightened-challenge-of-reaching-children-for-christ.
39. Lovett H. Weems Jr., *Focus: The Real Challenges that Face The United Methodist Church* (Nashville, TN: Abingdon Press, 2011), 2.
40. Travis Collins, in his description of the mixed-economy dynamic, coined the term *mecessary*—mess plus necessary. *From the Steeple to the Street: Innovating Mission and Ministry through Fresh Expressions of Church* (Franklin, TN: Seedbed Publishing, 2016), 42.
41. Weems, *Focus*, 4.
42. Ibid., 5.
43. Ibid., 8.

*Chapter 2: Post-Everything—Six Shifts*

1. Alan Hirsch, Tim Catchim, and Mike Breen, *The Permanent Revolution: Apostolic Imagination and Practice for the 21st Century Church* (San Francisco: Jossey-Bass, 2012), 162.
2. Paul Taylor, *The Next America: Boomers, Millennials, and the Looming Generational Showdown* (New York: PublicAffairs, 2015), 65.
3. Alan Kreider, *The Patient Ferment of the Early Church: The Improbable Rise of Christianity in the Roman Empire* (Grand Rapids, MI: Baker Academic, 2016), 9.
4. Elaine A. Heath and Scott T. Kisker, *Longing for Spring: A New Vision for Wesleyan Community* (Eugene, OR: Cascade Books, 2010), 16.
5. Darrell L. Guder, ed., *Missional Church: A Vision for the Sending of the Church in North America* (Grand Rapids, MI: W. B. Eerdmans Publishing, 1998), 6.
6. Stuart Murray, *Church after Christendom* (Milton Keynes, UK: Paternoster Press, 2004), 66.
7. Gregory A. Boyd, *The Myth of a Christian Nation: How the Quest for Political Power Is Destroying the Church* (Grand Rapids, MI: Zondervan, 2005), 13.
8. Walter Brueggemann, *God, Neighbour, Empire: The Excess of Divine Fidelity and the Command of Common Good* (Waco, TX: Baylor University Press, 2016), 1–2.
9. Ibid., 6.
10. Michael Moynagh and Richard Worsley, *Going Global: Key Questions for the Twenty-First Century* (London: A & C Black, 2008), 1–7.
11. Paul G. Hiebert, *The Gospel in Human Contexts: Anthropological Explorations for Contemporary Missions* (Grand Rapids, MI: Baker Academic, 2009), 118–19.
12. Robin R. Meyers, *Spiritual Defiance: Building a Beloved Community of Resistance* (New Haven, CT: Yale University Press, 2016), 85.
13. Brueggemann, *God, Neighbour, Empire*, 2.
14. Pamela Brubaker, *Globalization at What Price?: Economic Change and Daily Life* (Cleveland: Pilgrim Press, 2007), 39.

15. Yuval Noah Harari, *Homo Deus: A Brief History of Tomorrow* (New York: HarperCollins, 2017), 6.
16. Taylor, *The Next America*, 163.
17. Meyers, *Spiritual Defiance*, 103.
18. Boyd, *The Myth of a Christian Nation*, 12.
19. Hans Küng, *The Church* (Garden City, NY: Image Books, 1976), 12.
20. Alan J. Roxburgh, *Structured for Mission: Renewing the Culture of the Church* (Downers Grove, IL: InterVarsity Press, 2015), 79.
21. Gilbert R. Rendle, *Quietly Courageous: Leading the Church in a Changing World* (Lanham, MD: Rowman & Littlefield, 2019), 21–23.
22. David A. deSilva, *Honor, Patronage, Kinship & Purity: Unlocking New Testament Culture* (Downers Grove, IL: InterVarsity Press, 2000), 51.
23. Ibid.
24. Ibid., 218–19.
25. Paul Taylor, *The Next America: Boomers, Millennials, and the Looming Generational Showdown* (New York: PublicAffairs, 2015), 222, 230.
26. Taylor, *The Next America*, 51–52.
27. Anthony Brandt and David Eagleman, *The Runaway Species: How Human Creativity Remakes the World* (New York: Catapult, 2017), 7.
28. Robert Frank, "Richest 1% Now Owns Half the World's Wealth," https://www.cnbc.com/2017/11/14/richest-1-percent-now-own-half-the-worlds-wealth.html, last accessed January 2020.
29. Johan Norberg, *Progress: Ten Reasons to Look Forward to the Future* (London: Oneworld Publications, 2017), 78.
30. Taylor, *The Next America*, 39.
31. Brubaker, *Globalization at What Price?*, 46.
32. Graham Cray, *Mission-Shaped Church: Church Planting and Fresh Expression of Church in a Changing Context* (New York: Seabury Books, 2010), 2–3.
33. Roxburgh, *Structured for Mission*, 16.
34. Kevin Kelly, *The Inevitable: Understanding the 12 Technological Forces That Will Shape Our Future* (New York: Penguin Books, 2017), 120.

35. Kelly, *The Inevitable*, 120.
36. Ibid., 121.
37. Ibid.
38. Taylor, *The Next America*, 44.
39. Cray, *Mission-Shaped Church*, 3–4.
40. Taylor, *The Next America*, 150–53.
41. Ibid., 123.
42. Ibid., 210.
43. Ibid., 197.
44. Cray, *Mission-Shaped Church*, 3–4.
45. Taylor, *The Next America*, 38, 172.
46. Ibid., 163.
47. Ibid.
48. Ibid., 166.
49. Kenda C. Dean, *Almost Christian: What the Faith of Our Teenagers Is Telling the American Church* (Oxford: Oxford University Press, 2010), 7.
50. Ibid., 14–17.
51. Ibid., 14.
52. See http://www.unchurching.com/, last accessed January 2020.
53. David Goodhew, Andrew Roberts, and Michael Volland, *Fresh!: An Introduction to Fresh Expressions of Church and Pioneer Ministry* (London: SCM Press, 2012), 4–5.
54. Eddie Gibbs and Ryan K. Bolger, *Emerging Churches: Creating Christian Community in Postmodern Cultures* (Grand Rapids, MI: Baker Academic, 2005), 22.
55. Taylor, *The Next America*, 173.
56. Leonard I. Sweet, *Quantum Spirituality: A Postmodern Apologetic* (Dayton, OH: Whaleprints, 1991), 195.
57. George Hunter, "The End of the Home Field Advantage," *Epworth Review* (May 1992).
58. Taylor, *The Next America*, 12.
59. "Virtual Reality Church: Taking Church to the People," https://medium.com/virtual-reality-church/virtual-reality-church-7569baed4c2a; http://www.vr.church/.

60. Manuel Castells, *The Rise of the Network Society* (Oxford Malden, MA: Blackwell Publishers, 2000), xxix.
61. For more, see Susan Greenfield, *Mind Change: How Digital Technologies Are Leaving Their Mark on Our Brains* (New York: Random House, 2015).
62. Ryan K. Bolger, "Practice Movements in Global Information Culture: Looking Back to McGavran and Finding a Way Forward," *Missiology* 35, no. 2 (2007): 181–93 (188).
63. Robert D. Putnam, *Bowling Alone: The Collapse and Revival of American Community* (New York: Simon & Schuster, 2000), 27.
64. Castells, *The Rise of the Network Society*, 187.
65. Cray, *Mission-Shaped Church*, 4.

*Chapter 3: God of Recycling Bins, Not Dumpsters*

1. Simon Sinek, *Start with Why: How Great Leaders Inspire Everyone to Take Action* (New York: Portfolio, 2009), 37.
2. Lovett H. Weems Jr., *Focus: The Real Challenges That Face The United Methodist Church* (Nashville, TN: Abingdon Press, 2011), 12.
3. James A. Harnish, *You Only Have to Die: Leading Your Congregation to New Life* (Nashville, TN: Abingdon Press, 2004), 11.
4. Phil Potter, *Pioneering a New Future: A Guide to Shaping Change and Changing the Shape of Church* (Abingdon, UK: Bible Reading Fellowship, 2015), 33.
5. Thom S. Rainer, *Autopsy of a Deceased Church: 12 Ways to Keep Yours Alive* (Nashville, TN: B&H Publishing Group, 2014).
6. Ibid.
7. Samuel Wells, *Power & Passion: Six Characters in Search of Resurrection* (Grand Rapids, MI: Zondervan, 2007), 183.
8. Omer Yezdani, Louis Sanzogni, and Arthur Poropat, "Theory of Emergence: Introducing a Model-Centered Approach to Applied Social Science Research," *Prometheus* 33, no. 3 (2015): 305–22 (306).
9. Wells, *Power & Passion*, 183.
10. Vladislav Valentinov, Stefan Hielscher, and Ingo Pies, "Emergence: A Systems Theory's Challenge to Ethics," *Systemic Practice & Action Research* 29, no. 6 (2016): 597–610 (597).

11. Michael Moynagh, *Church in Life: Emergence, Ecclesiology and Entrepreneurship* (London: SCM Press, 2017), 11.
12. *Star Wars: The Last Jedi*, directed by Rian Johnson (San Francisco: Lucasfilm, 2017).
13. Yezdani, Sanzogni, and Poropat, "Theory of Emergence," 309.
14. Ibid., 308.
15. Lesslie Newbigin, *Foolishness to the Greeks: The Gospel and Western Culture* (Grand Rapids, MI: W. B. Eerdmans Publishing, 1986), 1.
16. Charles Taylor, *Modern Social Imaginaries* (Durham: Duke University Press, 2004), 23.
17. Wells, *Power & Passion*, 20.
18. John Drane, "Resisting McDonaldization: Will 'Fresh Expressions of Church Inevitably Go Stale,'" in *Walk Humbly with the Lord: Church and Mission Engaging Plurality*, eds. Viggo Mortensen and Andreas Nielsen (Grand Rapids, MI: W. B. Eerdmans Publishing, 2011), 154–55.
19. Samuel Wells, "Rethinking Service," in "Easter 2013," special issue, *The Cresset* LXXVI, no. 4 (2013): 6–14, http://thecresset.org/2013/Easter/Wells_E2013.html.
20. Ibid.
21. Ibid.
22. Ibid.
23. Samuel Wells, *Incarnational Mission: Being with the World* (Grand Rapids, MI: W. B. Eerdmans Publishing, 2018), 10–12.
24. Alister E. McGrath, *Christian Theology: An Introduction* (Chichester, UK; Malden, MA: Wiley-Blackwell, 2011), 241.
25. Michael L. Davis, "Spiritual Formation: Retrieving Perichoresis as a Model for Shared Leadership in the Marketplace," *Journal of Religious Leadership* 14, no. 1 (2015): 105–26 (117).
26. Wells, *Power & Passion*, 20–21.
27. Quoted in Louise Nelstrop and Martyn Percy, eds., *Evaluating Fresh Expressions: Explorations in Emerging Church: Responses to the Changing Face of Ecclesiology in the Church of England* (Norwich, UK: Canterbury Press, 2008), 92.

28. Luke T. Johnson, *The Creed: What Christians Believe and Why It Matters* (New York: Doubleday, 2003), 12.
29. N. T. Wright, *Surprised by Hope: Rethinking Heaven, the Resurrection, and the Mission of the Church* (New York: HarperOne, 2008), 18.
30. "Sure salvation is the end; heaven already is begun," quoted in Charles Wesley's hymn, "Let Us Plead for Faith Alone," 1740, public domain.
31. Dallas Willard, *The Divine Conspiracy: Rediscovering Our Hidden Life in God* (London: Fount, 1998), 33.
32. Ibid., 40.
33. Wright, *Surprised by Hope*, 184.
34. Ibid., 198.
35. "No angel tongues can tell thy love's ecstatic height, the glorious joy unspeakable, the beatific sight," quoted in Charles Wesley's hymn, "Maker, in Whom We Live," 1747, public domain.
36. "In Christ, your head, you then shall know, shall feel your sins forgiven; anticipate your heaven below, and own that love is heaven," quoted in Charles Wesley's hymn, "O for a Thousand Tongues to Sing," 1739, public domain.
37. T. Desmond Alexander and David W. Baker, eds., *Dictionary of the Old Testament: Pentateuch* (Downers Grove, IL: InterVarsity Press, 2003), 817.
38. Ibid., 813.
39. Alan J. Roxburgh, *Missional Map-Making: Skills for Leading in Times of Transition* (San Francisco: Jossey-Bass, 2010), 114.

*Chapter 4: Wild Branches—Fresh Expressions*

1. See Moot: A New-Monastic Community. http://www.moot.uk.net/.
2. Graham Cray, *Mission-Shaped Church: Church Planting and Fresh Expression of Church in a Changing Context* (New York: Seabury Books, 2010), 100, emphasis mine.
3. Michael Moynagh, *Church in Life: Emergence, Ecclesiology and Entrepreneurship* (London: SCM Press, 2017), 2.
4. Ibid., 27.

5. Ibid., 5–6.
6. Michael Moynagh and Philip Harrold, *Church for Every Context: An Introduction to Theology and Practice* (London: SCM Press, 2012), 28–50.
7. David Goodhew, Andrew Roberts, and Michael Volland, *Fresh!: An Introduction to Fresh Expressions of Church and Pioneer Ministry* (London: SCM Press, 2012), 20–21.
8. J. Todd Billings, *Union with Christ: Reframing Theology and Ministry for the Church* (Grand Rapids, MI: Baker Academic, 2011), 2.
9. Richard P. Heitzenrater, *Wesley and the People Called Methodists* (Nashville, TN: Abingdon Press, 1995), 99, italics mine.
10. For more, see Michael Beck with Jorge Acevedo, *A Field Guide to Methodist Fresh Expressions* (Nashville, TN: Abingdon Press, 2020).
11. John Wesley, "Reasons Against a Separation from the Church of England," 1758, http://anglicanhistory.org/wesley/reasons1760.html.
12. George Summer, "Wesley and Anglican Mission," 2014, https://livingchurch.org/2014/10/14/wesley-and-anglican-mission/.
13. Ibid.
14. Richard A. Hughes, "'Make Us One with Christ': Essay on the Anglican-Methodist Dialogue," *Journal of Ecumenical Studies* 49, no. 3 (2014): 443–57.
15. Chris Backert, "Fresh Expressions US Year-End Review 2018," Fresh Expressions, December 10, 2018, https://freshexpressionsus.org/2018/12/10/fresh-expressions-us-year-end-review-2018/.
16. See Michael Lipka, "Mainline Protestants Make up Shrinking Number of US Adults," Pew Research Center, May 18, 2015, https://www.pewresearch.org/fact-tank/2015/05/18/mainline-protestants-make-up-shrinking-number-of-u-s-adults/.
17. Heather Hahn, "U.S. Church Sees Numbers Slide in 2015," *United Methodist News Service*, November 18, 2006, https://www.mississippi-umc.org/newsdetail/u-s-church-sees-numbers-slide-in-2015-6749910.
18. Gregory Smith, "America's Changing Religious Landscape: Christians Decline Sharply as Share of Population; Unaffiliated

and Other Faiths Continue to Grow," Pew Research Center, May 12, 2015. http://www.pewforum.org/2015/05/12/americas-changing-religious-landscape/.
19. Michael Polanyi, *Personal Knowledge: Towards a Post-Critical Philosophy* (Chicago: University of Chicago Press, 1962), 127.
20. Data on all FLUM churches is accessible at https://www.flumc.org/congregationalvitality.
21. E-mail correspondence with Steve Loher, Florida UMC Manager of Knowledge & Information Services, April 9, 2019.
22. Executive Summary. Collected by the FLUMC for the NCD in the 2018 Imprint Report.
23. Douglas Wayne Balzer, "Positive Deviance: Empowering Ecclesial Contextualization with Theological Praxis" (DMin diss., Portland Seminary, 2012).
24. Executive Summary. Collected by the FLUMC for the NCD in the 2018 Imprint Report.
25. Verlon Fosner, *Dinner Church: Building Bridges by Breaking Bread* (Franklin, TN: Seedbed Publishing, 2017), 108–9.
26. Michael Moynagh and Richard Worsley, *Going Global: Key Questions for the Twenty-First Century* (London: A & C Black, 2008), 3.
27. Louise Nelstrop and Martyn Percy, eds., *Evaluating Fresh Expressions: Explorations in Emerging Church: Responses to the Changing Face of Ecclesiology in the Church of England* (Norwich, UK: Canterbury Press, 2008), 38.
28. Ibid.
29. Ryan K. Bolger, "Practice Movements in Global Information Culture: Looking Back to McGavran and Finding a Way Forward," *Missiology* 35, no. 2 (2007): 181–93 (182).
30. Nelstrop and Percy, *Evaluating Fresh Expressions*, 38.
31. Donald A. McGavran, *The Bridges of God: A Study in the Strategy of Missions* (Eugene, OR: Wipf & Stock, 2005), 1.
32. Vincent J. Donovan, *Christianity Rediscovered* (Maryknoll, NY: Orbis Books, 2003), 66.
33. Ibid., 64.

34. Ibid., 67.
35. Roland Allen, *Missionary Methods: St. Paul's or Ours?* (Grand Rapids, MI: W. B. Eerdmans Publishing, 1962), 52–53.
36. Ibid.
37. Ibid., 151.
38. McGavran, *The Bridges of God*, 8–11.
39. Ibid.
40. Ibid., 12–13.
41. Donald A. McGavran, *Understanding Church Growth*, ed. C. Peter Wagner, 3rd ed. (Grand Rapids, MI: W. B. Eerdmans Publishing, 1990), 222–23.
42. Ibid., 227–37.
43. Ibid., 240–56.
44. McGavran and Wagner, *Understanding Church Growth*, 240–56.
45. Bolger, "Practice Movements in Global Information Culture," 182.
46. McGavran, *The Bridges of God*, 49.
47. Bolger, "Practice Movements in Global Information Culture," 182.
48. Alan Hirsch, *The Forgotten Ways: Reactivating the Missional Church* (Grand Rapids, MI: Zondervan, 2006), 65 (footnotes).
49. Bolger, "Practice Movements in Global Information Culture," 186.
50. Ibid.
51. Ibid.
52. Arjun Appadurai, *Modernity at Large: Cultural Dimensions of Globalization* (Minneapolis: University of Minnesota Press, 1996), 296–97.
53. Bolger, "Practice Movements in Global Information Culture," 188.
54. Moynagh and Worsley, *Going Global*, 6.
55. Ibid., 2.
56. Bolger, "Practice Movements in Global Information Culture," 188.
57. Jenny Odell, *How to Do Nothing: Resisting the Attention Economy* (Brooklyn, NY: Melville House, 2019), xvii.
58. Ibid., 189–90.
59. Eddie Gibbs and Ryan K. Bolger, *Emerging Churches: Creating Christian Community in Postmodern Cultures* (Grand Rapids, MI: Baker Academic, 2005), 43.

60. Ibid., 43–44.
61. Bolger, "Practice Movements in Global Information Culture," 189–90.
62. Ibid.
63. Stuart Murray, *Church after Christendom* (Milton Keynes, UK: Paternoster Press, 2004), 71.
64. Ibid., 28–31.
65. Bolger, "Practice Movements in Global Information Culture," 189–90.
66. See critique in Nelstrop and Percy, *Evaluating Fresh Expressions*, 38. Also, see critique in Andrew Davison and Alison Milbank, *For the Parish: A Critique of Fresh Expressions* (London: SCM Press, 2010), 64–65.
67. Ibid., 38.
68. https://freshexpressions.org.uk/get-started/pioneer-ministry/.
69. Ray Oldenburg, *The Great Good Place: Cafés, Coffee Shops, Bookstores, Bars, Hair Salons, and Other Hangouts at the Heart of a Community* (Berkeley, CA: Marlowe, 1999), 16.
70. Nearly four in ten millennials (38 percent) have at least one tattoo; half of those have more than one. Gen Xers are not far behind, with 32 percent claiming to be inked up. See Paul Taylor, *The Next America: Boomers, Millennials, and the Looming Generational Showdown* (New York: PublicAffairs, 2015), 58.

*Chapter 5: Deep Roots—Blended Ecology*

1. Paul S. Minear, *Images of the Church in the New Testament* (Philadelphia: Westminster Press, 1970), 24.
2. Paul D. Avis, *The Oxford Handbook of Ecclesiology* (Oxford: Oxford University Press, 2018), 13.
3. Darrell L. Guder, ed., *Missional Church: A Vision for the Sending of the Church in North America* (Grand Rapids, MI: W. B. Eerdmans Publishing, 1998), 43.
4. Michael Moynagh, *Church in Life: Emergence, Ecclesiology and Entrepreneurship* (London: SCM Press, 2017), 143.

5. *Australia*, directed by Baz Luhrmann, Catherine Knapman, G. Mac Brown. Baz Luhrmann (Los Angeles: 20th Century Fox, 2008).
6. Michael Moynagh, *Being Church, Doing Life: Creating Gospel Communities Where Life Happens* (Oxford, UK; Grand Rapids, MI: Monarch Books, 2014), 20–21.
7. Michael Moynagh and Philip Harrold, *Church for Every Context: An Introduction to Theology and Practice* (London: SCM Press, 2012), 433.
8. Ibid., 435–41.
9. Lincoln Harvey, "How Serious Is It Really? The Mixed Economy and the Light-Hearted Long Haul," in Graham Cray, Ian Mobsby, and Aaron Kennedy, *Fresh Expressions of Church and the Kingdom of God* (Norwich, UK: Canterbury Press, 2012), 95–105 (98).
10. David J. Bosch, *Transforming Mission: Paradigm Shifts in Theology of Mission* (Maryknoll, NY: Orbis Books, 1991), 390.
11. Martyn Atkins, "What Is the Essence of the Church?," in *Mission-Shaped Questions: Defining Issues for Today's Church*, ed. Steven J. Croft (New York: Seabury Books, 2010), 17.
12. Alan J. Roxburgh, *Structured for Mission: Renewing the Culture of the Church* (Downers Grove, IL: InterVarsity Press, 2015), 39.
13. Alan Kreider, *The Patient Ferment of the Early Church: The Improbable Rise of Christianity in the Roman Empire* (Grand Rapids, MI: Baker Academic, 2016), 39–40.
14. Niall Ferguson, *Civilization: The West and the Rest* (New York: Penguin Press, 2011), 11.
15. T. Desmond Alexander and David W. Baker, eds., *Dictionary of the Old Testament: Pentateuch* (Downers Grove, IL: InterVarsity Press, 2003), 813.
16. Joel B. Green, Scot McKnight, and I. Howard Marshall, *Dictionary of Jesus and the Gospels* (Downers Grove, IL: InterVarsity Press, 1992), 782.
17. Ibid.
18. Geoffrey Barraclough, ed., *The Times Atlas of World History* (Edinburgh: Collins Bartholomew, 1978), 102–3.
19. Green, McKnight, and Marshall, *Dictionary of Jesus and the Gospels*, 782.

20. Leonard I. Sweet and Frank Viola, *Jesus: A Theography* (Nashville, TN: Thomas Nelson, 2012), 265.
21. Wayne A. Meeks, *The First Urban Christians: The Social World of the Apostle Paul* (New Haven: Yale University Press, 1983), 78–79.
22. Ibid., 75–81.
23. Ibid., 75–82.
24. Ibid., 107.

*Chapter 6: (Re)missioning—Time for a Remix*
1. Daniel L. Migliore, *Faith Seeking Understanding: An Introduction to Christian Theology* (Grand Rapids, MI: W. B. Eerdmans Publishing, 2014), 82–83.
2. Referencing John Zizioulas, *Being as Communion: Studies in Personhood and the Church* (1985) in Migliore, *Faith Seeking Understanding,* 274–75.
3. James Womack, "A Comparison of Perichoresis in the Writings of Gregory of Nazianzus and John of Damascus," quoted in Michael L. Davis, "Spiritual Formation: Retrieving Perichoresis as a Model for Shared Leadership in the Marketplace," *Journal of Religious Leadership* 14, no. 1 (2015): 105–26 (111).
4. Anthony Brandt and David Eagleman, *The Runaway Species: How Human Creativity Remakes the Word* (New York: Catapult, 2017), 47–48.
5. "What Is the Greatest Dance Track of All Time?" *Mixmag*, February 2013, http://mixmag.net/read/what-is-the-greatest-dance-track-of-all-time-features.
6. David J. Gunkel, "Rethinking the Digital Remix: Mashups and the Metaphysics of Sound Recording," *Popular Music & Society* 31, no. 4 (2008): 489–510 (490).
7. Ibid.
8. Dean McIntyre, "Did the Wesleys Really Use Drinking Song Tunes for Their Hymns?," https://www.practicapoetica.com/articles/did-the-wesleys-really-use-drinking-song-tunes-for-their-hymns/, last accessed June 10, 2020.
9. Ibid.

10. Kevin Kelly, *The Inevitable: Understanding the 12 Technological Forces That Will Shape Our Future* (New York: Penguin Books, 2017), 135.
11. Ibid., 136–43.
12. Ibid., 146.
13. Graham Cray, *Mission-Shaped Church: Church Planting and Fresh Expression of Church in a Changing Context* (New York: Seabury Books, 2010), ix.
14. Lincoln Harvey, "How Serious Is It Really? The Mixed Economy and the Light-Hearted Long Haul," in Graham Cray, Ian Mobsby, and Aaron Kennedy, *Fresh Expressions of Church and the Kingdom of God* (Norwich, UK: Canterbury Press, 2012), 97.
15. Cray, *Mission-Shaped Church*, x.
16. Tod E. Bolsinger, *Canoeing the Mountains: Christian Leadership in Uncharted Territory* (Downers Grove, IL: IVP Books, 2016), 64.
17. Tim Harle, "The Formless Void as Organizational Template," *Journal of Management, Spirituality, and Religion* 9, no. 1 (2012): 103–21 (117).
18. Benyamin B. Lichtenstein, Mary Uhl-Bien, Russ Marion, Anson Seers, James Douglas Orton, and Craig Schreiber, "Complexity Leadership Theory: An Interactive Perspective on Leading in Complex Adaptive Systems," *Emergence: Complexity & Organization* 9, no. 4 (2006): 2–12.
19. Ibid., 3.
20. Ibid.
21. Craig Pearce and Jay A. Conger, *Shared Leadership: Reframing the Hows and Whys of Leadership* (Thousand Oaks, CA: Sage Publications, 2003), xi.
22. Margaret J. Wheatley, *Leadership and the New Science: Discovering Order in a Chaotic World* (San Francisco: Berrett-Koehler Publishers, 1999), 39.
23. Ibid.
24. Michael L. Davis, "Spiritual Formation: Retrieving Perichoresis as a Model for Shared Leadership in the Marketplace," *Journal of Religious Leadership* 14, no. 1 (2015): 105–26 (106).
25. Ibid., 107.

26. Stephen J. Croft, "Formation for Ministry in a Mixed Economy Church: The Impact of Fresh Expressions of Church on Patterns of Training," in eds. Louise Nelstrop and Martyn Percy, *Evaluating Fresh Expressions: Explorations in Emerging Church: Responses to the Changing Face of Ecclesiology in the Church of England* (Norwich, UK: Canterbury Press, 2008), 48.
27. Sara Savage, "Fresh Expressions: The Psychological Gains and Risks," in *Evaluating Fresh Expressions*, 58.
28. Ibid., 60.
29. Ibid., 58.
30. Michael Moynagh, *Church in Life: Emergence, Ecclesiology and Entrepreneurship* (London: SCM Press, 2017), 22–23.
31. Bolsinger, *Canoeing the Mountains*, 82.
32. Alan J. Roxburgh, *Missional: Joining God in the Neighborhood* (Grand Rapids, MI: Baker Books, 2011), 176.
33. Moynagh, *Church in Life*, 34.
34. Peter J. Denning and Robert Dunham, *The Innovator's Way: Essential Practices for Successful Innovation* (Cambridge, MA: MIT Press, 2010), xxiii.
35. Ibid., xxiv.
36. Ibid., xxv.
37. Graham Cray, "Connecting the Centre to the Edge," Anglican Church Planting Initiatives, https://acpi2017.wordpress.com/2017/07/26/connecting-the-centre-to-the-edge-graham-cray/, last accessed June 11, 2020.
38. Graham Cray, Ian Mobsby, and Aaron Kennedy, *Fresh Expressions of Church and the Kingdom of God* (Norwich, UK: Canterbury Press, 2012), 22.
39. Verlon Fosner, *Dinner Church: Building Bridges by Breaking Bread* (Franklin, TN: Seedbed Publishing, 2017), 108–9.
40. Cray, Mobsby, and Kennedy, *Fresh Expressions of Church and the Kingdom of God*, 20.
41. Leonard I. Sweet, *Nudge: Awakening Each Other to the God Who's Already There* (Colorado Springs, CO: David C. Cook, 2010), 32.

42. Cray, Mobsby, and Kennedy, *Fresh Expressions of Church and the Kingdom of God*, 24.
43. Sweet, *Nudge*, 43.
44. Ibid.
45. Jürgen Moltmann, *The Church in the Power of the Spirit: A Contribution to Messianic Ecclesiology* (Minneapolis, MN: Fortress Press, 1993), 10.

## Chapter 7: Symbiosis—The Hybrid Organism

1. Leonard I. Sweet, *Quantum Spirituality: A Postmodern Apologetic* (Dayton, OH: Whaleprints, 1991), 195.
2. Steven J. Croft, *The Future of the Parish System: Shaping the Church of England for the Twenty-First Century* (London: Church House, 2006), 76–77.
3. Clark Gilbert, Matthew Eyring, and Richard N. Foster, "Two Routes to Resilience," *Harvard Business Review*, December 2012, https://hbr.org/2012/12/two-routes-to-resilience.
4. Scott Anthony, Clark Gilbert, and Mark Johnson, "Dual Transformation," https://www.innosight.com/wp-content/uploads/2017/04/Final_Dual-Transformation_Mini-Book.pdf, last accessed June 11, 2020.
5. Graham Cray, "A Test for the Whole Mixed Economy," in Croft, *The Future of the Parish System*, 26.
6. Michael Moynagh and Philip Harrold, *Church for Every Context: An Introduction to Theology and Practice* (London: SCM Press, 2012), 431.
7. Stuart Murray, *Church after Christendom* (Milton Keynes, UK: Paternoster Press, 2004), 122.
8. Michael Moynagh, *Church in Life: Emergence, Ecclesiology and Entrepreneurship* (London, UK: SCM Press, 2017), 22–23.
9. Peter J. Denning and Robert Dunham, *The Innovator's Way: Essential Practices for Successful Innovation* (Cambridge, MA: MIT Press, 2010), xxv.
10. Joseph Selbie, *The Physics of God: Unifying Quantum Physics, Consciousness, M-Theory, Heaven, Neuroscience, and Transcendence* (Wayne, NJ: Career Press, 2017), 136–37.

11. JR Woodward, *Creating a Missional Culture: Equipping the Church for the Sake of the World* (Downers Grove, IL: IVP Books, 2012), 184.
12. Angela Shier-Jones, *Pioneer Ministry and Fresh Expressions of Church* (London: SPCK, 2009), 90.
13. Ray Oldenburg, *The Great Good Place: Cafés, Coffee Shops, Bookstores, Bars, Hair Salons, and Other Hangouts at the Heart of a Community* (Berkeley, CA: Marlowe, 1999), 16.
14. Manuel Castells, *The Rise of the Network Society* (Oxford Malden, MA: Blackwell Publishers, 2000), xli.

*Closing Vision: Tree of Life (Re)mixed*

1. Yang Yingzhen, Mao Linyong, Yingyos Jittayasothorn, Kang Youngmin, Jiao Chen, Fei Zhangjun, and Zhong Gan-Yuan, "Messenger RNA exchange between scions and rootstocks in grafted grapevines," *BMC Plant Biology* 15 (2015): 1–14.
2. Linda Ly, "Grafting Gone Wild: Grow Your Ketchup and Fries on the Same Plate," *KCET*, February 26, 2015, https://www.kcet.org/home-garden/grafting-gone-wild-grow-your-ketchup-and-fries-on-the-same-plant, last accessed January 27, 2020.

CPSIA information can be obtained
at www.ICGtesting.com
Printed in the USA
LVHW020027090920
665210LV00002B/2